How To Rebuild PONTIAC V-8s

UPDATED!

Rocky Rotella

CarTech®

CarTech®

CarTech®, Inc.
6118 Main Street
North Branch, MN 55056
Phone: 651-277-1200 or 800-551-4754
Fax: 651-277-1203
www.cartechbooks.com

Edit by Bob Wilson
Layout by Hailey Samples
ISBN 978-1-61325-563-6
Item No. SA200

Library of Congress Cataloging-in-Publication Data
Names: Rotella, Rocky, author.
Title: How to rebuild Pontiac V-8s / Rocky Rotella.
Description: Updated edition. | Forest Lake, MN : CarTech, Inc., 2019.
Identifiers: LCCN 2019035080 | ISBN 9781613255636 (paperback)
Subjects: LCSH: Pontiac automobile--Motors--Maintenance and repair--Handbooks, manuals, etc.
Classification: LCC TL215.P68 R64 2019 | DDC 629.25/040288--dc23
LC record available at https://lccn.loc.gov/2019035080

Written, edited, and designed in the U.S.A.
Printed in China
10 9 8 7 6 5 4 3

DISTRIBUTION BY:

Europe
PGUK
63 Hatton Garden
London EC1N 8LE, England
Phone: 020 7061 1980 • Fax: 020 7242 3725
www.pguk.co.uk

Australia
Renniks Publications Ltd.
3/37-39 Green Street
Banksmeadow, NSW 2109, Australia
Phone: 2 9695 7055 • Fax: 2 9695 7355
www.renniks.com

Canada
Login Canada
300 Saulteaux Crescent
Winnipeg, MB, R3J 3T2 Canada
Phone: 800 665 1148 • Fax: 800 665 0103
www.lb.ca

CONTENTS

DEDICATION

I wish to dedicate this book to my mother, Carmen Rotella. She was excited for me when she learned that I was to author this book. She passed away mid-project, however, and wasn't able to see the completed book down here. Hopefully she's reading it from up there. Mom, this one's for you!

ACKNOWLEDGMENTS

Many people assisted in the compilation of information for this book. I couldn't have completed the project without their assistance. I extend thanks to the following:

Dave Anderson, Ken Anderson, Kevin Beal, Rich Benolken, Dave Bisschop, Ken Brewer, Armin Brown, David Butler, Brian Carson, Chris Casperson, Wade Congdon, Ken Crocie, Paul Delfield, Tom DeMauro, Alan Fanning, Bob Florine, Bart Foreman, Eric Gardner, Kevin Gertgen, Dick Glady, Rick Gonser, Jim Hairston, Dave Hall, Jim Hall, Floyd Hand, Jim Hand, Joe Hand, Tom Hand, Jon Hardgrove, Jill Hepp, Mike Hicks, John Glasgo, Dan Jensen, Paul Johnson, Terry Johnson, Jeff Kauffman, Don Keefe, Ken Keefer, Shawn Kniesly, John Kryta, Jim Lehart, Robert Loftis, Robert Martin, Jim Mattison, Jim Mazzei, Pete McCarthy, Skip McCully, Malcolm "Mac" McKellar, Bill McKnight, Robert McMackin, Chase Milner, Fred Mittan, Randy Moore, Hailey Naylor, Kerry Novak, Joe Oldham, Scott Parkhurst, Christopher Phillip, Mike Randal, Chris Ritter, Nunzi Romano, Tony Romano, Jim Rotella, Cliff Ruggles, John Sawruk, Steve Schappaugh, Fred Simmonds, Ann Skrycki-Mohler, Smitty Smith, Paul Spotts, Kevin Studaker, Scott Sulprizio, Kevin Swaney, Scott Tiemann, Joe Tonietto, Jim Wangers, Mike Wasson, Mark Weymouth, Chuck Willard, Jeff Williams, and George Zapora.

I extend special thanks to my dad, Jim Rotella. He is the reason behind my passion toward the Pontiac hobby. Because of his profound love for Pontiacs, we always drove Pontiacs while I was growing up. And because of him, I learned my way around the Pontiac V-8 at an early age. He was very willing to lend a helping hand many times on this project.

I extend special thanks to my wonderful wife, Jennifer, for the confidence and support to write a book and for being so understanding while my head was buried in a camera viewfinder or a computer keyboard so often during the past year.

   HOW TO REBUILD PONTIAC V-8s

FOREWORD

There are few objects in this world as beautiful to behold as a trimmed-out Pontiac V-8. With its light-blue paint, chrome valve covers and 4-barrel, or even better, three 2-barrel Rochester 2GC carbs sitting under three small chrome pots, it is truly a stunning sight—in my opinion, the best-looking car engine of all time.

Even more exciting than looking at a Pontiac V-8 is stomping on the throttle of one. I have had that pleasure many times over the years in the course of road-testing Pontiacs for various magazines, and in owning some. I'd had a few clunkers before, but my first real car was a 1959 Pontiac Bonneville convertible—Tri-Power, Royal Bobcat kit, and 4.55:1 gears. Later I bought a 1968 GTO—400 H.O., 4-speed, and 3.90:1 gears. I still own a 1976 Trans Am.

I can say with certainty that there is something unique about the wail of a Pontiac V-8 under full throttle. It starts out as a low moan. As the revs climb and the secondaries fully open, the sound changes to a banshee-like wail that promises to suck up and spit out any nearby competitor. It's absolute music to an enthusiast's ear.

Pontiac engines also possess inner beauty. For one thing, they're relatively easy to work on. All the components are pretty much straightforward and easily bolt on and off. There are no tricks involved.

For another thing, they're responsive. Want to build a Poncho that screams? That's easy. Pontiac V-8s respond, and quite well, to just about any modification or improvement you wish to bestow upon them. All the usual stuff makes any Pontiac run better—increased carburetion, a hotter cam, headers, headwork, etc. You can hardly make a mistake if you're working with a Pontiac.

Finally, there is the interchangeability. Just about any component from any year—heads, intake manifolds, camshafts, etc.—fits to just about any other year block. So, if you want to put a 1966 389 Tri-Power intake manifold on a 1970 400 block and use a number-068 H.O. cam from a 1968, go right ahead. It all works—and well. Thank you, Pontiac engine design engineers, wherever you are.

In this book, renowned Pontiac tech expert Rocky Rotella takes you through the ubiquitous 400 Pontiac V-8, from a stock rebuild with mild modifications that increases horsepower to nearly 400. But what he shows and tells you applies to your Pontiac engine too, be it a 1958 347 or a 1976 455. Rocky's tech articles appear regularly in Pontiac publications such as *High Performance Pontiac* magazine and the Pontiac-Oakland Club International's official mag, *Smoke Signals*. He knows Pontiacs. He knows his stuff. You're in good hands with Rocky.

—Joe Oldham, author of *Muscle Car Confidential*

WHAT IS A WORKBENCH® BOOK?

This Workbench® Series book is the only book of its kind on the market. No other book offers the same combination of detailed hands-on information and revealing color photographs to illustrate engine rebuilding and modifying. Rest assured, you have purchased an indispensable companion that will expertly guide you, one step at a time, through each important stage of the rebuilding process. This book is packed with real-world techniques and practical tips for expertly performing rebuild procedures, not vague instructions or unnecessary processes. At-home mechanics or enthusiast builders strive for professional results, and the instruction in our Workbench® Series books help you realize pro-caliber results. Hundreds of photos guide you through the entire process from start to finish, with informative captions containing comprehensive instructions for every step of the process.

The step-by-step photo procedures also contain many additional photos that show how to install high-performance components, modify stock components for special applications, or even call attention to assembly steps that are critical to proper operation or safety. These are labeled with unique icons. These symbols represent an idea, and photos marked with the icons contain important, specialized information.

Here are some of the icons found in Workbench® books:

Important!

Calls special attention to a step or procedure, so that the procedure is correctly performed. This prevents damage to a vehicle, system, or component.

Save Money

Illustrates a method or alternate method of performing a rebuild step that will save money but still give acceptable results.

Torque Fasteners

Illustrates a fastener that must be properly tightened with a torque wrench at this point in the rebuild. The torque specs are usually provided in the step.

Special Tool

Illustrates the use of a special tool that may be required or can make the job easier (caption with photo explains further).

Performance Tip

Indicates a procedure or modification that can improve performance. The step most often applies to high-performance or racing engines.

Critical Inspection

Indicates that a component must be inspected to ensure proper operation of the engine.

Precision Measurement

Illustrates a precision measurement or adjustment that is required at this point in the rebuild.

Professional Mechanic Tip

Illustrates a step in the rebuild that non-professionals may not know. It may illustrate a shortcut or a trick to improve reliability, prevent component damage, etc.

Documentation Required

Illustrates a point in the rebuild where the reader should write down a particular measurement, size, part number, etc. for later reference or photograph a part, area, or system of the vehicle for future reference.

Tech Tip

Tech Tips provide brief coverage of important subject matter that doesn't naturally fall into the text or step-by-step procedures of a chapter. Tech Tips contain valuable hints, important info, or outstanding products that professionals have discovered after years of work. These will add to your understanding of the process, and help you get the most power, economy, and reliability from your engine.

RESTORATION RESOURCES

To many Pontiac hobbyists, it's difficult to find a more impressive sight than a fully detailed Ram Air V-8. The subtle contrast created by a light-silver-blue block, natural cast-aluminum intake manifold, and highly polished chrome valve covers can be breathtaking for any enthusiast. Engines such as this 1969 Ram Air IV are full of small details that require careful attention.

There are several companies, organizations, and publications that specialize in the preservation and restoration of Pontiacs. While vehicle restoration is a topic large enough to fill its own book, many of these sources can help identify and document Pontiac engines, so you can correctly restore your Pontiac engine to a factory-fresh appearance and they can provide you with an exhaust system to make your Pontiac look and sound as it did the day it was delivered.

Reproduction Parts Suppliers

The hobby is full of restoration parts suppliers, and high-quality reproductions can be purchased from any number of them. It's unlikely that the Pontiac hobby finds stronger support than in two of the companies: Ames Performance Engineering (APE) and Max Performance. True Pontiac enthusiasts founded and operate both companies, which specialize in Pontiac restoration components. Both companies bring parts trailers to serve customers at various Pontiac events across the country.

APE has supported Pontiac hobbyists with top-quality reproduction components for the past 30 years. In addition to a number of suspension components, interior pieces, and body panels, APE offers a complete line of reproduction engine components. It has even created a number of its own proprietary reproductions. Those include small brackets, chrome valve covers, and a cast-aluminum timing cover and oil filter housing. APE can fulfill all your Pontiac restoration needs.

In its 20 years of supporting the Pontiac hobby, Performance Years (PY) has made a name for itself as a premier reproduction-parts supplier, providing hobbyists with high-quality reproduction body, interior, and suspension pieces. Its engine

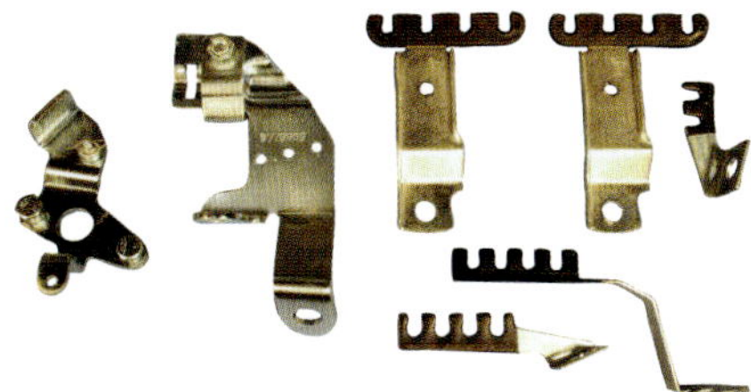

Ames Performance Engineering offers exact reproductions of many small engine brackets to replace missing originals during a restoration. These particular units retain the throttle linkage and spark plug wires. Certain examples are even marked with the proper part number just like an original.

component line includes a wide array of quality reproductions, some of which are exclusive to PY. Those include small brackets, throttle linkages, fuel filters, and vacuum hose harnesses. In 2015, Performance Years consolidated its retail operation with Ames Performance Engineering and rebranded itself as Max Performance to focus on its specialty lines such as Pypes Performance Exhaust, which is a high-performance line of complete exhaust systems, and Cold-Case Aluminum Radiators. Max Performance also hosts one of the most popular online forums on its website.

Reproduction Exhaust Systems

Gardner Exhaust Systems has long been considered a premier reproduction exhaust company. It specializes in exhaust systems that are authentic reproductions with careful attention given to exact appearance and sound. Gardner Exhaust Systems products fit and function just like factory pieces and even include exact reproductions of the hangers, clamps, and tailpipe extensions for installation. Complete systems are readily available for most 1967–1974 Firebirds or a 1964–1972 LeMans or GTO.

Waldron's Exhaust reproduces exhaust systems for Pontiac applications with mufflers specifically designed to recreate the original Pontiac sound. Unlike some of its competitors, Waldron's Exhaust has the ability to customize certain pieces for an application. It can modify its mufflers internally to attenuate a specific sound without compromising the factory look.

When it comes to pre-bent fuel lines, Inline Tube is considered an industry leader. It also offers reproduction exhaust systems that look and fit like the originals. In some instances, the reproduction mufflers are modified internally to improve airflow and performance without compromising the factory look. To complement its reproduction exhaust systems, Inline Tube also offers reproduction exhaust hangers, clamps, and tailpipe extensions for many models.

Pontiac Engine Colors

Pontiac engines were always painted some shade of green or blue over the years. The most popular colors seem to be the light blue and light metallic blue hues that Pontiac used during the 1960s and 1970s. While some colors are available in spray cans and easily found at local auto parts stores, those colors are usually just close to that used by Pontiac, not exact.

Supercar Specialties restores all types of Pontiacs, and owner Scott Tiemann has spent a great deal of

When it comes to exact reproductions of popular Firebird and GTO exhaust systems, many agree that Gardner Exhaust Systems is an industry leader. Gardner used original exhaust pieces as templates to produce its complete reproductions, which look, fit, and function just like the originals. Gardner also reproduced the original hangers and clamps. If you seek a factory exhaust system, then Gardner Exhaust Systems may be the answer. (Photo Courtesy of Eric Gardner)

The rubber grommet used to seal a Pontiac's system have often rotted from years of underhood heat. Replacements may be only as far away as the HELP section of your local auto parts store. HELP number 42054 is the PCV valve seal that presses into the valley pan, while number 42055 is the small grommet that slips into the valve cover. If your local parts store doesn't stock either piece, it can likely have them for you in a day or two.

Pontiac's 301 received forced-induction when a turbocharger was added in 1980, adding more than 50 hp to the naturally aspirated 4-barrel mill. To accommodate the added cylinder pressure, the block received additional material in high-stress areas and the crankshaft was specially prepared. Availability was limited to the Firebird Formula and Trans Am.

time researching and mixing colors to produce exact matches to the colors that Pontiac used. Supercar Specialties offers any Pontiac-type blue that an owner many need in a quart can. Bill Hirsch Auto is one company that offers several Pontiac engine enamels in aerosol cans or quart containers. And Inline Tube has recently released its own line of Pontiac engine paints.

OEM Paints specializes in reproducing all types of automotive finishes. The company has documented original colors and offers a wide variety of Pontiac engine paints in easy-to-use aerosol cans. Unlike other conventional engine enamels, however, OEM Paints' engine colors are uniquely formulated to increase heat dissipation and resist grease and grime, keeping its engine colors looking new longer. I found OEM Paints' products to be an excellent choice when attempting to correctly detail a Pontiac engine.

I found that the complete line of Pontiac engine colors from OEM Paints are a close match to Pontiac originals. OEM Paints engine paint is specially formulated and contains ceramic and other proprietary materials. The company states the materials deliver increased bonding strength that flexes during thermal expansion and contraction and actually get stronger with use. OEM Paints engine colors resist gas, oil, rust, and grease and are dyno proven to withstand intermittent engine temperatures up to 500°F. OEM Paints has any shade of Pontiac blue available in an easy-to-use aerosol can.

Documentation

Documenting certain vehicles can be impossible without original paperwork. It usually wasn't saved by the original owner or passed on to the next. That can leave the authenticity of many vehicles in question. That's not the case for Pontiac hobbyists. Pontiac saved the vehicle billing history or invoices that it sent to its dealerships for many years. Enthusiast Jim Mattison was fortunate enough to take possession of the documents up to the 1986 model year.

Mattison's company, PHS Automotive Services, provides hobbyists with production data, technical information, and detailed

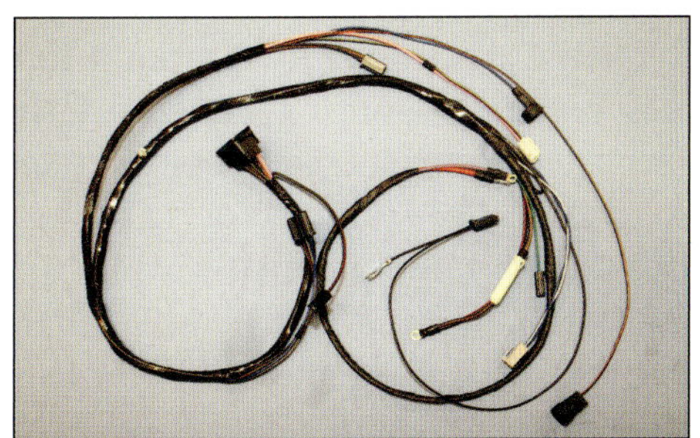

An engine rebuild presents the perfect opportunity to correct any underhood issues. Often the original wiring harness has weathered from years of use, which can cause it to deteriorate or fray. M&H Electric Fabricators reproduction wire harnesses fit and function just like an original, and even contain original-type connectors for correct appearance and easy installation. M&H can also replace the original resistor wire in points-type harnesses with a 12-volt source when converting to HEI.

paperwork that can be used to document a specific Pontiac from 1961 to 1986 for a nominal fee. It's an excellent resource that can verify the authenticity of a certain Pontiac or its optional equipment and possibly prevent a potential buyer from purchasing a misrepresented example. General Motors of Canada offers a similar service for any Canadian-built or Canadian-shipped Pontiac from 1945 forward.

Publications

There is one Pontiac-specific magazine available to subscribers today. In addition to providing various vehicle features, *Don Keefe's Poncho Perfection* has been delivering detailed articles on the technical aspects of the Pontiac V-8, new components and product reviews, and high-performance engine build-ups to its readers since the demise of *High Performance Pontiac* magazine in 2015. It is an excellent monthly publication available in print or web-based formats.

National Clubs

In addition to local owners clubs, there are several national clubs that serve the Pontiac hobby. The three major Pontiac organizations host annual national conventions, drawing attendees from across the country. The clubs distribute publications, have major shows where vehicles are judged for complete correctness, and provide members with knowledgeable advisers who are willing to provide detailed technical support. For those just beginning in the hobby, joining such a club may be a very worthwhile investment.

The Firebird was Pontiac's most popular vehicle in the late 1970s. More than 211,000 were produced in 1979 and more than half of them were Trans Ams. Several thousand 400s were stockpiled during 1978 model year production for use as T/A 6.6 engines in 1979 Trans Ams. These were the last 400-powered Pontiacs ever produced.

The GTO Association of America (GTOAA) is comprised of a large group of GTO owners sharing a common interest: preserving and promoting GTO heritage. Its award-winning publication, *Legend*, contains technical information about GTOs, club and hobby news, and member features. The annual GTOAA convention is an event that any Pontiac enthusiast—even more specific, any GTO enthusiast—should attend. The show field is routinely comprised of several hundred GTOs, some of which are the rarest and most desirable ever produced.

The National Firebird and Trans Am Club (NFTAC) is an organization comprised solely of Firebird enthusiasts. The club provides a wealth of technical information about Firebirds of all years for its members. Its annual convention, the Trans Am Nationals, is held in Dayton, Ohio, each August and attracts several hundred Firebirds from around the country. The show includes specific classes where Firebirds can be judged for correctness. The NFTAC is an excellent organization for any Firebird enthusiast.

The Pontiac-Oakland Club International (POCI) boasts the largest membership of any Pontiac-related club. Its goal is to pool resources to provide members with the best opportunity to preserve and restore any Pontiac. Its publication, *Smoke Signals*, is an excellent resource full of club and hobby news, technical information, member features, and classified ads. The annual POCI national convention features several hundred Pontiacs gathered in a single location. Many of the individual specialty chapters hold their own events throughout the year as well.

The Cruisin' Tigers Pontiac Club was once a regional GTO club that recently relaxed its membership rules to include all Pontiac models and has become a national organization. In addition to a bimonthly publication containing hobby news, technical and feature articles, and classified ads, its annual event—the Indian Uprising held in the greater Chicago area—draws several hundred Pontiacs with attendees traveling several states away to attend.

Internet Web Forums

The internet information age is upon us and it has fueled the Pontiac hobby to some degree. A quick web search on a Pontiac topic provides a number of links to enthusiasts' personal web pages. While those personal pages are only as accurate as its owner's knowledge, there are several web-based forums where hobbyists can interact—posting real questions and receiving accurate replies.

There are a number of web forums that can provide information on how to improve your Pontiac's appearance or performance. I regularly visit Bill Boyle's pontiacstreetperformance.com, Chris Casperson's maxperformanceinc.com, and Rich Miller's classicalpontiac.com. There are many others that are model specific such as Mike Barefoot's transamcountry.com and Joe Richter's 301garage.com. Any of these online forums and many more can be an invaluable resource when rebuilding, restoring, or modifying any Pontiac. I also have my own website, Pontiac V8.com, that I use for blogging and to post past articles that I've penned over the years.

The 1968–1972 A-Body vehicles remain an excellent foundation for performance enhancements. Unique GTOs and those with The Judge package are likely too valuable to modify, but entry-level Tempest and LeMans models can be purchased reasonably. The aftermarket abounds with restoration and suspension components.

PREPARING FOR THE REBUILD

When Pontiac designed its V-8 packages, each engine type was subjected to an endurance test, which consisted of static operation at 4,500 rpm on a dynamometer for 100 consecutive hours without shutdown. The engine was then completely disassembled and inspected for any signs of abnormal wear. If nothing of significance was detected, it was one step closer to reaching production.

Through durability testing, Pontiac's goal was to develop a V-8 engine that could endure 100,000 miles of normal use before requiring a rebuild. Extra material was cast into the components so that each could easily accommodate being moderately machined at least once.

Modern passenger car engines are designed to last 150,000 miles or more, and there are a number of factors that allow it to accomplish this. Modern machining and finishing techniques, piston ring technology, and engine oil quality are generally considered better than ever before. Modern fuel injection ensures instant start-up and improved cold-weather operation and prevents excessive fueling to wash the oil film from the cylinder walls.

In addition to those advancements, most modern cars are typically lighter and can accelerate with less resistance to motion, lessening the overall load an engine sees on a daily basis. The use of overdrive

An engine dynamometer is an excellent tool for breaking in an engine and measuring output under full-throttle load. The best machine shops or engine builders use a dyno to ensure a completely assembled engine operates properly before delivering it to a customer. Measured output values can tell you if your engine meets your performance expectations.

Any engine may require a rebuild for any number of reasons, even one that had a rebuild recently performed. Abnormal thrust bearing wear is evident in this particular Pontiac engine, which might indicate improper bearing main cap alignment or insufficient thrust clearance. In either instance, it requires a rebuild.

transmissions equates into reduced engine RPM during normal conditions. Even without these advantages, but with routine maintenance and general care, it's common to find a Pontiac V-8 that exceeded the 100,000-mile mark by many thousands of miles.

Rebuild Basics

Neglect often results in an engine that falls well short of its intended lifetime. There's no telling what type of lifestyle your Pontiac led prior to your taking possession of it. If your Pontiac V-8 operates smoothly, doesn't use oil, and doesn't smoke, chances are that it's in relatively good operating condition. But it may not be in perfect health and may benefit from a complete rebuild.

The newest Pontiac V-8 was produced in 1981, so it's quite possible that your engine has already been rebuilt at some point in its life, but there's also a chance that it's never been apart before. There's no way of knowing an engine's internal condition without complete disassembly, and unless you've owned it for a number of years, you really have no way of verifying originality. No matter your engine's circumstances, now might be the opportune time to give your Pontiac a complete refresh.

The purpose of any engine rebuild is to eliminate the internal wear that results from normal operation and restore any lost performance. A typical rebuild should include machining each contact surface, replacing all sacrificial components, and installing new bearings, seals, and gaskets. If properly executed, the effort should produce a Pontiac that runs at least as well as the day it rolled off the assembly line, and the use of high-quality gaskets and seals should prevent any annoying oil or coolant leaks.

There are other factors beyond normal wear that might force an owner to rebuild an engine. Those might include incorrect assembly by a shop during a prior rebuild, significant damage from component failure after exceeding the engine's intended operating range, or simply bad luck. The machining performed during the rebuilds, or the extent of damage that occurred when a component let go, determines how useable your existing components are.

Creating a Plan

One of the first steps to any successful rebuild is creating a sound plan of action. You need to determine which category your rebuild best falls within. Is your engine a strictly stock rebuild, a mildly modified street engine, a significantly modified street/strip setup, or something in between the previous descriptions? After you've identified the type of engine you want and the application for the engine, you need to establish a fairly certain horsepower and torque target. This helps you and a machinist select the parts to meet your goal and then establish the budget for build project.

Each type of rebuild requires a different rebuild plan and different machine shop services. Is your vintage Pontiac driven often and you simply feel it's time to rebuild its engine back to near-stock specs? Are you performing a frame-off restoration and looking to rebuild and restore your Pontiac's numbers-matching engine? Or are you less concerned with originality and simply looking to increase your Pontiac's performance while maintaining a relatively stock appearance?

You need to identify the vintage of your Pontiac V-8 and determine if the existing components are capable

When looking for an engine to rebuild, you can tell that an engine has been rebuilt if it has been freshly painted and is relatively free of heavy grease deposits. I prefer an engine that is completely covered in grime because it generally indicates it is a complete original that hasn't been tampered with over the years. This particular 1966 389 4-barrel could be an excellent foundation for a restoration application.

of meeting your performance expectations in stock or mildly modified form. If your machinist is unfamiliar with the various Pontiac castings and the capacity of each, then it may be best to use one of the many proven combinations found in chapter 9, or contact one of the many Pontiac builders listed in the source guide. The answers you receive should include recommendations for total engine displacement, which pistons, connecting rods, rings and bearings should be used, and the camshaft specifications and cylinder heads that help you reach your performance goal during your rebuild.

There are two other important questions that you must ask yourself when planning your engine rebuild. How much money do I have to spend on the entire project? And how much of the actual engine assembly work am I willing to perform myself? Only you can answer all these questions, and it is common to be undecided at this point of the rebuild. You do, however, have to take a realistic approach and need to stick close to your plan once you commit to it.

When considering all that's involved in a complete engine rebuild, some hobbyists are more content taking a complete engine to an engine builder and returning when it's ready for reinstallation; others enjoy performing some or all of the assembly process themselves. Be realistic when assessing your experience and skill level when tackling your engine rebuild because small errors can result in significant consequences and ultimately lead to engine failure. But attention to detail and proper guidance can keep you from making costly mistakes, and that's the purpose of this book.

Setting Performance Expectations

I know of very few hobbyists who wouldn't want their Pontiacs to run better. However, most hobbyists don't gauge "better" by using a drag strip or engine dyno. To most, "better" means the amount of tire spin that occurs upon a brisk takeoff. Depending upon the application and what you're beginning with, simply performing a basic rebuild to a tired engine may be enough to accomplish that, but some applications might not contain the ideal components to achieve that.

Pontiac designed the components of a given combination to complement one another and perform suitably for its intended application. A particular low-performance engine may have used a 2-barrel carburetor, small-valve heads, and a mild camshaft, but for the most part, its remaining components were the same as those on a similar 4-barrel offering. By simply swapping parts around, generally speaking, it's quite possible and cost effective to increase the power output of a 2-barrel to match that of a similar 4-barrel offering.

Significantly increasing an engine's power output almost always requires using high-performance factory pieces, such as those from Ram Air engines, or significantly modifying 4-barrel pieces to extract maximum potential from them. Either of these approaches can be quite costly. Though still expensive, it's often easier and more cost effective to purchase some aftermarket components designed as replacements for the desirable stock pieces. Additional information on parts selection and power levels are covered in later chapters.

Gathering Required Equipment

If you've been wrenching on cars for any amount of time, you likely understand that using the most expensive tools doesn't make a mechanic great. The absolute best tool for any job is the one that helps complete a given task at a given time, and it doesn't matter if it was purchased off a name-brand tool truck or from a reputable retailer. Snap-on, Mac Tools, and other brands make professional hand tools for working mechanics. These fine instruments are a pleasure to use and should last a lifetime or longer. However, the at-home mechanic can competently rebuild an engine with Craftsman, Husky, and other high-quality consumer tools. But I don't advocate using low-quality tools that can damage fasteners, round-off bolt heads, and generally make a mess of a basic job.

Before any engine can be rebuilt, it must be completely disassembled, and tearing it down before delivering it to a machine shop can often save you a few bucks. Fortunately for Pontiac hobbyists, V-8 disassembly doesn't require much beyond basic hand tools for the majority of it. If you don't presently own such equipment and future plans include additional engine rebuilds or repairs, then you might consider investing in them as they can be handy for most automotive repairs. A list of the tools you'll need at this time includes:

- Standard 6-point socket set in 3/8- and 1/2-inch drive
- A 1/2-inch breaker bar
- Variety of combination wrenches
- Variety of flathead and Phillips screwdrivers
- Flared wrenches for fuel lines

- Small variety of pry bars
- Soft-faced hammer
- Various taps for thread cleaning
- Digital camera and notebook for documentation

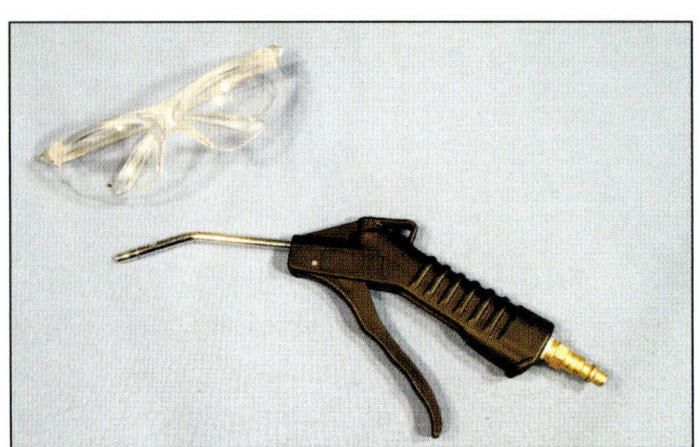

Though generally not regarded as a tool, compressed air is great to have available for a myriad of reasons. An air blow gun can be used to remove decades of dust and grime, especially after being loosened with solvent and a wire brush. Though the use of eye protection is suggested throughout the entire rebuild process, it is mandatory when using compressed air.

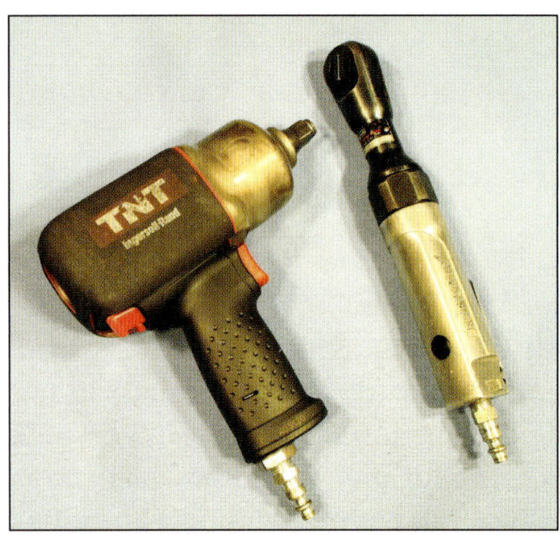

Air-operated tools seem to make any job easier. While I often use such equipment for more common repairs, I prefer hand tools when rebuilding an engine. It allows me to feel just how much effort is required to remove or install a fastener, and that can be a telltale sign of thread or fastener damage. A pneumatic impact wrench can be used to remove high-torque harmonic balancer and main cap bolts.

Some specialized equipment, such as a valve spring compressor, engine hoist, and engine stand, are required. But keep in mind: The tools mentioned above are for disassembling and assembling your Pontiac V-8, as well as several other task-specific tools. You might look into renting or borrowing them from friends or parts stores for a single engine rebuild. If additional engine rebuilds are possible down the road, then now might be the best time to add them to your toolbox. However, they are usually more costly and can quickly deplete a budget. The list of those specialty tools includes:

- Engine stand (1,000-pound capacity)
- Engine hoist (cherry-picker type)
- Torque wrenches
- Micrometers and calipers
- Various dial indicators
- Feeler gauges
- Piston ring compressor

One of the most important resources to have on hand during your entire rebuild is a Pontiac service manual that's specific to the year of your engine. You're probably wondering why I'd make such a recommendation if you're reading a book entitled *How to Rebuild Pontiac V-8s*. Well, there's a simple answer for that. Though the Pontiac engine family is so closely related, most individual engine models contain at least a few characteristics

that are unique to certain model years, and a Pontiac Service Manual should address an area if it varies from what's shown in this book.

A digital camera is another excellent resource that can be used throughout the entire project. It's beneficial when documenting the position of specific components during assembly. But it also allows you to provide your machinist with detailed pictures of any suspect areas you might have found in the disassembly process. With the relatively low cost of high-resolution point-and-shoot digital cameras and high-volume memory cards, it's a wise investment for the project and one that can be used for personal use too.

A gasket scraper of some sort is an inexpensive tool that's used to remove the gasket paper or sealant that's generally left behind on mating surfaces during disassembly. This unit uses a conventional razor blade that can be changed as often as necessary.

A Pontiac service manual is an excellent resource that can provide information about specific details for a particular model year. Costly reprints are commonly available from various sources, but worn, lower-priced originals are often available on popular internet classifieds or auction sites. A service manual for the model year of the engine being rebuilt is a must-have item for every enthusiast.

Planning Your Rebuild

The owner of a 1967 GTO had complained that the car's original 400 suffered from a number of operating issues. It had been rebuilt several years before by a reputable area shop. But the engine simply never lived up to the owner's expectations in several ways.

The engine was rebuilt with dished pistons to reduce compression ratio, so the original 10.25:1 mill operated suitably on lower-octane fuel, which was ideal for the owner because he planned to frequently take it on long trips to various car shows across the country. After the rebuild, the engine's coolant temperature sometimes soared; it audibly detonated on occasion and commonly ran-on after shutdown. Though the owner was told the engine could operate on 87- or 89-octane fuel, he found the issues seemed to worsen while using fuel under 91 octane. The engine appeared down on power, it struggled to operate past about 4,000 rpm, and it leaked and consumed oil regularly.

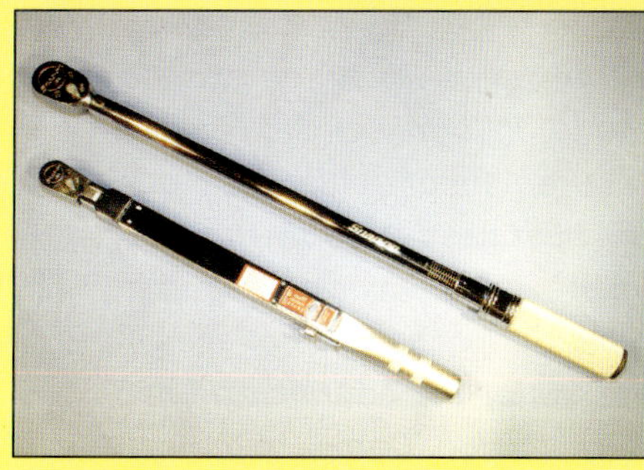

A torque wrench accurately measures the amount of torque applied to a fastener during installation and indicates effective clamping load. Adjustable versions like this one give an audible click when the selected amount of torque is reached. A torque wrench is useful most of the time during an engine rebuild but is absolutely required when installing connecting rods, main caps, and cylinder heads. The price sometimes reflects quality and accuracy, so I suggest buying a name brand unit.

Over the course of several thousand miles operating in this condition, the owner received a number of suggested solutions from fellow hobbyists. Though each was tried with hopes of a miraculous result, none ever really improved the situation, and the owner's frustration worsened. He approached me and asked for my opinion on the matter, and I agreed to assist.

The first step I took was an initial test drive to better understand the GTO's operating condition and gather a basis to determine the effects of any adjustments I'd make. Keeping in mind that this particular GTO featured functional air-conditioning, a Turbo 400 automatic transmission, a stock-stall torque converter, and a 2.93:1 rear axle ratio, my initial test drive revealed the owner's perception of lackluster performance was not exaggerated. This particular 400 ran about as well as a typical low-compression Pontiac 350!

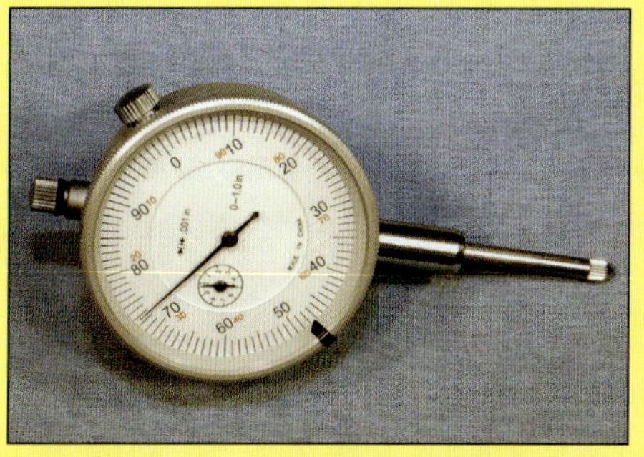

A dial indicator is a useful tool that, when combined with the proper mounting base, can provide useful measurements when rebuilding an engine. This unit was purchased from a local discount tool retailer, and its accuracy is more than adequate for this task.

When torque is applied to a fastener, its overall length increases as it stretches a certain amount, and that stretch can be used to determine its clamping force. Comparing your measurements to the manufacturer's predetermined values can tell you when a fastener has fatigued, which could otherwise result in failure. A stretch gauge is a valuable tool to measure the length of any bolt after tightening, and it's most commonly used to measure connecting rod bolts.

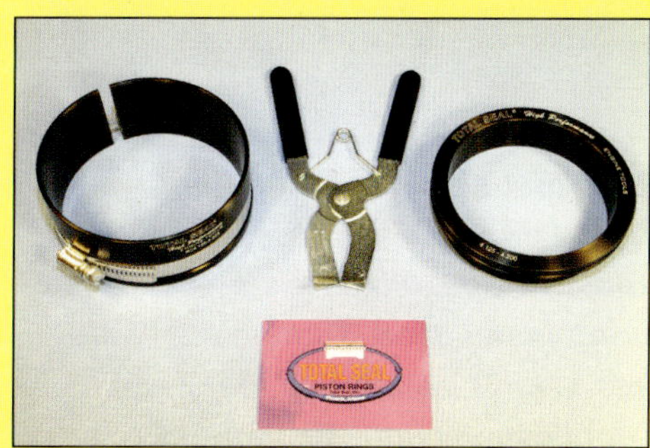

A variety of specialized tools are required to fit piston rings to a bore, install rings onto a piston, and insert a piston assembly into a cylinder. Total Seal offers such products in a wide and affordable array of cylinder sizes.

Planning Your Rebuild *(Continued)*

Plastigauge is an extruded plastic thread designed to uniformly crush, giving a fast and accurate measurement of actual main and rod bearing clearances. It's best used to verify that your machinist's measurements were accurate and that clearance actually exists. Simply cut a small piece and lay it on a clean journal, install the bearing and cap, and torque it to the correct value. Compare the spread Plastigauge to the graduated marks on the cover to determine clearance. It should be wiped from the journal surface and bearing coating, but any residue quickly dissolves when in contact with oil.

My attention was first directed toward the carburetor and distributor in an attempt to improve engine efficiency at every point. Though part-throttle drivability had significantly improved, the effect on full-throttle performance was limited, and many of the same issues remained. A compression check proved that cylinder pressure varied throughout the engine. It indicated to us that something was amiss somewhere within the combination and the only way to accurately determine the cause and find a solution was complete engine disassembly followed by a proper rebuild.

Having had several positive experiences with a local machinist, I knew that with his help, we could make this 400 run the way it should. I discussed with him the engine's existing operating condition, the goals that the owner and I sought, and the time frame we were working within. I explained that, because this was the GTO's original engine and that it was entered into shows often, original appearance was a key factor. And because of time constraints and for ease of photography, we also needed to have him assemble the Pontiac for us.

A camshaft installation tool attaches to the front snout of a camshaft and provides the assembler with additional control and leverage, ultimately preventing bearing damage during installation. Though available for many other makes, a cam installation tool wasn't offered for Pontiac applications until Tin Indian Performance began offering this unit, which retails for less than $25.

When dealing with camshafts, a few degrees of valve timing can make a significant difference in the way an engine idles and operates. A quality camshaft degree kit, such as this from Comp Cams (number 4936), allows the assembler to accurately install a camshaft at the desired position in relation to the crankshaft angle. A complete kit like this costs a well-spent $200 dollars.

This lifter bore fixture from Comp Cams (number 4925) is designed to be used in conjunction with its camshaft degree kit. When inserted into the lifter bore, the small extensions, which are intended to replicate a roller and flat-tappet lifter face, ride on the camshaft lobe for maximum accuracy.

Planning Your Rebuild *(Continued)*

The experience leading to the decision to rebuild your Pontiac V-8 may be similar to the example above, or it could be completely different. Nothing changes the fact that this 400 was running so poorly it was basically asking for a rebuild. Your Pontiac may not be quite as bad, but a tired engine needs attention too. Once you arrive at that point, you need to sort out your expectations and goals, set a realistic budget that allows you to achieve them, and prepare to get your hands dirty! ■

Valvetrain geometry can be affected anytime a block is surfaced or a cylinder head is machined. The easiest way to restore proper alignment of the valve stem and rocker arm is to utilize a specific-length pushrod. Comp Cams offers adjustable pushrods like this, which can be used to determine the required length of the replacements.

A dyno simulator computer program can never take the place of an actual engine dyno, but it can be a useful tool when determining the effects certain components can have on an engine's performance. Performance Trends Engine Analyzer v3.4 is among the best programs available. It allows hobbyists to compare how different camshafts, intake manifolds, cylinder heads, and exhaust systems can affect engine operation, and it contains excellent displacement and compression calculators. I have used one for years and have found it to be an excellent learning tool.

Selecting a Machine Shop

Once you've laid out the rebuild path you plan to follow and have the proper equipment on hand, the next step is to locate a reputable machine shop in your area that can satisfy all of your needs. The best choice is one that comes recommended by fellow Pontiac hobbyists who have had direct experience with a shop. You may find some shops with several caveats and others with several attributes.

In my opinion, a reputable, professional shop should be clean and able to perform such tasks as sonic testing, magnetic-particle inspection of components for cracks, fully machine a block and crankshaft, rebuild cylinder heads, prepare connecting rods, and completely balance a rotating assembly. It should also be able to procure replacement components, such as pumps, gaskets, and seals. Specialized procedures, such as nitride or cryogenic treatments, are often beyond the resources of typical engine building shops.

If a machine shop must send any component to an outside company for specific machining processes, then the machinist should assume full responsibility for any failure that occurs and is found to be related to the component that was outsourced. Just the same, you can't expect a machinist to stand behind any complete component you bring to the rebuild from an outside vendor. A machine shop technician must be able to work with a complete selection of compatible and complementary components because all the components

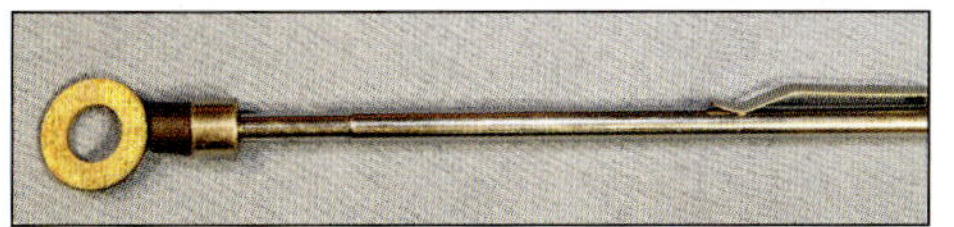

A magnetic pick-up tool is handy if you've dropped something like a nut or washer into a crevice or the tight confines of the crankcase. A telescoping tool like this or one with a flexible head is an inexpensive purchase at your nearest parts store.

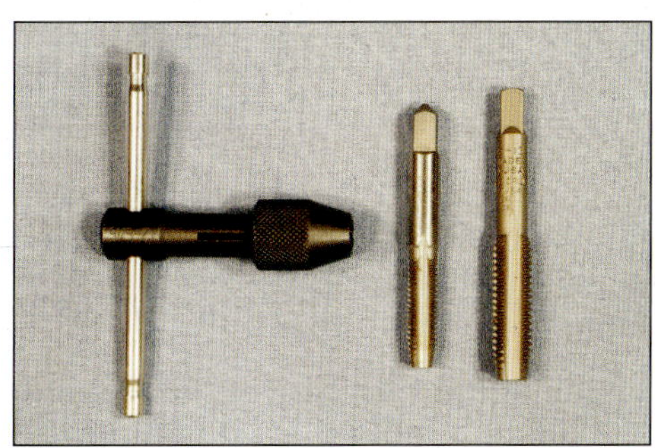

A complete tap and die set can be a valuable asset when cutting new threads into metal or restoring the shape of an existing one, but they're generally rather pricy. Only a handful of basic taps of various sizes and thread pitches are needed during an engine rebuild to chase the threads found on any cylinder head or block.

---

must work in harmony to complete a strong, reliable engine. In addition, the machinist must be able to fully inspect each component and verify its parts, function, dimensions, and overall quality. If the machinist is not able to do this, the slightest problem or mistake can lead to a catastrophic failure. An example of this might be valvetrain failure related to cylinder heads that were improperly prepared by an outside vendor.

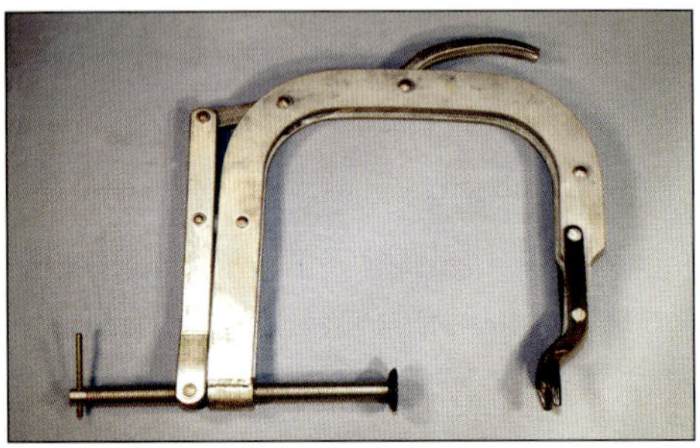

A valve spring compressor is required to completely disassemble and reassemble cylinder heads. Though units of various arrangements are available, I prefer a C-clamp style like this. It's better to spend a few more bucks for a high-quality unit like this one from Snap-on that won't flex under pressure.

This valve spring micrometer and other similar units determine the installation height of a valve spring when combined with the particular length of valve and retainer that's being used. Available within specific ranges, this Comp Cams unit measures from 1.4 to 1.8 inches.

Most machine shops can assemble certain components you're unable to handle yourself for whatever reason. For instance, cylinder head assembly includes measuring valve spring pressure and installing valve springs at the proper height. Allowing your machinist to assemble them is often a wise move. If you're concerned with the critical measurements and minute clearances associated with the rotating assembly, or if correct rod and piston orientation is intimidating, your machinist may be able to assemble the short-block for you at a reasonable cost or suggest a certain engine assembler for you.

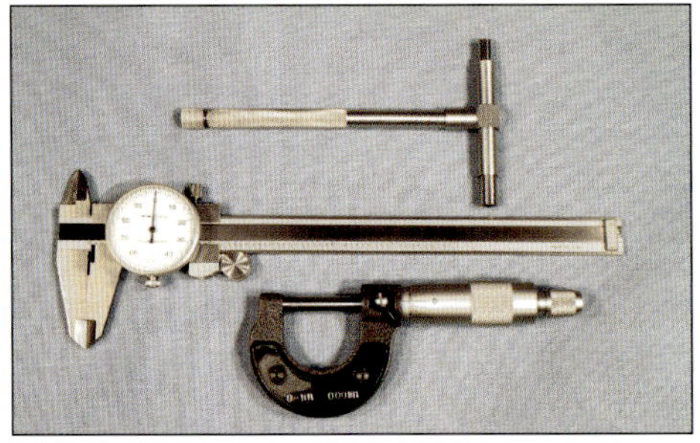

Various telescoping gauges, calipers, and micrometers are essential tools when performing any engine rebuild. They can be used to verify the measurements of most components. Units like these can be purchased at a reasonable cost from a local discount tool retailer. They're accurate for engine-build measurements.

No matter how much or how little of the engine rebuild you intend to perform yourself, you need to find a machine shop that can meet your machining requirements. You want to find a shop that has rebuilt and/or machined many Pontiac V-8 engines because you don't want a shop to make mistakes. If they have to learn the specs and machining processes while working on your engine, the chances of making mistakes are much greater. If you don't have one already in mind, finding the best choice for you can be as easy as asking around to gather opinions. This may be as simple as attending local car shows and asking fellow Pontiac owners who they'd recommend for an engine rebuild.

After striking up a conversation with a Pontiac owner, clearly ask if the Pontiac's engine has ever been rebuilt and if so, by which owner. Remember, you're looking for first-hand experience with a machine shop. Here are some general questions to ask:

- Why did you select this machine shop?
- What was considered a complete engine rebuild?
- Was any portion of it sent out to another shop?
- How long did it take to complete your project?

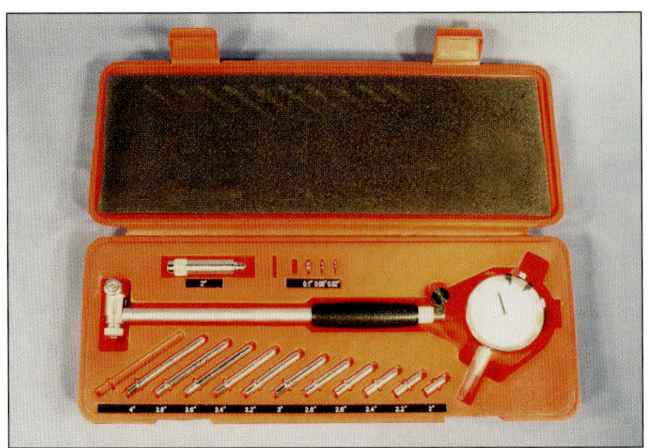

A dial-bore gauge can be used to measure areas of the block, such as the bore diameter, cylinder wall taper, and diameter of the camshaft tunnel and main caps. This unit was purchased from Summit Racing Equipment, cost less than $100, and has been very useful.

- How long were you told it would take?
- How much work did you perform yourself?
- Were you completely satisfied with the results?
- Did the cost seem reasonable for what you received?
- Have you had any issues with your engine since the rebuild?
- Would you use this machine shop again?

If you're satisfied with the answers to these questions, simply consider that machine shop as a possibility and move on to the next Pontiac owner for another opinion. Remember, when dealing with the minute tolerances associated with an engine rebuild, one can go wrong from time to time. A quality machine shop stands behind its work, however. Once you're completely confident in one shop's ability, you're ready to contact them to inquire about the services offered.

The term "machine shop" is often interpreted as a business that can rebuild an engine for a customer, but there's a major difference between the services offered by an actual machine shop and engine assembling and building shops.

While modern machine shops often offer both machining and assembling services, some machine shops have no interest in assembling an engine after the machining portion a rebuild is complete. In these instances, it is your responsibility to completely assemble your engine or enlist the services of an engine assembler.

An engine assembling shop in simplest terms is just that: a shop or a person that assembles engines for customers. Some or all of the component machining is outsourced and the entire combination is assembled with little regard toward maximizing performance. The engine is typically fully assembled and ready for installation into a vehicle, but it may or may not have been fired prior to customer delivery and usually does not include any form of tuning.

An engine builder is best described as a person or a shop that designs and assembles a customer's combination. It includes performing

With so many affordable aftermarket crankshafts for other makes available today, there aren't many modern machine shops that grind crankshafts in-house anymore. If your rebuild requires this, and if the machine shop you select subcontracts the task, ask for the name of the company.

A high-quality machine shop should possess the equipment required to properly machine a Pontiac block. That includes using a Pontiac-specific torque-plate for boring and honing cylinder walls and a line hone to restore main journal geometry.

A feeler gauge is used to measure the clearance between two perpendicular mating surfaces. And when combined with any precision straight edge, it can be used to measure cylinder head or deck surface warping. Units like this are available at any parts store and generally cost less than $20.

Balancing the reciprocating assembly involves attaching stationary weights to crankshaft journals, which replicates the effects of the piston-and-rod assemblies. The crankshaft is spun at low RPM and a strobe light is used to determine where counterweight mass should be added or removed to ensure smooth operation.

or arranging machining by one or more competent machine shops and selecting the proper combination of components to help a customer achieve his or her performance expectations. Engines are typically delivered to the customer completely assembled and fully tuned, and the output should be documented with the results of dyno testing.

There are distinct markets for all three services, and that's something to consider if you're going to have a shop assemble any part of your engine for you. No matter which route is chosen, have a clear understanding of how your components are being machined and which machine shop is handling the task. It may be worthwhile to visit that machine shop before making a decision on moving forward.

In my opinion, a good machine shop is one that can completely rebuild any engine in a timely manner with its own in-house equipment. I feel that outsourcing any part of a rebuild can compromise a project. The machinist tends to lose control of time and quality, and that can negatively affect the outcome. A quality machine shop to consider for your project should possess the following equipment:

- Parts cleaning equipment
- Cylinder honing equipment and a Pontiac-specific torque plate
- Line-hone equipment
- Vertical mill
- Surfacing equipment for heads and block
- Rod preparation equipment
- Crank grinding and polish equipment
- Balancing equipment
- Valve refacing equipment
- Valve guide and seat equipment

The high numbers of low-cost aftermarket crankshafts currently on the market has limited the number of cranks that a machine shop must prepare on a regular basis, and the high cost of such equipment can prevent newer shops from purchasing a crankshaft grinder. Unless your plans include an aftermarket Pontiac crankshaft, however, the machine shop you choose should have that ability to perform that task or confidence in the company it outsources it to.

I also feel that the best shops are those that offer engine break-in with a test stand or engine dyno. This allows you to verify that your engine starts immediately, idles and revs smoothly, is free of oil and coolant leaks, and ultimately confirms that your engine has been broken-in properly before ever leaving the machine shop. If you chose to spend the extra money, a dyno tune can be a great tool to measure your Pontiac's output and ensure that it's performing reliably and optimally under full-throttle conditions.

Before contracting a shop for your rebuild, clearly discuss your expectations and specifically disclose the wear parts (valve springs, bearings, gaskets,

Any quality machine shop should have modern valve guide and seat equipment to precisely prepare its customer's cylinder heads. This equipment from Serdi can cut multiple angles into a valve seat in a single pass, using the valve guide to properly locate the cutter in relation to the seat.

If new valves are part of your rebuild, then there's a chance that your machine shop does not need to use this piece of equipment. If you're planning to reuse your existing valves, however, a valve grinder like this is required to restore the surface of the seat angle or add other cuts that could possibly improve airflow.

A surface mill is required when removing material from the mating surfaces of a block or cylinder head. Other uses include resurfacing a manual-transmission flywheel, or intake or exhaust manifold flanges. It's a valuable piece of equipment that any machine shop should have.

etc.) you'll be expected to buy from them. Most businesses have some type of policy in place that allows it to add a certain percentage onto the cost of the project if a customer supplies parts, and at that point, any warranty against failure is void. Some shops may even go so far as to simply refuse to assemble anything they didn't supply. Some shops just aren't willing to take this risk of failure.

Once you have selected the machine shop you feel most comfortable working with and your rebuild project begins, it's advisable to check in often to follow your engine's progress. Asking questions and being visible is an easy way to learn and to be sure your project is on track. But you must also understand that, in business, there's a fine line between being inquisitive and being a pest!

When Rebuilds Go Bad

A good machinist takes pride in the work and sincerely feels that what leaves the shop is as functionally sound as if it were as good as or better than new. Just because a machinist has good intentions doesn't mean that accidents can't happen, however. A good machinist can have a bad day, but the best machinists routinely check their work throughout the course of any task to prevent any associated failure.

For any number of reasons, it's sometimes easier to allow a shop to assemble your engine for you, and careless assembly can have a catastrophic outcome. If you choose to handle your own assembly, as a smart owner you can check your engine's tolerances just before assembly to be sure your machinist wasn't having a bad day when machining your components. That might help you gain trust in the machinist and the shop if future engine rebuilds or various projects are on the horizon.

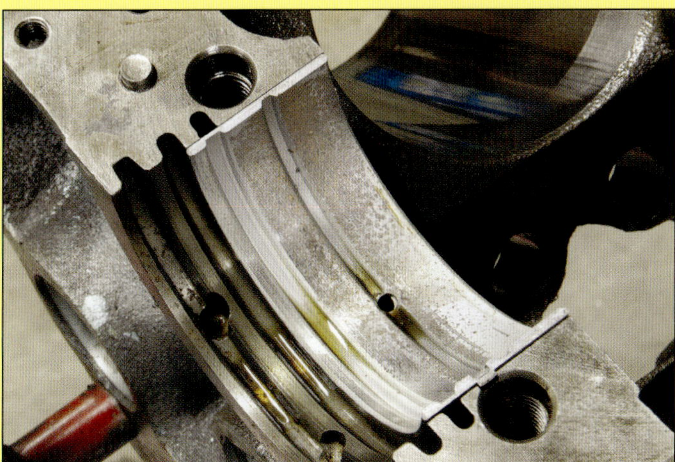

It's obvious that a significant amount of material has embedded into this bearing. As bad as this might look, it actually performed its intended task. There was almost no major wear on the corresponding crankshaft journal.

By design, bearings are sacrificial components. Minute particles passing through the lubrication system embed into them, saving the crankshaft journals. Once a bearing is no longer able to perform that task, distinct wear patterns can begin appearing on the corresponding crankshaft journal surface. This crankshaft was reused after removing 0.020 inch of its surface.

When Rebuilds Go Bad *(Continued)*

This connecting rod bearing has experienced complete failure. Metallic particles in the lubrication system and extreme heat wore through all of the Babbitt layer and most of the copper layer, exposing the metal backing.

A local assembler rebuilt this Pontiac 455 for its owner. It was a very basic rebuild like many of the Pontiacs the assembler rebuilt before. But it wasn't broken-in on a test stand before it was returned to the owner. The owner simply installed it into his Pontiac, and it immediately started showing signs of significant internal issues. After a handful of miles, it was evident the freshly rebuilt engine required an immediate teardown. These photos reveal what was found.

Working with an independent machinist to gain an understanding of what occurred, the best guess seemed to be that the rear camshaft plug was driven in a bit too far, and when the camshaft thrust plate was installed, all camshaft clearance was lost. It appears unlikely that the engine assembler had checked for any clearance during the rebuild.

With the camshaft's first revolution after immediate start-up, it's evident that it churned into the steel plug, which sent metallic filings into the oiling system, where material was distributed throughout the entire engine. The metallic particles quickly damaged the piston skirts and bearings, several of which failed completely.

This steel plug was driven too far into the rear opening of the camshaft bore, and when the camshaft and thrust plate were installed, the engine assembler neglected to check for proper clearance. The wear that followed sent metallic particles throughout the engine, causing a significant amount of damage and effectively destroying a freshly rebuilt engine.

After removing the bottom plate from the oil pump body, there's no question that metallic particles were being carried throughout the engine by its oiling system.

Unfortunately, another set of new pistons is required during the rebuild. The deep grooves and embedded material can prevent the piston from properly maintaining cylinder seal.

Unfortunately, examples like this are common. Though it may have looked like this 455 would never run again, it was completely disassembled and the reusable components were thoroughly cleaned. Several new components were purchased and the entire engine was properly rebuilt by another machinist shortly after these photos were taken. It has since given its owner a number of issue-free miles, but it was a rebuild that cost this owner twice as much as it should have. ■

Found while rebuilding a different engine, the dark areas on the deck surface of this block are soot trails. This indicates that the cylinder head bolts used on this engine were not torqued properly or fatigued from over-use, or that the head gasket didn't crush properly during cylinder head installation. Regardless of the cause, it eventually resulted in head gasket failure.

DISASSEMBLY

With all of the necessary tools and equipment on hand, it's time to begin complete engine disassembly. Though it might seem relatively easy, it's a methodical process that should be considered to be as important as any other portion of the rebuild and shouldn't be performed haphazardly. It not only provides a firsthand look at how engine components interact during typical operation and the slight tolerances between them, it also reveals just how well your engine is functioning overall.

Using your engine's operating characteristics just prior to the decision to rebuild as a guideline, you might consider more closely inspecting suspect components or those potentially related to the issue for a possible cause during disassembly. For instance, if oil consumption is an issue, check for worn valve guides or irregular piston and/or ring wear. If the engine uses coolant, check the head gaskets for signs of seepage. And if your engine routinely detonates under moderate load, check the piston crowns and combustion chambers for excessive carbon buildup.

Disassembly also provides the opportunity to gauge the level of care an engine received from its previous owners. Sludge or deposits in areas where oil typically puddles might indicate a lack of regular oil change intervals. Scored cylinder walls or scuffed piston skirts could indicate tight tolerances or careless high-speed operation. Worn main and rod bearings could indicate an oil-distribution or pressure-related issue or possibly improper machining. The list goes on.

Pulling the Engine

For this book, the owner prepared his GTO for engine removal at home by working a few hours each night for several days. Detailed pictures of the entire engine compartment were taken from every imaginable angle to use as a visual aid during reassembly. The hood was unbolted, the coolant and oil were drained, and the radiator was removed. The accessories were unbolted and moved aside, the carburetor and exhaust manifolds were removed, the engine wiring harness was disconnected, and masking tape and a permanent marker were used to note each wire's exact location.

The transmission was supported from beneath by a hydraulic jack,

This engine's external appearance doesn't lend any clue to its internal operating condition. It wasn't until complete disassembly that I gained a better understanding of why it ran so poorly. A countless number of detailed photographs like this were taken before and during teardown. Such photos can be a great asset when determining where components go during reassembly.

After deciding to completely rebuild this GTO's 400, the owner and a helper pulled the engine in the comfort of his home garage. Anything bolted to the engine that could be easily damaged or impede extraction was removed and set aside. Engine removal is different for each vehicle. It typically includes draining the coolant and oil and removing the carburetor, fuel lines, wiring, vacuum hoses, distributor cap and coil, accessory brackets and pulleys, and radiator. Some prefer to remove the transmission with the engine, but that can add several more steps and could make separating the engine and transmission more difficult while it is suspended. I recommend unbolting the transmission bellhousing from the engine, and the torque converter from the flexplate if equipped with an automatic transmission and leaving the transmission in the car. Remove the clutch countershaft from the engine or frame rail on cars equipped with a manual transmission. Unbolt the exhaust manifolds from the engine or the head pipes, whichever is easier. Then, remove the engine mount bolts. Connect a section of heavy tow chain to the cylinder heads or a carburetor flange adapter to a cherry-picker hoist. Lift the engine up and away while the helper watches closely for anything that might snag the engine during lift-out.

Before disassembly begins, remove the flexplate from the engine while it is suspended from the hoist. This prevents damaging it or the ring gear while bolting it to an engine stand. It can be difficult to apply sufficient torque to remove the bolts while the engine is hanging loose. If you have a helper who can prevent the engine from rotating by using a flywheel-holding tool, you can use a long 1/2-inch breaker and 5/8-inch socket. However, I prefer using a 1/2-inch-drive pneumatic impact wrench as opposed to hand tools for this task. Note the orientation of the flexplate in relation to the engine and place the bolts and star washer in a clearly marked bag. If the engine is equipped with a flywheel and clutch assembly, remove the pressure plate first. Watch that the clutch disk doesn't fall onto your feet as the pressure plate is pulled away! Remove the flywheel in a manner similar to removing a flexplate. Inspect the ring gear for signs of excessively worn or missing teeth. If a flywheel, inspect the clutch contact surface closely for heat cracks. While some can be removed with milling, it's sometimes easier to start with a new flywheel.

While suspended from the cherry-picker hoist, mount the engine from its bellhousing flange to a high-quality engine stand with Grade-8 hardware. To prevent it from falling over and causing significant damage to itself or anyone standing nearby, have a helper gently lower the hoist while you watch that the engine sets down easily on solid pavement. Units similar to this retail for less than $100, while used stands in good condition can be found for about half that at local swap meets or internet classifieds. A complete Pontiac engine typically weighs around 700 pounds, so you're safest using an engine stand with a capacity rating of at least 1,000 pounds.

and the torque converter, transmission bellhousing, and motor mount bolts were removed. Using a high-quality engine hoist and a length of heavy chain, the engine was lifted up and out of the vehicle while closely watching for any snagged electrical wires, additional pieces that needed to be removed, and sufficient clearance in every direction. Expect to perform a similar process if you're pulling your Pontiac's engine.

Since this 400 operated normally and didn't experience catastrophic failure, I didn't treat its disassembly different from any other. Once the engine was secured to a suitable engine stand, I worked toward the center of it. My first goal was to remove the cylinder heads, which tends to make the engine more balanced, more maneuverable, and much easier to rotate on the stand. I then focused on removing the oil pan, camshaft, and rotating assembly in that order.

Though each example in the Pontiac V-8 engine family shares common characteristics, it seems each variant contains something that's slightly different. For instance, early engines utilized a reverse-flow coolant system, and the rocker system of engines through the mid 1960s was oiled through its studs. This particular 400 contains neither, and as such, the disassembly steps shown do not touch on them. If your particular engine has one or more characteristics not covered here, I recommend that you consult a factory service manual for that portion.

Component Inspection

As the components were removed from the engine, I closely inspected each for signs of abnormal wear and photographed and noted anything that looked suspect. Each component was stored in a safe and dry location and placed in close proximity to others as it was removed to prevent losing anything. I stored small parts and hardware in clearly marked Ziploc-type bags, photographed each bag, and placed them in a dedicated box or container that remained with major components throughout the process.

I found several issues that I considered areas of great concern during component inspection, and each instance was noted for the machinist. The pistons and combustion chambers were heavily coated with carbon, indicating that the engine was not burning cleanly. At least one of the lifters was irregularly worn, and the camshaft was difficult to remove from the block. The piston skirts had some visible scuffing, and some of the connecting rod bearings were worn to the copper.

The owner and I discussed what was found in his engine and agreed that the decision to rebuild was very timely. It seems that significant damage or complete failure could have occurred at any time without much warning or indication, and that certainly would have cost him even more time, money, and aggravation. The next step was to choose a machinist whose ability was one that we were equally comfortable with to correctly rebuild this 400 and determine exactly what it needs.

Top End Removal

An engine is much more balanced and easier to maneuver when its cylinder heads are removed. That process first involves disassembling the engine's top end components.

1 Drain Remaining Fluid

Though the fluids were drained before removing the engine from the vehicle, a certain amount inevitably remains in its internal passageways. Just before beginning disassembly, remove the oil filter (if still installed) and the oil filter housing bolts (using a 9/16-inch wrench), and drain the remaining coolant from the water jacket surrounding each cylinder bank by removing the drain plug on both sides. The type of wrench required to remove the drain plugs varies. Drain the oil pan in a similar manner with an 11/16-inch wrench.

2 Remove Valve Covers

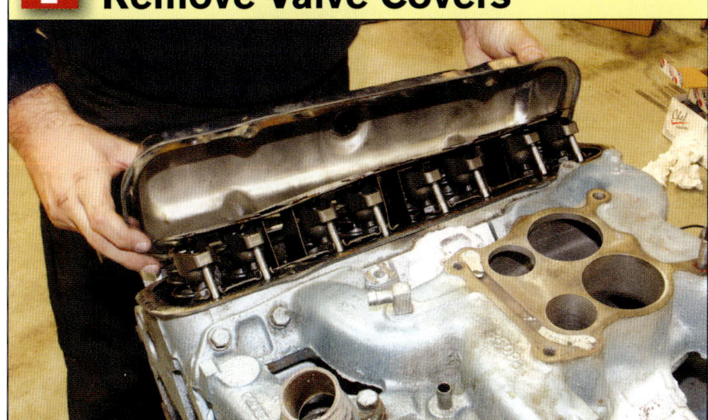

Remove the valve cover bolts with a 7/16-inch socket. Lift the valve covers. Place units with a chrome-plated finish into a cloth or in a safe location where they cannot be scratched or damaged. Place the bolts and wire-harness retainers into a clearly marked bag.

Important! 

3 Remove Coolant Bypass Bolt

Pontiac intake manifolds are sealed to the timing cover and use a rubber O-ring and a long bolt. The intake is used as a bypass to circulate coolant throughout the engine while the thermostat is closed during warm-up. Remove the bypass bolt with a long 7/16-inch box-end wrench for maximum leverage. Rust and corrosion can make the bolt difficult to remove. To avoid possibly breaking it, exercise patience during the process.

4 Remove Intake Manifold Bolts

Remove the 10 bolts that secure the intake manifold to the cylinder heads with a 9/16-inch wrench and place them in a clearly marked bag. Many later engines use studded bolts on either side of the water crossover that serve to secure various accessory brackets. This 400 didn't use any.

5 Remove Intake Manifold

Use a pry bar to separate the intake manifold from the cylinder heads. Lift the intake manifold up and away from the engine. A typical cast-iron Pontiac intake manifold weighs at least 40 pounds, so be sure to have a firm grip on it during removal.

6 Remove Valley Pan

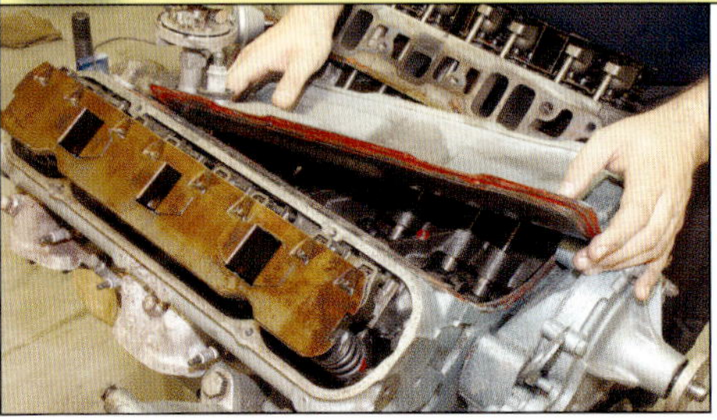

Remove the two bolts that secure the valley pan to the block with a 9/16-inch socket, and then walk a pry bar around the perimeter of the valley pan. Gentle pressure may be required to break the silicone seal bond. Use care to prevent bending the pan's thin lip because that could impede its ability to seal if it is reused during reassembly.

7 Remove Distributor

Remove the distributor cap and external coil of a points-type system before removing the engine from the car. Remove the single bolt securing the distributor hold-down with a 9/16-inch socket. The bolt and hold-down are placed in a clearly marked bag. Lift the distributor up and out of the block. Rotate the distributor housing while lifting it; this can make removal a bit easier.

How to Remove a Stubborn Distributor

Distributor removal should be as easy as grasping the housing and gently lifting it upward and out of the block. But years of sludge buildup around the base can make the process much more difficult and make extraction seem practically impossible.

Some hobbyists have tried prying, twisting, or hammering on the distributor housing, only to find that it's bound in the block even more than before. Or worse, it's inflicted major damage to the distributor itself. There's a very simple solution that can remove much of the frustration surrounding a stuck distributor, and it includes a $2 can of brake component cleaner and some patience.

This trick isn't limited to an engine that's on a stand; it can be performed in the same manner on an engine that's still in the vehicle. Just remember to change the engine oil to remove any contaminants before starting the engine. ■

Brake component cleaner is a powerful solvent, and a can of it is useful when removing a distributor that's stuck in a block. Instead of prying on the distributor housing and risking damage, simply lift the distributor out of the block as far as reasonably possible and spray a liberal amount of brake component cleaner around the base. Wait a few minutes for it to soak in, push the distributor back into the block, and try removing it again. It may take a few attempts and a few applications of brake component cleaner, but persistence and patience pays off. The distributor eventually comes out and can be cleaned up appropriately.

Valvetrain Disassembly

1 Remove Oil Dripper

Most production Pontiac V-8s produced through the early 1970s used a bolt-on oil dripper to lubricate the rocker arms, while a version that was welded on to the valve covers was used later on. The bolt-on type is fastened to the studded head bolts and is commonly discarded or forgotten during rebuilds that lack attention to small details. Remove the retaining nuts with a 9/16-inch socket.

Aftermarket Rocker Arms

Pontiac developed the stamped steel rocker arm assembly for the new V-8 it introduced in 1955. Comp Cams produced these roller-tip rocker arms, which were a popular upgrade during the 1990s. The roller tip is intended to reduce the side loading that causes valve guide wear. The roller tip rocker otherwise installs and functions just like an original.

2 Remove Rocker Arms

Remove the nut securing the rocker arm pivot ball with a 5/8-inch socket. Inspect the contact surfaces of each rocker arm and pivot ball for pitting or galling. Because the rocker arm and pivot ball wear in together and self-adjust to each other, it's best to keep each pair united to prevent potential issues during future use. Like all pieces of the valvetrain, I prefer to keep the rocker arm assemblies in sequential order for inspection purposes.

Professional Mechanic Tip

Valvetrain Organizer

PRO TIP

A valvetrain organizer, such as this from Comp Cams, is an excellent way to maintain the order of the valvetrain components for each cylinder during disassembly. It allows for complete inspection of each complementing component after the entire valvetrain has been removed. The high-quality plastic tray is impervious to oil and solvents and cleans up easily.

3 Remove Pushrods and Lifters

Remove the pushrods and organize them in sequential order. Then remove and organize the lifters in a similar fashion. Two hands are required for removal, so use one to push the lifter upward and the other to lift it from the bore. Quickly inspect each lifter face for immediate signs of abnormal wear, such as grooving, pitting, or cracking. Organize them in a manner so each lifter can be inspected closely along with its corresponding lobe when the camshaft is removed.

4 Remove Cylinder Head Bolts

The 10 bolts securing the cylinder heads were likely torqued in a specific pattern during assembly. It generally includes working in a spiral pattern outward from the center bolt. A spiral pattern is not necessary for bolt removal during disassembly. I tend to pick an outside bolt, unloosening each as I work toward the center in a spiral pattern. The head bolts are very tight. I use a long 1/2-inch-drive breaker bar for maximum leverage and I squarely seat a quality 3/4-inch socket against the cylinder head to prevent rounding the edges. Some bolts on this 400 required noticeably less effort to remove than others, which possibly indicates improper torque during install or a head gasket that didn't crush evenly. I recommend loosely reinstalling one or two head bolts. It keeps the cylinder head from falling off the block during the next step.

5 Remove Cylinder Heads

Dowel pins locate the cylinder heads on the block. In most cases, you need to use a forceful upward tug to break the cylinder head free from any sealing compounds or corrosion. Place a pry bar into an intake port and smoothly apply pressure until the cylinder head pops up against the two remaining head bolts. If the cylinder head does not move after a fair amount of prying force has been applied, stop prying! Closely inspect for any hidden head bolts that may still be installed. Once the cylinder head is loose, remove the remaining head bolts and inventory them all, and lift the head up and away from the engine. I prefer grabbing the loose cylinder head near its exhaust ports and lifting it toward the center of the block, where I can carefully slide my fingers beneath and grasp it firmly. Fully assembled iron cylinder heads weigh nearly 60 pounds each, so be prepared. It can inflict damage and serious pain if dropped on your feet.

6 Inspect Cylinders

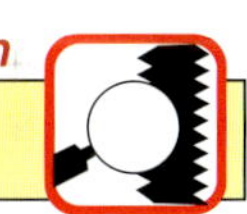

Visually inspect the pistons and cylinder walls to gain an insight on the engine's over-all operating condition. The dish found on these pistons reveals that the engine's static compression ratio was much lower than its original rating of 10.25:1. The heavy deposits indicate that oil was entering the combustion chamber and that irregular combustion was occurring. The cylinder walls have a defined ridge at top but otherwise look fine.

7 Inspect Block and Head Gasket

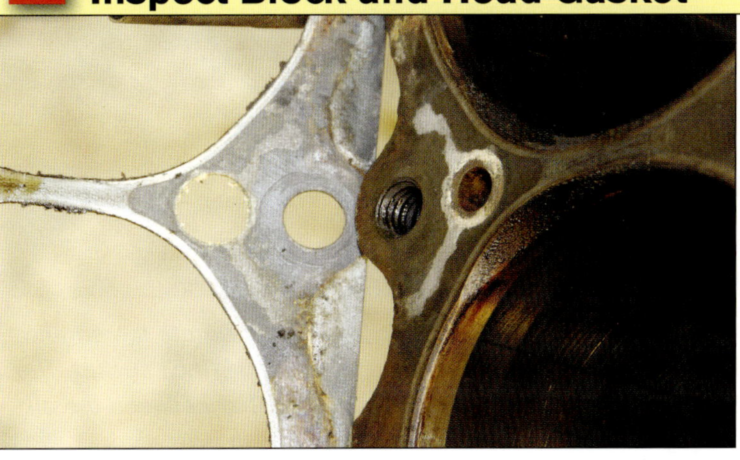

Closely inspect the block deck and head gaskets for any signs of coolant and cylinder pressure seepage. If seepage is identified, there could be an underlying issue. If the head gaskets are in good condition, they can be reused if you're on an extremely tight budget, but I strongly recommend using new, high-quality gaskets because a well-sealed head is essential. In this case, the coolant found leaking outward around this cylinder head bolt has clearly ruined this gasket. The leak was likely the result of an under-torqued head bolt, and we found several during cylinder head removal. Soot trails found between cylinders are further indication that the head bolts were not properly torqued.

Camshaft Removal

1 Remove Harmonic Balancer

Unbolt the water and fuel pumps, and remove the lower pulley from the harmonic balancer with 1/2-inch and 9/16-inch sockets. Inventory and set aside the hardware and accessories. You now have clear access to the harmonic balancer bolt, which should be extremely tight. I prefer a pneumatic impact wrench if compressed air is available. A very long 1/2-inch-drive breaker bar and a 15/16-inch socket can be used to remove the bolt, but crankshaft rotation must be prevented. Thread a long, hardened steel 1/2-inch x 20 stud into a flywheel bolt hole on the flywheel register. The stud locks the crankshaft when it contacts the engine stand so the balancer bolt can be removed.

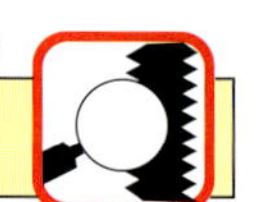

2 Inspect the Harmonic Balancer

On a Pontiac V-8, the harmonic balancer is used to damp harmonic vibrations, and not necessarily balance the front end of the crankshaft as its name suggests. Pontiac actually corrected its name in later years, referring to it as a "harmonic damper" in factory literature. It is designed to be an integral part of the crankshaft, is located on the front snout by a large keyway, and is secured to the crankshaft by a bolt torqued to 160 ft-lbs. A common cause of harmonic balancer failure is improper bolt torque. That allows the balancer to shimmy on the keyway, which causes it to crack. If not caught quickly, it can cause the balancer to separate at speed or complete crankshaft failure. The harmonic balancer should be replaced if there is any sign of fatigue.

3 Remove Oil Pan

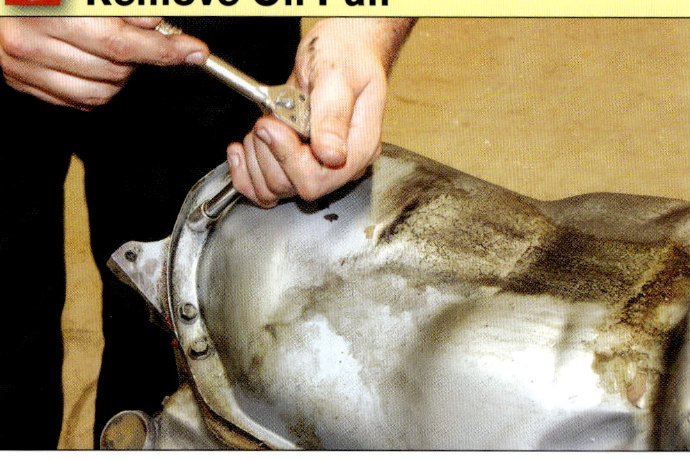

After the cylinder heads have been removed, an engine is much easier to rotate on an engine stand. Rotate the engine 180 degrees and remove the 18 bolts that secure the oil pan to the block and timing cover with a 7/16-inch socket. The oil pan should lift up and away, but it is usually bonded to the block with RTV sealer. Position a pry bar between the oil pan lip and the block rail. Apply gentle pressure and walk the pry bar around the pan until the oil pan is free.

4 — Remove Timing Cover

Rotate the engine 180 degrees, returning it to right side up. Remove the two bolts and two nuts that secure the timing cover to the block with a 9/16-inch socket and inventory the parts. RTV sealer is often used to prevent leaks during rebuilds, and it was clearly used in this instance. Persuasion with a rubber mallet and pry bar is sometimes required to break the sealant's bond on the timing cover.

5 — Remove Timing Gear Set

Remove the fuel pump eccentric retaining bolt with a 3/4-inch socket, and then set it aside for later use. Walk the cam gear off of the camshaft snout with a pry bar. The crankshaft gear should slide off but could also require some gentle prying. Inspect the entire timing set for signs of abnormal wear, such as excessive chain stretch or worn gear teeth. None were found here.

6 — Remove Camshaft

Remove the camshaft thrust plate with a 1/2-inch socket. Inventory the bolts and inspect the thrust plate for abnormal wear. If you don't have a camshaft installation tool available, thread the fuel pump eccentric bolt back into the camshaft snout. It serves as something to grasp while pulling the camshaft outward from the engine. Position the camshaft far enough out so it can be firmly grabbed with one hand. The rear journal can be supported with the other hand and the cam guided through the bearings.

Critical Inspection, Documentation Required

7 — Inspect Camshaft and Lifters

Some of the valuable anti-wear additives have been removed from modern-spec oil, and it can negatively affect flat-tappet camshaft life. Even though this camshaft showed no signs of lobe failure, the lifters tell a different story. A flat-tappet camshaft lobe is designed to rotate its lifter during normal operation, and the lifter face should gain a distinct polishing pattern immediately after the break-in process. The unit on the left is an excellent example of ideal lifter condition after long periods of normal operation. The lifter at right never rotated and complete failure was in the very near future. It's possible that this resulted from incorrect camshaft lobe finishing, improper camshaft break-in, or tight lifter-to-bore tolerances. It's something that must be noted and communicated to the machinist.

Labeling the Connecting Rods

The connecting rod assembly is a precisely machined component. Its main body and cap are precision-fit pieces that aren't intended to interchange without additional machining. It's advisable that each rod and cap be marked during disassembly so the two can be reunited and orientated correctly during the machining process.

This practice wasn't typically performed at the factory, so if your engine hasn't been previously rebuilt, the connecting rods likely have no marks on them. If you find your rods lack any identifiable characteristics during disassembly, it can be performed with a steel stamp set, an engraving pencil, or even a permanent marker. Perfection isn't required while stamping; the machinist is likely to remove or replace these marks during the machining process anyway. ■

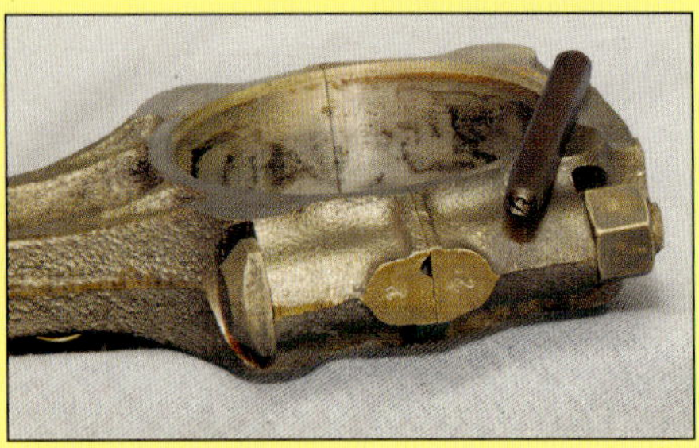

Identifying each connecting rod and its corresponding cap during disassembly ensures that the matched pair remains together during the machining process. It's good practice even if the set is not reused. A steel stamp set, like this, can be used to mark each pair with a different number for quick identification.

The steel stamp is firmly whacked with a dead-blow hammer, leaving behind a numeric indentation. Since the rods are to be machined, it isn't important to note which rod is from which cylinder. I prefer to mark them in that fashion, however, which gives me the ability to inspect for collateral damage if an issue is found later. Remember, the number-1 cylinder is on the driver's side, and number-2 is actually ahead of it because of cylinder offset. So if you're using a similar method, your rods should be marked 2-1-4-3-6-5-8-7 from front to rear.

Someone used a center punch on the balance pad of each rod to note its cylinder position during a previous rebuild. This is required to pair certain rods on a crankshaft journal to maintain proper connecting-rod side clearance and proper piston-to-rod orientation during assembly. It doesn't necessarily take the place of marking the rod and cap in your preferred manner, however, but can be considered another form of identification.

Bottom End Disassembly

1 Remove Oil Pump and Driveshaft

Pontiac used at least three different oil pumps for its V-8 engines, and they're typically categorized by approximate pressure ratings. The oil pump is secured to the block by two bolts and is driven by an intermediate shaft captured between the distributor and oil pump. There is a loop cast into the block and two tabs are pinched near the top of the driveshaft so the driveshaft does not disengage from the oil pump tang during distributor removal. The oil pump bolts are removed with a 9/16-inch socket, and the driveshaft simply lifts up and out once the oil pump is removed.

2 Remove Oil Pan Baffle

Many Pontiac V-8s were equipped with an oil pan baffle secured to the number-2 and -4 main caps. Also referred to as a windage tray, it combats oil aeration during high-speed operation and also captures the lower oil dipstick tube. Remove the windage tray retaining bolts with a 1/2-inch socket and then inventory them. After it has been removed, then lift and remove the tray. Inventory the lower dipstick tube parts and other small parts.

3 Remove Connecting Rod Caps

Important!

 *Address each connecting rod separately. Use a long 1/2-inch-drive breaker bar and a 9/16-inch socket to back off several threads on the nuts. The nuts are not totally removed at this time, however. They are used to keep the rod and cap together while separating the two. It may take several gentle smacks from a soft-face hammer on the side of the connecting rod to separate them. Another method is to tap downward on the nuts, which drives the connecting rod away from the cap. After the cap is loose, the nuts are completely removed and the cap and bearing are removed, inventoried, and set aside. Because the connecting rod and cap is a matched pair, however, the two are reunited immediately and the nuts loosely reinstalled after removing the piston-and-rod assembly from the block.*

Important!

4 Remove Pistons

Position a long wooden handle under the piston crown and drive the piston toward the top of the cylinder bore and into an awaiting hand. Use caution when catching the piston-and-rod assembly! It can be difficult to hold because the connecting rod swings free under its own weight after pulling it from the bore. A helper may be required if an excessive buildup has created a ridge at the top of the cylinders. The ridge can cause the pistons to bind up in the bore during removal. If the pistons cannot be easily removed, use a specialty tool, called a ridge reamer, to remove the ridge close to the deck. This should allow the pistons to pass through the bores. If your rebuild includes new pistons, you can also use a hammer to tap on the wooden handle, forcing the piston outward and into a helper's hands. The connecting rod cap is immediately reunited with the connecting rod.

Machinist Tip Number 1

Cam bearing removal requires a special tool, and removing these bearings in any other manner can be difficult and possibly damaging. Our local machinist suggests that this be left to a professional possessing the proper equipment. He's seen several blocks with cam journal bores that were dinged or damaged by owners attempting to remove cam bearings with a normal punch or irregular object.

It also allows the machinist to inspect for abnormal bearing wear, which might indicate some type of alignment issue with the cam bore. Our machinist's experienced eye saw something in two consecutive bearings that attracted his attention. The bearings seem to show some irregularity at the number-3 and -4 journals, which is addressed during machining. It might have otherwise gone unnoticed if we had removed them at home. ∎

A cam bearing removal tool typically consists of a stepped collar mounted onto an arbor. The bearing is driven from its bore as the arbor is tapped with a dead-blow hammer. Though any number of methods for cam bearing removal may exist, using proper equipment, like this, is the best way to keep from damaging the block.

Critical Inspection, Documentation Required

5 Inspect Rod Bearings

The condition of an engine's bearings usually tells of its general operating condition. These rod bearings are something no owner wants to find. The lower rod bearings (left) show above-average wear, while the upper rod bearings (right) are clearly worn to the copper. Engines with this wear pattern have typically experienced significant detonation. Each of the eight upper and lower bearings showed the same level of wear. It's very possible that this 400 was on the verge of significant failure.

Critical Inspection

6 Inspect Pistons

The pistons appear to be forged-aluminum Sealed Power replacements with a dish cut into the crown to reduce compression. The amount of carbon built up in and around the dish further indicates that some type of irregular combustion had occurred. The scuffing on the piston skirts appears to be mostly cosmetic and may have possibly occurred when coolant temperature was too high to maintain sufficient skirt lubrication.

7 Remove Main Caps

Important!

Large bolts retain and dowel pins locate the main caps of a Pontiac V-8. The main cap bolts are very tight, and the bolts of the first four caps are removed with a long 1/2-inch-drive breaker bar and 3/4-inch socket, while the last main cap bolts are removed with a 15/16-inch socket. Remove the main cap bolts and place them into a clearly marked bag. The tight fit of the dowel can make main cap removal impossible without a bit of persuasion. The main cap is alternately tapped on its sides with a soft-faced hammer to walk it off the dowel pins while carefully pulling the cap upward. Once free, the cap and bearing are set aside for inspection.

8 Main Cap Identification

Professional Mechanic Tip

Pontiac cast sequential numbers into the first four main caps for identification purposes, so there wasn't a need to label them like we did the connecting rods. The number-5 main cap is visually different than the others and subsequently does not interchange, so there's no real way of mistaking its identity with any other.

9 Remove Crankshaft

Important!

With the main caps removed, firmly grasp the crankshaft by its front snout and flywheel register, and lift it up and out of the block. Set it aside for inspection. The crankshaft is extremely heavy and quite slick; handle it with extreme care. Dropping it on the ground could inflict irreparable damage to it or you!

10 Inspect Rear Main Seal

Critical Inspection

The owner complained of a significant oil leak coming from the rear of the engine, and this explains why. This replacement rope-type rear main seal had spun shortly after the last rebuild had been completed because it had likely been improperly installed. It was either not packed into the groove correctly or not lubricated sufficiently for initial start-up. As a result, its functional ability had been severely compromised. The seal was simply pried out of the block and rear main cap using a screwdriver until it could be removed by hand.

11 Remove Main Bearings

After the crankshaft has been removed, it's common to find the upper main bearings still in the block main saddles. To remove the main bearings, push on the end opposite of the bearing tang, and rotate each by hand until there is enough of it exposed to grab it and lift it out. A flathead screwdriver can also be used to persuade stubborn bearings.

Critical Inspection

12 Inspect Main Bearings

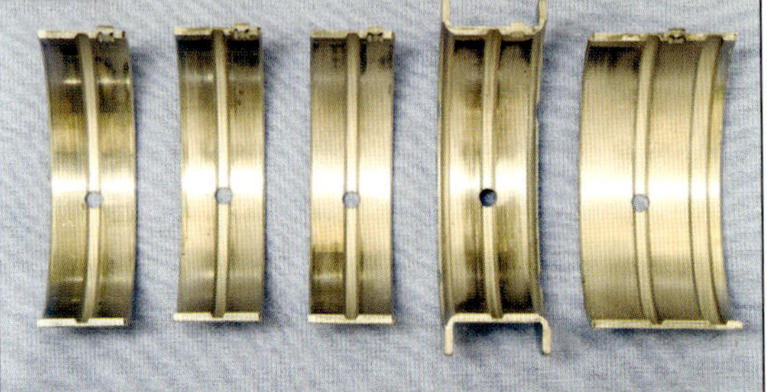

The main bearings of this 400 showed no real wear, which indicates ideal tolerances between the crankshaft and block. Consistent copper could reveal an oil supply issue, while scoring may indicate that some type of debris had once circulated throughout the oiling system.

Critical Inspection

13 Inspect Crankshaft Journals

The main bearings show no signs of any pending issue, and the crankshaft main journals appear to be in excellent condition. Though the upper rod bearings showed significant wear, we didn't find any sign of complete bearing failure, so we didn't expect there to be any significant crankshaft rod journal damage. The machinist inspects for deep scores or scratches and measures for journal irregularities to determine if any journal grinding is required.

Cylinder Head Disassembly

1 Loosen Valve Locks

With a cylinder head on the workbench, threaded rocker studs are removed with an 11/16-inch socket. Inventory and set aside the studs and guide plates. Place a large socket onto the retainer and each valve spring, and give it a forceful jolt with a hammer to loosen the retainer and locks. This should make valve spring removal easier.

2 Remove Valve Springs

The cylinder head has been fastened to a homemade cylinder head stand for convenience, but one isn't required for cylinder head disassembly. Use a high-quality valve spring compressor to compress a valve spring, and use a magnet to remove the locks. Once decompressed, the retainer, valve spring, and any seat shim beneath are lifted away. The entire assembly is inspected for abnormal wear.

3 Inspect Valve Springs

Pontiac originally used a dual valve spring package (left) on its V-8 engines. The single-spring package found on this 400 (right) was a popular stock-replacement that Crane Cams sold in the 1990s. Inspect the valve guide area and the condition of spring shims. In this case, nothing kept Crane's single-spring replacement from dancing about the guide. And the pronounced wear found on several of this 400's spring shims clearly indicates significant valvetrain instability. It corroborates the owner's report of a valve float condition at high RPM and is likely the cause behind a number of hobbyist reports of broken coils over the years. Dual springs are an excellent option with a rebuild. In addition to better pressure control, dual springs maintain the spring's position around the guide.

Machinist Tip Number 2

The coolant system and oil gallery passages left exposed after casting or machining were sealed at the factory with metal plugs. Some were press-fit while others were threaded. Any high-quality rebuild includes removing all of them to flush the entire block of any contaminants that might've accumulated behind them over the years. Failing to do so could result in significant bearing damage if any of the material dislodges and passes throughout your fresh engine.

While the pressed plugs are easily removed, the threaded plugs can sometimes be downright difficult to remove. If you don't have access to the correct equipment, or any of them resists reasonable efforts, it might be best to leave plug removal to an experienced professional. Distorting the center of a threaded plug or losing a pressed plug inside the block simply creates more work, and that can be reflected in the labor portion of your bill. ■

You can easily remove the pressed plugs sealing the coolant system by tapping them inward by using a punch and then prying them out. After the threaded oil plugs have been removed at the rear, a long rod is inserted into the block and used to drive out the pressed plugs at the front of the block that seal the oil gallery. Plug removal isn't too difficult, but you can always leave it for your machinist if you have any reservations.

Three threaded plugs seal the oiling system at the rear of the block. They require oddly sized square-key or hex-head sockets and can sometimes be difficult to remove. If you don't have the proper equipment, it's best to let your machinist remove them. An unsuccessful attempt by you can make more work for your machinist later, costing you extra money spent on labor.

4 Remove Valves

While removing the valves from a cylinder head, each valve was pulled out slightly and shifted in every direction to assess the condition of its valve guide. If there's more than a slight amount of free play, it's likely that the valve guide is excessively worn and needs to be replaced. Your machinist uses a valve guide dial bore gauge to accurately measure the valve guide and determine if that action is required, however.

5 Inspect Combustion Chambers

Critical Inspection

A visual inspection of the combustion chamber and valve seats is performed after the cylinder head is completely disassembled. Inspect for burn pattern consistency within the combustion chambers and for irregular valve seat wear or pitting. If seat wear isn't concentric, it might indicate excessive spring pressure, unhardened valve seats, a machining error during the last valve job, or even a bent valve. Nothing of any immediate concern was found on these cylinder heads.

6 Inspect Valves

The valves are visually inspected in a similar fashion. The stems are checked for signs of irregular wear and gummy deposits, which could indicate leaky valve guides. Each valve stem is checked for straightness. Unworn portions of the stem are measured against areas that are in direct contact with the guide to determine if any stem wear is present. The seat angles are also checked for inconsistent wear, which may reveal an underlying issue. These valves are high-quality aftermarket units installed during a previous rebuild. They look very normal and are likely reusable, but the machinist has the final say.

Professional Mechanic Tip

Cylinder Head Organizer

A cylinder head organizing tray like this from Comp Cams makes cylinder head disassembly much easier. It includes cups for practically everything that's removed, and the components can be positioned to maintain consistent order for disassembly and inspection purposes. It is a worthwhile investment that can help keep your workbench organized.

FACTORY PARTS

The Pontiac V-8 block is constructed of cast iron, and though its displacement increased from 287 to 455 ci by enlarging the bore and lengthening the stroke over the years, the external dimensions didn't waiver far from the original design. A number of changes occurred during the course of its production run, however, and some limit component interchangeability. Included among them are revised engine mounting points and differences in the transmission bellhousing bolt pattern, starter location, main bearing diameter, and cooling system.

The basic block features a relatively tall deck height of 10.24 inches, which is measured from the crankshaft centerline to the deck. The deck surface is very thick and rigid. Cylinder head bolt holes are drilled and tapped through the deck surface and into individual bosses within the water jacket walls. Unlike many other makes, traditional Pontiac V-8 bolt holes do not extend into the water jacket, so no thread sealer is required during installation. The 301 (and 265 variant) is the only exception.

The symmetrical 90-degree design features large main bearing saddles, which adds overall rigidity and allows for using long connecting rods for good rod-to-stroke ratio. The main bearing caps are fastened to the block by two large bolts in most cases and by four bolts in certain high-performance applications. In either instance, the main caps are located by dowel pins, which are intended

The block casting number contains several digits and, depending on the year, is sometimes found on the passenger's side of the block or at the rear of the block on a ledge near the number-8 cylinder. This 9790079 block is a 1968–1969 350 casting. Depending on the application, Pontiac sometimes ground off several or all of these numbers and stamped others into place.

The block's casting date is generally located on the distributor pad, and "L186" found on this unit translates to December 18, 1966 (L = Dec, 18 = 18th day, 6 = last digit of 1966). The block casting number is also found in this area on most 1964–1967 castings. The visible digits in this example are what remain of the original "9786133" after machining. It indicates that this block is a 1967 400.

Pontiac blocks featured two freeze plugs per side through 1966. Another was added in 1967, bringing the total to three. This is a quick and easy way to narrow down the vintage of a particular block when hunting for possible options at salvage yards or swap meets.

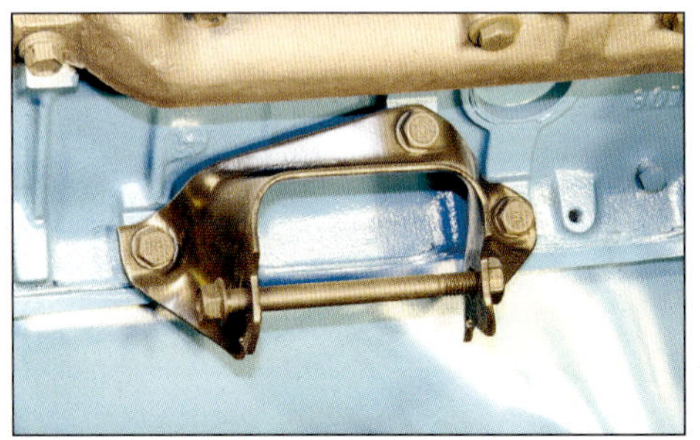

The motor mounts were moved to the side of the block in 1959, where they remained throughout the duration of Pontiac V-8 production. Some blocks contain two, three, or five motor-mount bosses, depending on the year and chassis application. In some instances, they are not drilled and tapped. Most quality Pontiac engine builders and restoration parts suppliers offer adapter kits if one is required.

To identify the block, the 2-digit engine code, "XU" in this instance, denotes its original application. It is located on the front of the block, just below deck surface of the passenger's side. The six- or seven-digit numeric stamp just above it is the engine serial number (ESN), which is the engine's sequential build number. It does not directly correlate to the vehicle identification number (VIN) of the vehicle in which it was originally installed.

to prevent the caps from wandering during high-speed operation.

When searching for a block to use in a project, one from the model year of the vehicle is ideal since the engine and transmission mounts should correspond with those of the chassis. If that's of no real concern, then any 1965 to 1979 block generally makes a suitable choice since these engines are the most supported by OEM and aftermarket parts suppliers. The engine mounts may be different for certain years, but most engine builders and restoration parts suppliers offer specific adapter kits for such situations.

Oiling System

The oil pan is on the same plane as the crankshaft, and it contains a large sump at the rear. Oil drawn from the sump is pressurized by the oil pump and filtered before being dispersed throughout the engine. Oil travels across the rear of the block to a gallery that runs adjacent to the crankshaft on the left side. It feeds the camshaft, crankshaft, and left-side lifter bores as it travels toward the front of the block. It then crosses to the right side, feeding those lifter bores.

The Pontiac V-8 oil pump is a rotary gear–type that's driven by the distributor shaft. Pressure is regulated by a spring-loaded check valve, and the pickup contains a mesh screen that filters out debris that could damage the gears or keep the check valve from properly seating. Pontiac generally used oil pumps capable of generating a maximum pressure of 40 or 60 pounds per square inch (psi), depending upon the application. The SD-455 used a specific 80-psi unit.

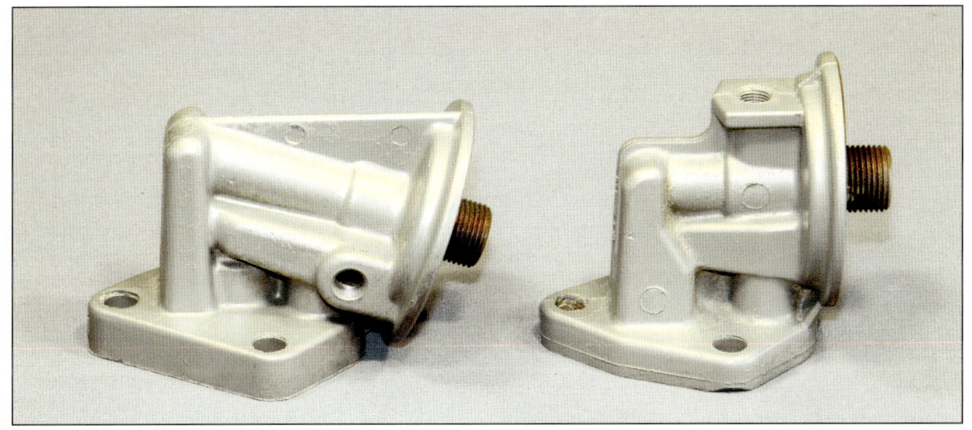

The Pontiac V-8 uses a bolt-on oil filter adapter, and the type most hobbyists are familiar with comes in two distinct variations. One places the filter at about a 70-degree angle from the block (left), while the other places the filter at a 90-degree angle. The original application depends on the type used to assemble a particular Pontiac. The 75-degree unit seems to be the most common and tends to provide the best exhaust system and chassis clearance.

A relatively large filter is used to keep the oil as clean as possible. It mounts to a cast-aluminum adapter that's bolted to the right side of the block toward the rear. Depending upon the model year and application, a small variety of oil filter adapters were used throughout the course of V-8 production. It's best to use the filter and adapter that was originally installed on your engine, unless a suitable replacement is available.

Crankshafts

The stock Pontiac crankshaft is a durable and well-balanced unit. It features large counterweights and relatively large 2.25-inch-diameter connecting-rod journals. As stroke was added to increase displacement, main bearing diameter was increased to maintain sufficient crank pin overlap for adequate strength.

Crankshafts produced through 1958 were steel forgings, while castings were used exclusively in later years. Because of main journal diameter differences, the early production forged-steel units do not directly interchange with later units without significant modification. The heat-treated steel forgings used in specific high-performance applications during the late 1950s and early 1960s

Pontiac placed displacement callouts on each side of the block in 1968 and cast the last two digits of the displacement size into the center of the lifter valley. The "00" found on this block indicates that it's a 400. Other examples include "50" or "55," which indicate a 350 or 455, respectively. These features allow quick and easy determination of displacement.

are some of the strongest crankshafts Pontiac ever produced and fit later blocks but are quite rare.

The first production cast crankshafts, which appeared in the late 1950s, were constructed of a material referred to in Pontiac literature as ArmaSteel. ArmaSteel is a GM trade name for its Pearlitic Malleable Iron (PMI) alloy, which possesses some strength qualities similar to certain steels. The crankshafts were constructed of cast-nodular iron in later years. ArmaSteel cranks can be identified by the ArmaSteel name cast in them, while a large "N" was

often used to signify nodular-iron composition in later years. A crankshaft of either type is quite durable and completely adequate for regular production engines and even high-performance applications.

In most instances, the cast crankshafts directly interchange if the main bearing diameter is the same. Depending upon the original application, there are slight differences in the length of the front snout, diameter of the rear flywheel register, and counterweight shapes. So, if at all possible, comparing a potential replacement to the original is highly suggested.

The 500557 Block

During the mid 1970s, Pontiac was seeking ways it could lighten its vehicles. This not only increased fuel economy, but each pound removed put a vehicle one step closer to the next lowest weight bracket, which translated into different EPA standards. In addition to body and chassis modifications, the engine was thoroughly inspected for areas that material could be removed without compromising integrity.

Pontiac introduced a new block casting during the 1975 model year to replace 481988. Number-500557 was designed with less material in certain areas to reduce weight. That feature makes it slightly weaker when compared to its former counterpart. But it's plenty strong for a street-driven Pontiac making around 400 hp.

Dowel pins are typically used to prevent the Pontiac V-8 main caps from wandering at high engine speed. Solid pins exert stress on the thin main saddles of the 500557 block, and they became susceptible to failure in certain applications. Hollow roll pins replaced the solid dowels in September 1976 on the 1977 T/A 6.6 engine only.

The combination of low compression, a mild camshaft, an exhaust catalyst, an automatic transmission with a low full-throttle upshift speed, and a high-ratio rear axle meant that engines wouldn't likely be subjected to high-speed operation. The block no longer needed much of the extra material that was originally included to maximize rigidity.

In mid 1975, Pontiac released a new 400 block that was externally identical to the preceding 481988 casting but was internally different. The new 500557 casting had cylinder wall thickness reduced to as little as 0.125 inch in some areas, and the main saddle and oil pan rail areas were thinned considerably. Though slightly weaker than a 481988, the 500557 was completely adequate for normal production vehicles, and was used through 1977 in all 400 applications, including the 200-hp T/A 6.6.

Concerns arose that the traditional main cap dowel pins exerted too much pressure on the main saddles at high engine speed and could cause block failure. In September 1976, Pontiac began using sprung roll pins in place of the solid dowel pins in all T/A 6.6 engines. As T/A 6.6 output increased to 220 hp for 1978, the 481988 casting was revived for that application only. All other 400 applications used the 500557 casting that year.

The reintroduced 481988 block was identical to the former and the main caps again used solid dowel pins. Most likely for easy assembly line identification, a large

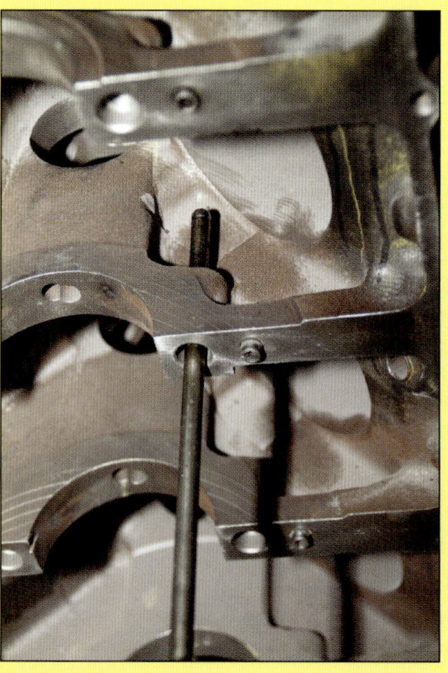

In an attempt to lighten the casting, material was removed from the cylinder walls, oil pan rail, and main saddle area. One characteristic of the new casting is that the main-cap bolt holes actually break through the main saddles. A common push-rod is used in this photograph for illustration purposes.

The 500557 Block *(Continued)*

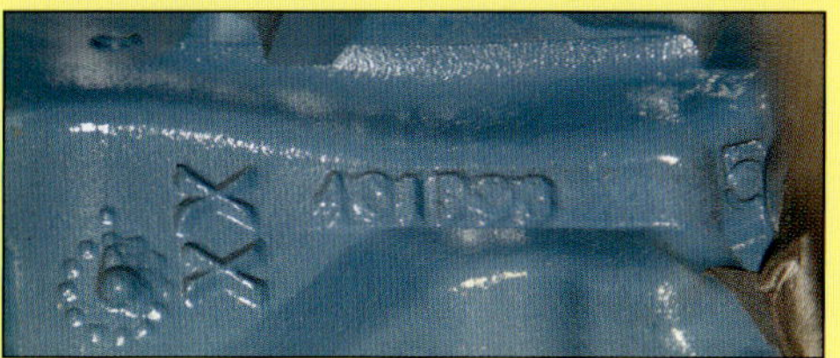

The beefier 481988 returned in 1978 for T/A 6.6 applications only. A large "XX" was added to the block, and it's a unique characteristic that makes identifying this block easier than using the casting number, which can sometimes be difficult to read, as proven with this example. The "XX-481988" block is an excellent foundation for a performance rebuild.

"XX" was cast into the block in several locations. The "XX" is found near the casting number, in the lifter valley, and on each water jacket. The "XX-481988," as it is generally referred to, was used for the 1979 T/A 6.6 as well.

Pontiac sold tens of thousands of 400-powered cars in the 1970s, and there are countless used 400s on the market today. The 500557 block should be adequate for a power level up to and possible slightly above 400 hp. If your rebuild includes output levels that might exceed that amount, then it may be best to begin with another 400 casting, such as any earlier unit or the XX-481988. ∎

Connecting Rods

A connecting rod is one of most highly stressed components within an engine. The inertial force placed upon it during normal operation requires that it be constructed of a sturdy material that's elastic enough to not fatigue during normal operation. Steel forgings are tough, but the process is somewhat expensive. The rod must be properly heat treated to be able to withstand the additional force associated with greater power amounts or high engine speeds, which makes it even more costly.

Pontiac introduced its common cast connecting rod in 1963 for 389 applications. The ArmaSteel unit was then used in all production engines from 1967 through 1979. It's an excellent piece that is quite reliable when operated within its intended limit. Adding modern fasteners and proper preparation is an easy way to increase its durability during any rebuild.

Cast connecting rods are much cheaper to produce. Cast iron is generally very strong up to its elastic point but tends to shatter once surpassed. Pontiac constructed its cast rods of ArmaSteel, a specific iron desirable for its steel-like strength qualities. If an engine is operated within its intended limit, a properly designed cast connecting rod should provide a long service life in a given application, which makes it ideal for typical production engines.

Pontiac's basic I-beam connecting rod was introduced in 1955. The block's tall deck height allows the use of a relatively long connecting rod with a center-to-center length of 6.625 inches, which produces a good rod-to-stroke ratio. This tends to lessen the amount of side loading placed on the cylinder wall, reducing cylinder wear and overall operational friction.

Though a low-grade steel forging, Pontiac's 1955 connecting rod is completely adequate for its intended application of stock street performance, but the lack of heat treating limits its strength for high-performance applications. A floating-piston wrist pin, which consists of a slip-fit wrist pin retained in

the piston by snap rings on either end, was used through 1957. The pin was pressed into a fixed position beginning in 1958. Forged-steel connecting rods were used in all applications through 1962 and in select 421 applications through 1966.

The Super Duty engines of the era used a moderate-grade steel forging that was heat treated to various standards, producing a noticeably stronger piece. These are quite rare today. The most common Pontiac connecting rod that hobbyists are familiar with is the cast unit introduced in 1963 for 389 applications. It was used in all production Pontiac V-8s from 1967 through 1979, except for the SD-455.

Pontiac developed a beautiful forged-steel connecting rod for the 1973 Super Duty 455. Retaining the stock 6.625-inch length, the quality steel forging was heat treated and blasted with metal shot to improve strength while being magnetic-particle inspected for minute cracks several times during the manufacturing process. The SD-455 rod is an excellent piece that was the best available option for several years, and the price reflected it.

The 1973–1974 Super Duty 455 received a beautiful forged steel connecting rod, which was a direct replacement for the cast unit. When hobbyists learned of its availability, orders poured into dealership parts departments. By mid-year 1974, more than 1,350 orders for complete sets were on bank, yet Pontiac assembled fewer than 1,300 complete orders! A bulletin was issued stating that a valid VIN was required when placing any order and only four were supplied if the claim was accepted. Modern forgings have lessened their desirability, but they remain fairly valuable.

Though Super Duty connecting rods remain quite valuable today, the common forged-steel units from the 1950s and 1960s are far less desirable. Typically selling at a reasonable price, some hobbyists have improved rigidity by having them heat treated. The cost of that process along with the cost of adding modern fasteners and having them correctly sized can make them an unreasonable choice.

Reusing your Pontiac's original cast rods during your rebuild is certainly possible. A simple upgrade is the addition of modern fasteners, which tends to improve clamping force. However, the units are generally 50 years old or more and have endured countless miles and thousands of heating and cooling cycles during normal operation. There's also no telling how close they've been pushed toward their elastic limit in the past. If there's even a remote chance of a questionable past, consider upgrading to a modern forging. It's cheap insurance.

were used in essentially all production Pontiac V-8s, except for some of the unique maximum-performance engines. These engines, such as the Super Duties and R/A-IV, received forged-aluminum units.

The factory cast piston is an excellent design. Its wrist pin is offset slightly toward the thrust side of the piston, which is intended to lessen thrust load on the cylinder wall and provide quiet operation. Depending upon the application, a valve relief was specifically positioned to provide maximum piston-to-valve clearance in most engines. A dish was machined into the crown to reduce compression in a limited number of others, such as the 428.

Mickey Thompson supplied Pontiac with forged-aluminum pistons for early Super Duty engines, while TRW Automotive provided forgings for the R/A-IV and SD-455. The TRW pieces were precisely machined and quite reliable. TRW began offering a wide array of stock-replacement forged-aluminum pistons for Pontiac applications based on the R/A-IV design, and several of the high-volume offerings are presently available under the Federal-Mogul Motorparts Sealed Power line.

Pistons

Pontiac developed its own cast-aluminum pistons, which were cam ground for precise fit. Cast pistons

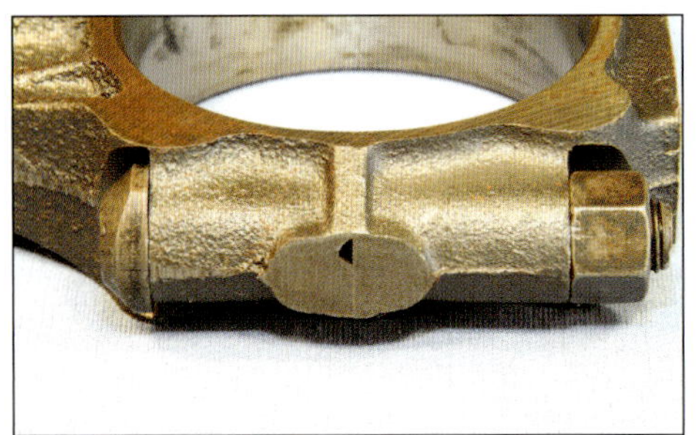

The cast connecting rod includes a machined groove that serves to direct a jet of lubrication toward the camshaft and cylinder wall. Most likely because of emissions concerns, it was eliminated in September 1972. Factory literature states that the two rod types can be freely interchanged. Your rebuild can include either, but modern bearings do not include the required feedhole, which renders the feature useless.

Most Pontiac engines were assembled with cast-aluminum pistons similar to this. Some applications have the valve relief in a different position, while others feature a dish in the center or a machined lip around the edge to reduce compression. It was an excellent design that was relatively strong and was made to run with tight piston-to-wall clearance. The piston pin is offset approximately 1/16 inch toward the thrust side to reduce side load and ensure quiet operation.

Harmonic Balancer

A harmonic balancer is located on the front snout of a crankshaft. It generally consists of a center hub and floating outer ring isolated by rubber. It's designed to damp the irregular torsional vibrations that occur during combustion. It also contains a top dead center (TDC) timing mark for conveniently setting spark timing and is flanged to accept a pulley that drives the engine accessories. For many other makes, it was slightly imbalanced and can be adjusted to balance the reciprocating assembly, but it was neutral balanced in nearly all Pontiac applications.

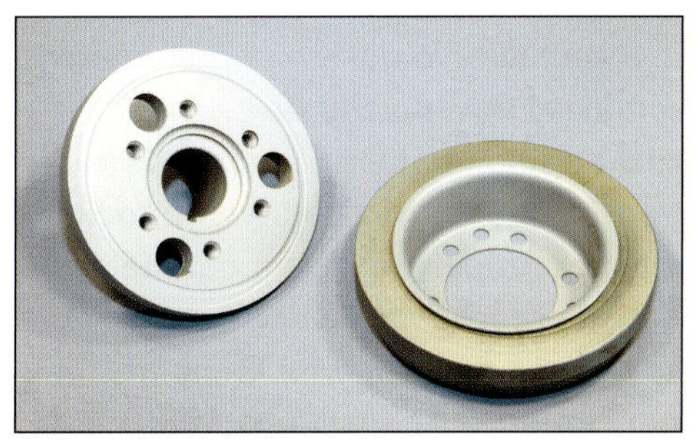

The Pontiac harmonic balancer generally bolted together through 1967, and this two-piece unit was introduced in 1964. The inertia ring is pressed onto the stamped steel housing, which then gets bolted to the crankshaft hub. The accessory drive pulley is sandwiched between them.

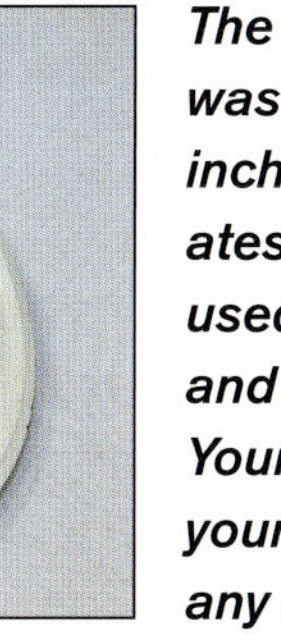

The most common Pontiac harmonic balancer was introduced in 1968 and measures 6.75 inches across. An excellent design that operates reliably when properly installed, it was used in all applications through midyear 1976 and then in select applications through 1979. Your machinist can verify its accuracy during your rebuild. It should be replaced if it shows any signs of inaccuracy or pending failure. New units were available through GM parts departments for many years, so NOS units may still be available. Aftermarket units are also available from your favorite Pontiac vendor.

Early Pontiac units bolted together and were somewhat complex. The design grew simpler over the years and eventually evolved into the unit that most hobbyists are familiar with today. Introduced in 1968, the common Pontiac harmonic balancer measures 6.75 inches in diameter and was used on select applications through 1979. It was quite reliable and rarely failed when installed properly. New old stock (NOS) units were still available from GM dealers for quite some time, so examples shouldn't be very difficult to locate. If a used balancer in good condition isn't readily available, there are several companies that can rebuild them for you.

Crankshaft Hub

The same initiative aimed at reducing overall vehicle weight that resulted in material being removed from the block led to the introduction of a modified harmonic balancer. Pontiac knew that most of its mid-1970s engines wouldn't rev quickly and that the internals wouldn't be exposed to heavy inertial drag, so engineers determined that a traditional harmonic balancer wasn't required for most production engines.

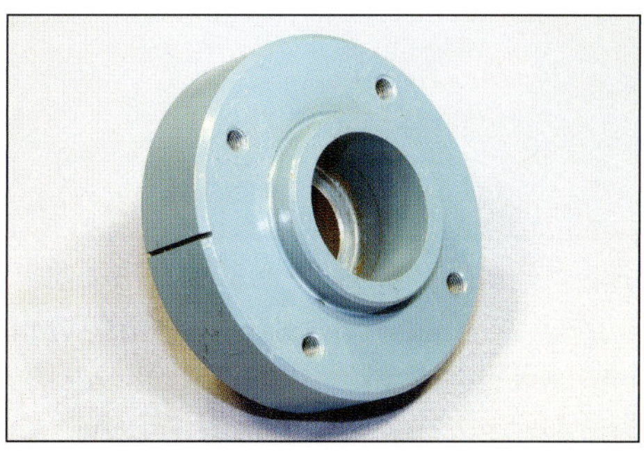

This crankshaft hub appeared in midyear 1976 on most 350- and 400-ci engines backed by an automatic transmission, including the 400 used in the Trans Am. It offers no damping quality whatsoever. Its primary purpose is driving engine accessories and providing a Top Dead Center mark for setting spark timing. It should be replaced with a traditional harmonic balancer during any rebuild.

In mid 1976, Pontiac replaced the harmonic balancer on select applications with a crankshaft hub that offered no damping ability whatsoever. It simply used drive engine accessories and contains a TDC timing mark. Engines unaffected by the running change include the long-stroke 455, any Pontiac engine backed by a manual transmission, and the T/A 6.6. These exceptions received a traditional balancer to ensure operational longevity. It's highly recommended that a conventional harmonic balancer be used during any rebuild.

Valvetrain

When Pontiac developed its V-8 package during the 1950s, the lifter bores were designed to deliver a sufficient amount of pressurized oil for hydraulic lifter operation. Save for a few Super Duty applications, which used mechanical camshafts for maximum performance, Pontiac specified

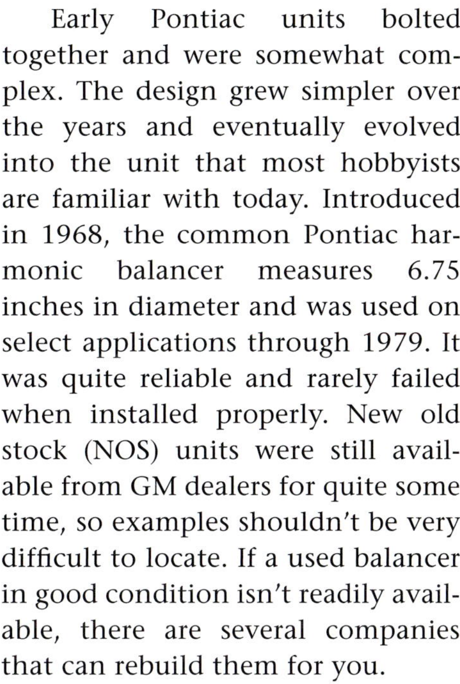

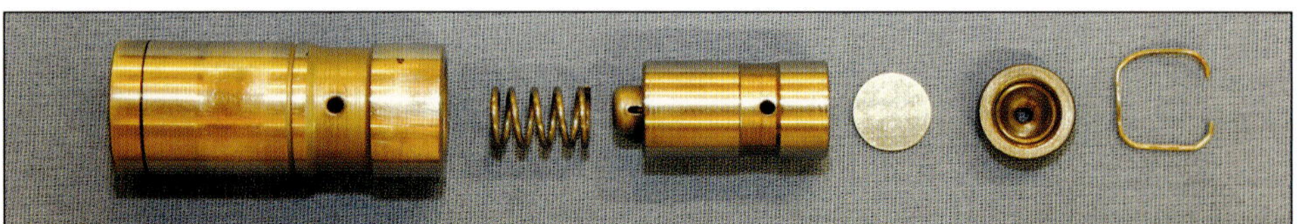

The Pontiac V-8 block was designed to supply the lifter bores with additional oil flow to accommodate hydraulic valve lifters. All regular production Pontiac engines received flat-tappet camshafts and used hydraulic lifters similar to this. The hydraulic action allows the lifter to continually adjust to keep all valvetrain components in constant contact for quiet and consistent operation. This lifter has been completely disassembled to show the complex inner workings.

hydraulic camshafts in every production engine to produce a valvetrain that operated reliably and quietly with very little maintenance required.

A typical hydraulic lifter in an overhead-valve engine is quite complex, but the functional design is a technological marvel. A hydraulic lifter is comprised of a main body and an internal plunger-and-valve assembly that relies on pressurized engine oil to continually adjust valve lash, so all the valvetrain components are constantly in contact with one another.

While on the base circle of the camshaft lobe, pressurized oil enters a feed hole and fills a cavity in the lifter body that's located beneath the plunger. As the lifter body follows the cam lobe and begins rising, valve spring pressure transmitted through the pushrod compresses the plunger against its spring-loaded check-ball, immediately isolating the lifter from the engine oil supply. As the cam lobe travels toward peak lift, the lifter and plunger rise as a unit, lifting the pushrod, which in turn lifts the valve off its seat.

Resistance from the valve spring pressurizes the oil within the lifter body, which causes a small amount to bleed outward between it and the plunger. It is generally referred to as "leakage." Once the lifter trav-

els up and over the entire cam lobe and is back on the base circle, internal spring pressure causes the lifter to expand and force the plunger upward, which eliminates valve lash, opens the check-valve, and allows pressurized oil to refill the lifter body cavity before the next lift cycle starts.

Leakage rate is controlled by using various degrees of lifter body-to-plunger clearance. Pontiac used specific-rate hydraulic lifters for certain applications over the years. In nearly all its production engines, plunger depth was preset by using a tapered rocker arm stud and a corresponding adjuster nut. The combination ensured that the lifter functioned correctly by continually adjusting in any condition and with normal valvetrain wear. The R/A-IV may be the most well-known production engine to use special limited-travel hydraulic lifters that required manual lash adjustments.

As hydraulic lifter leakage occurs during normal operation, a small amount of pressurized oil is sent through a hollow pushrod to lubricate the contact end of the stamped steel rocker arm. Through the early 1960s, the rocker arm pivot was lubricated by pressurized oil that was fed to the cylinder head rocker studs from the camshaft journals. In later years, the system was revised and

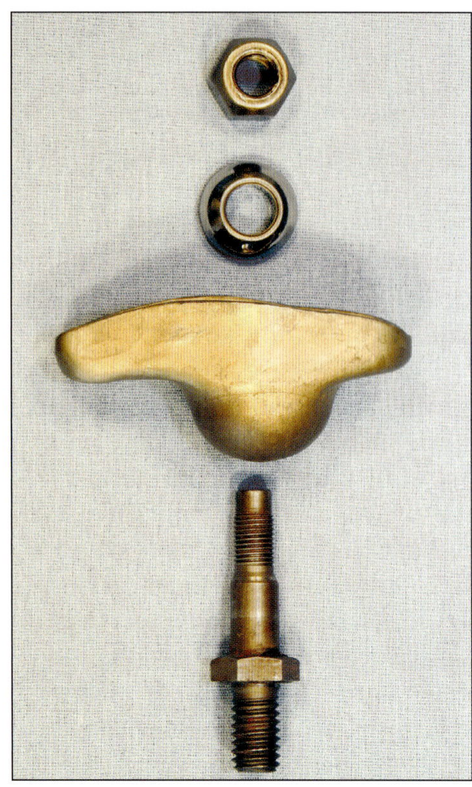

The ball-stud-type rocker arm system is a very simple design that contains relatively few moving parts. The rocker stud contains a tapered shoulder that's used to position the rocker arm for proper valvetrain geometry. It was pressed into place in early years and was screwed into place in performance applications from 1967 through 1973. A running change was made in midyear 1973 that eliminated pressed rocker studs entirely.

the pushrod supplied all lubrication exclusively.

The stamped-steel rocker arms were somewhat adjustable in 1955 and in a fixed position in most 1956-and-later regular production engines. The R/A-IV required manual lashing, however. All engines received pressed rocker arm studs through 1967, and threaded rocker studs were used in performance applications beginning that year. A pushrod diameter of 5/16 inch was used in most production engines, while the R/A-II and R/A-IV used 11/32-inch-diameter units for additional stability.

Many Pontiacs were originally assembled with a timing set that used a cam gear with nylon teeth. Intended to provide quiet operation and less operational load, it was prone to failure because the unit aged and the nylon teeth grew brittle. Any that broke off almost always ended up in the oil pan sump, where it posed no threat. A steel cam gear is always recommended during any rebuild.

The camshaft identifier stamp was sometimes a shape instead of an alphanumeric character during the late 1970s. These three camshafts are 1977–1979 T/A 6.6 units. The valve events of each vary slightly. They are, from left to right, 1977 T/A 6.6 automatic transmission, 1977 T/A 6.6 manual transmission, and all 1978–1979 T/A 6.6.

Camshafts

Pontiac Engineering took camshaft design very seriously. During the late 1950s and early 1960s, the production camshafts were so technologically advanced that the factory-installed units performed as well as many of the aftermarket camshafts available at that time. Pontiac attained maximum performance for its production vehicles by adding several degrees of exhaust duration to compensate for the somewhat flow-deficient exhaust port and complete exhaust system. Also, the intake lobe center was delayed to make engine performance livable on questionable-quality fuel.

Malcolm "Mac" McKellar was one of Pontiac's top camshaft designers, and he once said that gross valve lift was limited to just over 0.400 inch in most instances because the cylinder heads generally contained larger valves and that the small ports promoted good velocity. High valve lift simply wasn't needed to achieve good performance from most of Pontiac's passenger car engines. That moderate valve lift provided customers with a durable valvetrain while maximizing service life.

Pontiac found it easier to increase rocker arm ratio than to modify the actual camshaft lobe if additional lift was required for a particular application. McKellar reasoned that adjusting rocker arm ratio is less stressful on the valvetrain while increasing all aspects under the lift curve, and it can make the camshaft appear slightly larger to the engine at the same time. Pontiac generally used 1.5:1 rocker arms, but 1.65:1 rockers were specified in certain high-performance applications, such as the SD-421 and R/A IV.

Many of Pontiac's most popular camshafts were developed during the mid-to-late 1960s. The 066 and 067 were considered the workhorses, offering the best combination of street manners and performance. The 068 and 744 were specified for high-performance street applications. The high-lift 041 was introduced in 1968½ for the R/A-II and was combined with 1.65:1 rockers to produce nearly 0.520-inch lift for the R/A-IV in 1969 and 1970.

Various camshafts were compared during the performance era to find the grind that best complemented a particular engine's operating characteristics for a given application. A manual-transmission engine generally

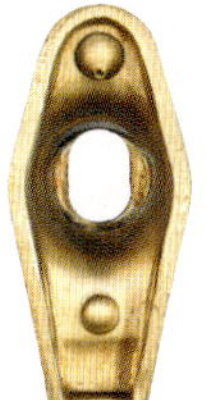
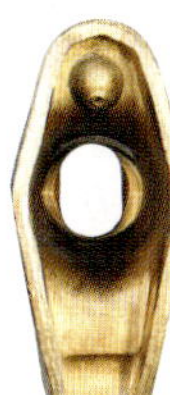

Pontiac used 1.5:1 ratio stamped steel rocker arms in nearly all its V-8 applications. A 1.65:1 ratio rocker arm was developed to increase gross valve lift of early Super Duty and R/A-IV engines by 10 percent over its 1.5:1-ratio counterpart. Moving the pushrod cup toward the rocker stud increases the ratio. The difference is virtually undetectable unless the original units are compared side by side. A 1.5:1-ratio stamped steel rocker arm is on the left, while a 1.65:1 ratio unit is on the right. Both are original Pontiac units.

Common Pontiac Camshaft Specifications

Pontiac used a wide variety of hydraulic flat-tappet camshafts for its production engines, and while some are stamped with a complete part number, the majority are identified by a single character stamping. The exact location depends on the model year. The identifier is stamped on the snout of the first journal through the mid 1970s, and it's usually hidden under the timing chain gear if installed. The stamping was relocated on the face of the rear bearing journal in later years.

Common Pontiac camshafts are generally identified by a single character stamp on the front snout. Pontiac also used a paint marking in later years, at which point the stamp moved to the rear face. The "P" found on this unit indicates that it is number-9779067, or "067" as it's commonly referred to.

The chart in the appendix contains the part number, identification stamp, and valve specifications of the Pontiac's more common camshafts, including several of its performance grinds. None of these are available from GM any longer. But if you're looking for a Pontiac-spec grind for your rebuild, Melling Tool Company currently produces a limited number of direct replacements, while virtually any camshaft manufacturing company can provide you with a customized grind to your desired specification. ■

received a camshaft that was slightly more aggressive than its automatic-backed counterpart because it could generally tolerate a little more duration, and buyers opting for a manual transmission were generally performance minded. Once emissions regulations became a greater concern, camshafts were mostly chosen based on emissions compliance.

Cylinder Heads

Pontiac's basic overhead-valve cylinder head with D-shaped exhaust ports was introduced in 1955. The same general intake and exhaust port configurations were used on most production engines through the end of V-8 production in 1981.

In all instances, the cylinder heads were retained to the block by a total of ten 1/2-inch-diameter bolts, which allows any Pontiac cylinder head to be installed onto any Pontiac block.

The small intake and exhaust ports were designed to maximize port velocity, which is critical when attempting to maintain good throttle response and low-speed street manners. The combustion chambers were fully machined for several reasons, among which was to maintain good chamber volume consistency and reduce the risk of detonation. As the engines grew larger and were designed to operate at higher engine speeds, the intake and exhaust valves were enlarged and the ports were reshaped to increase airflow.

During the late 1950s and again in the 1960s, Pontiac revised the method in which the intake manifold bolts to the cylinder heads. The original reverse-flow design was replaced by the conventional-path system. The oiling system was also slightly revised. A pushrod-oiled system replaced the stud-oiled rocker arm. Most of these changes can be overcome relatively easily if you're attempting to use a block and cylinder heads from different years.

Casting numbers, generally located on the center exhaust port, identify Pontiac's D-port cylinder heads. It typically consists of two or three-digits but is sometimes a complete part number located on the valve cover rail. This particular 6X casting was used from mid-1975 to 1978. The appendix of this book should help you identify any popular castings you might come across.

Pontiac's D-port head was introduced in 1955, and airflow was generally increased over the years by enlarging valve diameters. The 2.11-inch intake and 1.77-inch exhaust debuted in 1967 for performance applications. A number of castings were used in the following years. Exhaust valve size decreased to 1.66 inches in 1973, but airflow much wasn't affected much. Smog-era castings, such as this 6X, can be purchased quite reasonably and make excellent performance cylinder heads in stock form.

What Does "CWC" Mean?

Many factory-original and aftermarket Pontiacs have "CWC" and some numbers cast into the core between the first journal and lobe. The number is simply a camshaft core identifier and has no bearing on actual valve events. Many people believe that "CWC" is actually "CMC" for Camshaft Machine Company, a camshaft finishing company in Jackson, Michigan. It actually represents the Campbell, Wyant, and Cannon (CWC) Foundry, which is presently located in Muskegon, Michigan.

When CWC first opened in 1908, it produced components for marine applications and four-cylinder passenger car engines. Camshaft cores were among them. The raw cores were purchased and finished to exact specification by auto manufacturers. Textron purchased the company in 1956 and it now operates as CWC Textron, producing more than 10 million cam cores annually for all major auto manufacturers and aftermarket camshaft companies. ■

Pontiac performed its own camshaft finishing, ensuring that the lobes were ground to the proper specifications and heat treated correctly. But it didn't produce the camshaft cores. The Campbell, Wyatt, and Cannon (CWC) foundry provided camshaft cores to many auto manufacturers over the years and continues to do so. The "CWC" found on many original or aftermarket camshafts simply indicates that the raw cam core was sourced from the CWC foundry.

The cylinder head design used from 1965 through the end of traditional V-8 production in 1979 allows for directly interchanging any casting. Castings of this era are generally easiest to find and work with any block configuration. There's a wide variety of options if you need to replace your Pontiac's existing castings. Simply educate yourself on the major casting differences and how they could affect the outcome of your project.

All Pontiac cylinder heads produced in 1965 and 1966 feature 1.92/1.66-inch valves and pressed rocker studs. Mild port work can increase intake airflow beyond the stock range of roughly 190 cfm at 28 inches of pressure, and larger valves can be installed. Unless limited to such castings for originality purposes, cylinder heads from 1967 or later may be a better option.

In addition to the displacement increase for 1967, Pontiac improved piston-to-valve angle and increased valve diameters to 2.11/1.77 inches in performance applications. This improved peak airflow by about 20 cfm to an approximate total of 210 at 28 inches of pressure, while intake port volume remained around 153 cc. Mild street applications through the mid 1970s continued using small intake valves (1.96-inch) and 1.66-inch exhaust valves were common from 1973 forward.

A running change eliminated the pressed rocker studs entirely in 1973.

Beginning in 1973, a secondary application stamp appeared on cylinders heads, and it denoted such variables as the original application, valve sizes, and combustion chamber volume. The stamp is located on the vertical accessory boss located between the left and center exhaust port. As with this casting, the stamp is sometimes off-center and can be difficult to read. The "8" shown on this 6X casting indicates that it was originally intended for a 400 engine and features 100-cc chambers.

Threaded rocker arm studs became standard equipment in all applications in May of the model year. Pontiac began using only 2.11-inch intake valves for its 350, 400, and 455 engines, regardless of application. Because of these common characteristics, virtually any mid-to-late 1970s D-port casting is suitable for any performance rebuild, and they can usually be purchased quite reasonably.

While most D-port cylinder heads with large intake valves make an excellent choice for any high-performance street application, Pontiac produced a series of castings in the late 1960s and early 1970s that aimed to take the top-performance engines to the next level. Featuring unique round exhaust outlets, these "round-port" castings possess well-designed intake and exhaust ports and their excellent airflow characteristics can extend an engine's maximum operating speed by several hundred RPM.

The 1968½ R/A II castings share the same basic intake port as the number-670 D-port cylinder head from 1967, which measures roughly 153 cc and flows roughly 210 cfm. The intake port was enlarged by nearly 30 cc for the 1969 R/A-IV, and as a result, peak airflow increased to about 240 cfm at 28 inches of pressure. Combustion chamber volume of approximately 72 cc allows the engine to achieve its intended compression ratio of just greater than 10:1 on the 400. That feature makes these castings all but unusable for larger engines operating on modern pump fuel.

The round-port casting was revised slightly for the 1971 and 1972 455 H.O. The combustion chamber was enlarged to more than 110 cc to reduce the compression ratio to 8.4:1, and the intake port floor was raised to accommodate the large chamber, which took about 10 cc of intake port volume with it. This change reduced peak intake airflow to roughly 230 cfm at 28 inches of pressure. The SD-455 cylinder head was completely redesigned. Its intake and exhaust ports are aimed at maximizing port efficiency and peak airflow increased to just over 240 cfm in similar test conditions.

In general, the cost for a pair of usable D-port cylinder heads can range from less than $100 to several hundred, depending upon the casting. Beyond combustion chamber volume and its effect on resultant compression ratio, however, there's very little functional difference among them. Even small-valve castings, once considered worthless, can be retrofitted with larger valves, making them functionally equivalent to an original 2.11-inch casting. The round-ports generally start at more than $1,000, however, and can approach several thousand, depending upon the casting application.

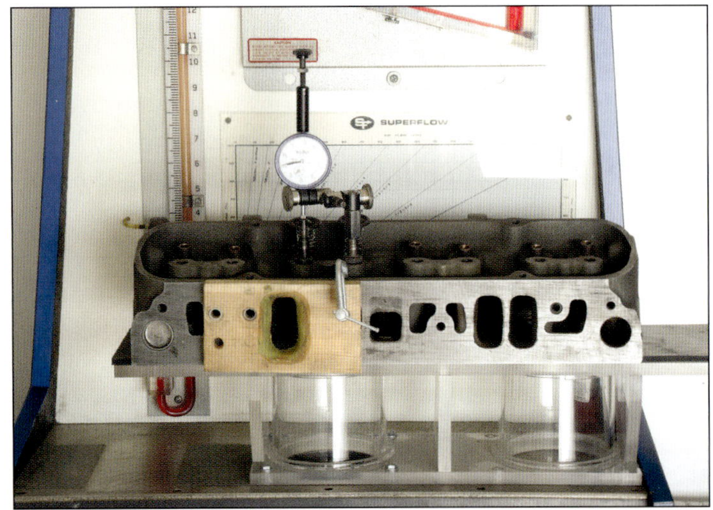

All D-port cylinder heads with 2.11-inch intake valves feature an intake port volume of approximately 153 cc. Peak airflow is somewhere around 210 cfm at 28 inches of pressure regardless of the casting number. Common small-valve castings with 1.92 to 1.96-inch intake valves generally peak around 190 cfm in similar conditions. Testing shows maximum airflow occurs around 0.450-inch valve lift in either instance.

Pontiac developed a series of cylinder heads for high-performance applications that featured round exhaust port outlets and boasted of improved airflow. Introduced in 1968 and used through 1974 in various forms, casting numbers found on the center or end exhaust ports generally identified the "round-port" heads. They were originally installed on some of the rarest and most desirable Pontiacs ever produced and remain very valuable.

What about the 301?

You may have noticed that you haven't read much about the 301. It was introduced in 1977 and was the last Pontiac V-8 ever produced. So why hasn't it been discussed more? Well, there's a pretty good reason for that.

The 301 (and its 265 variant) is considerably different from the traditional Pontiac V-8. In an attempt to shed weight, Pontiac removed a significant amount of material from the 301, which makes it less rigid and fairly undesirable for high-performance applications. The deck height is nearly an inch lower, which requires unique-length connecting rods and pushrods. The cylinder heads and intake and exhaust manifolds are also unique and may not directly interchange with those of the traditional Pontiac V-8.

To save weight, the 301 crankshaft is void of its central counterweights and contains only the large units at opposite ends. This requires the use of a specific flywheel and harmonic balancer, both of which serve to balance the reciprocating assembly. Although both have an appearance much like that of the traditional pieces, and despite the fact that both actually bolt onto a traditional Pontiac V-8 crankshaft, the 301-specific harmonic balancer and flywheel should not be used in any other Pontiac application.

The 301 contains some parts that are common to any Pontiac V-8. They include the carburetor and distributor, valve covers, some of the accessory brackets, and the front cover. Because the 301 isn't commonly rebuilt, and it lacks strong support from OEM and aftermarket suppliers, it isn't often mentioned in this book. But a vast majority of the machining and assembly procedures still apply. If you're rebuilding a 301, it may be best to use a factory service manual for tolerances and specifications. Another excellent resource is to confer with fellow 301 owners at 301garage.com. ∎

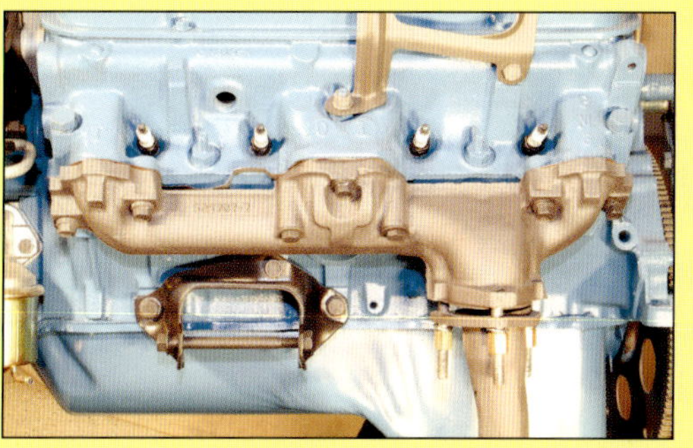

The 301 was introduced in 1977 as Pontiac's economy V-8. Designed entirely for maximum weight reduction, performance was secondary. It was, however, quite reliable if operated within its intended limits. The 301 (and the 265 variant introduced in 1980) uses many unique components that do not interchange with the traditional Pontiac V-8. The block and all its internals, the cylinder heads, and intake and exhaust manifolds are all specific to the 301.

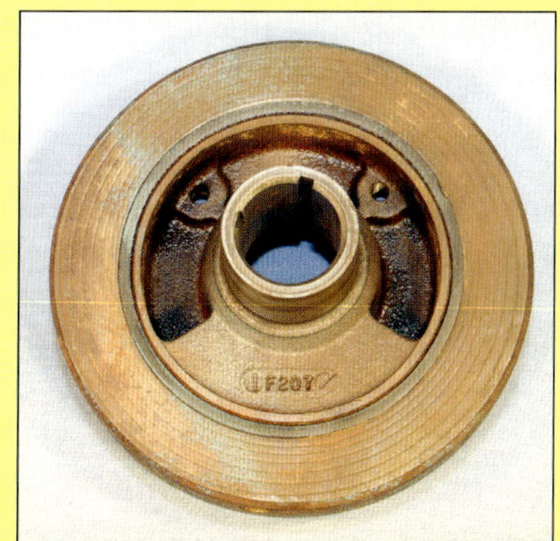

The 301 (and 265 variant) harmonic balancer looks virtually identical to the conventional Pontiac V-8 balancer when installed. This view shows that it's vastly different, however. The large weight is required to counterbalance the unique 301 crankshaft, which features only two large counterweights. The harmonic balancer should not be used on any other Pontiac engine.

Intake Manifold

The intake manifold is generally one of the first items replaced when modifying an otherwise stock engine for improved performance. Often, factory manifolds are at best a design compromise with more focus on low-speed efficiency and emissions-friendly economy than high-RPM performance. Aftermarket units tend to produce greater amounts of peak power but don't always provide optimal street manners. However, that's not necessarily the case with Pontiacs.

The Pontiac intake manifold features a divided plenum, which creates a dual-plane (180-degree) design. Four runners draft from one half of the carburetor while the other four runners draft from the opposite side of the carburetor. Half the cylinders see only one half of the carburetor. This design typically accentuates low-speed street manners and favors torque production, and it perfectly complements the intended operating range of the 1955 Pontiac V-8.

The basic 2-barrel intake manifold designed in 1955 was used through 1974 with minor modifications over the years. The basic

In 1955, Pontiac unveiled its V-8 with a 2-barrel intake manifold. The basic intake casting continued through 1974 with minor modifications. Runner dimensions are generally smaller than the 4-barrel unit. Therefore, it is intended to promote maximum velocity (increasing low-speed performance), but it limits top-end power. While a 2-barrel setup is certainly capable of providing plenty of performance, a 4-barrel should be considered during any performance rebuild.

Tri-Power was introduced in 1957 to provide Pontiac's top performance street engines with a performance boost over the 4-barrel carburetor. The trio of Rochester 2-barrel carburetors became a Pontiac trademark. It was a wise marketing move that truly gave Pontiac a more youthful appeal with America's hot rodders and generated a high volume of customer traffic at dealerships.

The popular cast-iron 4-barrel intake manifold was introduced in 1967, and it was used in performance applications that year. It was used in all 4-barrel applications beginning in 1968. It saw minor changes to such areas as bracket mount points and exhaust crossover dimensions over the years. It's arguably the best performance intake manifold available for any street-driven Pontiac that's shifted below about 5,500 rpm.

4-barrel design was introduced in mid-1955 and was used through 1966 on all 4-barrel engines, and in select 1967 applications. A dual 4-barrel intake manifold was used in certain maximum-performance applications in the 1950s and early 1960s. When Tri-Power was introduced in 1957, it was intended to offer additional performance over the 4-barrel and was available on all high-performance street engines through 1966.

General Motors banned the use of multiple carburetion on all 1967 vehicles, except the Corvette. Pontiac developed a beautiful cast-aluminum single 4-barrel intake manifold for the early-1960s Super Duty, and it featured long, smoothly contoured runners. It proved to offer an excellent combination of low-speed torque and high-speed horsepower. A modified version of this intake manifold was used with the new Rochester Quadrajet to produce an induction package that performed as well as,

and quite possibly better than, the Tri-Power it replaced in 1967.

The cast-iron 4-barrel intake manifold used from 1968 forward is among the best performing units available for a street-driven Pontiac. Independent flow testing reveals that even with the addition of exhaust gas recirculation (EGR) in 1973, and the unsightly appearance of a unique carburetor flange in 1975, its airflow characteristics and performance potential weren't grossly affected.

The carburetor flange of the 4-barrel intake manifold was significantly modified in 1975 to accommodate the rerouted EGR system. It required a dish directly under the carburetor primaries, which gave the secondary openings a pronounced "D" shape. From looks alone, this manifold should significantly restrict airflow, but independent testing reveals otherwise. It is completely adequate for a strong-performing street engine.

The basic casting received several minor changes over the years, which can affect direct interchange. This includes exhaust crossover port size, and various methods of mounting the automatic choke, throttle linkage, and rear bracket for the air-conditioning compressor. These are small obstacles that can create difficulty when combining an intake manifold of a certain vintage with a vehicle of another, but they are relatively easy to overcome.

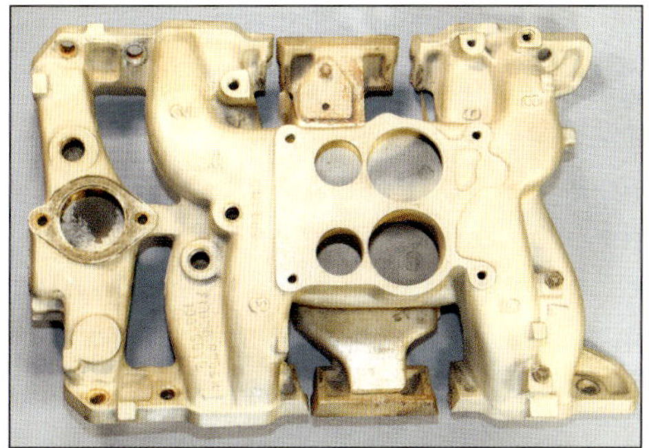

High-flow R/A-IV and 455 H.O. cylinder heads feature intake ports that are taller than those of a conventional D-port casting. A specific intake manifold was developed for those applications. With an appearance identical to the standard manifold, its runners were enlarged internally to support additional airflow. Instead of using cast iron, however, the high-flow units were aluminum and contained a separate cast-iron heat crossover.

The most desirable factory units are the cast-aluminum versions used on 1969 to 1972 R/A-IV and 455 H.O. engines and the cast-iron 1973–1974 Super Duty 455 manifold. They feature enlarged runners to complement the increased airflow capacity that the larger cylinder head intake ports offer. These manifolds are quite valuable, and while capable of sustaining greater amounts of peak horsepower, the performance effects are negligible on a street-driven Pontiac.

Carburetors

A carburetor's role is to provide an engine with precise amounts of fuel and air at a particular RPM or engine load. A throttle valve controls the volume of air passing through the bores and past the fuel discharge nozzles, which draw atomized fuel from the float bowl and through the nozzles. The goal is to produce peak performance in all

Flow testing an intake manifold can predict the effect it may have on total performance. The task is somewhat tedious and requires using a cylinder head and measuring each runner separately, but the results allow hobbyists to accurately determine the flow differences among various castings. Testing proves that there's very little flow variance from any 1968–1979 cast-iron 4-barrel intake manifold.

driving conditions from light part-throttle to wide open.

When developing a carburetor for a specific application, carburetor engineers use a mathematical equation to determine the amount of air a particular engine must ingest to effectively operate at its intended RPM peak. It may seem easiest to simply increase carburetor size when the required airflow capacity is greater than the carburetor can supply. But doing so has consequences. A larger carburetor bore can lessen air velocity, subsequently reducing nozzle signal, and ultimately degrading throttle response and low-speed performance.

To retain maximum performance in all conditions, carburetor engineers developed a dual-stage carburetor with four nearly equal sized bores (or barrels). Airflow is directed through two primary barrels for maximum low-speed performance. As engine workload increases, a progressive throttle linkage opens the

remaining two barrels for maximum heavy-throttle performance.

The Pontiac V-8 was introduced with a Carter 2-barrel carburetor. A Carter 4-barrel was made available in mid-1955 for customers seeking to improve performance. The 2- and 4-barrel options remained for 1956. A unique Rochester dual 4-barrel setup was created for hobbyists looking for a complete maximum-performance package intended for various forms of competitive racing.

Part of Pontiac's goal during the 1950s was to change its image and produce equipment that was favorable with young performance enthusiasts. Many aftermarket manufacturers were offering a single-intake manifold that allowed the use of a trio of 2-barrels for various makes. Pontiac was among the many manufacturers that offered and marketed such an option for its performance vehicles beginning in 1957. Heralded as "Tri-Power," it was Pontiac's top regular-production performance option through 1966.

The mechanical fuel pump was mounted on the front of the engine, where it received airflow wash from the cooling fan. Canister units like this began appearing on production vehicles during the 1960s. AC was the original supplier in most instances, and direct replacements are still available for many popular applications.

The Rochester 2-barrel was a simple design that worked quite well. It remained the carburetor of choice from 1957 through 1974 in all 2-barrel and Tri-Power applications except for a lone 1972 350-ci manual-transmission engine, which specified a Carter 2-barrel. Finding used units isn't too difficult today, but finding specific castings for certain engines can be time consuming and costly. Two competent companies that presently support the Rochester 2-barrel are The Carburetor Shop and Cliff's High Performance.

During the early days of 4-barrel production, Rochester carburetors received a bad reputation when compared to Carter. Rochester was perceived as a carburetor company that simply produced carburetors to auto manufacturer specifications for production vehicles. Carter went a step beyond, however, and offered a limited line of tuning parts available on the aftermarket. When placed in service, the Rochester Model 4GC and Carter WCFB 4-barrel carburetors performed much the same. Beginning in 1957, Pontiac started using the Carter

The Carter AFB was a popular 4-barrel carburetor during the late 1950s and 1960s. Pontiac used it in most 4-barrel applications from 1958 through 1966. Carter even offered tuning parts to improve performance beyond the factory setting. But finding replacement and performance parts can now be difficult.

AFB for its performance applications and it remained a regular-production carburetor through 1967.

The Carter AFB was an excellent performance carburetor when tuned properly, and it was able to rival the performance of the Tri-Power in certain Pontiac applications. The Tri-Power was quite profitable for Pontiac, and it was a key feature with enthusiasts. To maintain its performance advantage over the 4-barrel, Pontiac specified that a "wing" be added inside certain AFB castings, which limited airflow and subsequently affected full-throttle performance.

Rochester engineers discovered that throttle response and fuel economy could be improved by decreasing primary size while the

engine's maximum flow requirement could be fulfilled to maintain strong full-throttle performance by incorporating in a larger secondary size. Named "Quadrajet," the design was a highly efficient, well-balanced unit that was practical for virtually any driving condition.

The Model 4M Quadrajet first appeared on select 1965 Chevrolet applications, and by 1968 it was the only 4-barrel used by the GM divisions, except for those specialized Chevrolet applications that used a Holley. The primary bores supplied each engine with a fixed amount of airflow while the secondary circuit featured a vacuum-operated air valve, which was factory preset, supplied just enough total airflow to fulfill a particular engine's requirements.

The 1971 455 H.O. Quadrajet

Rochester developed a unique Model 4M in conjunction with Pontiac for the 1971 model year. Designed to increase airflow, the typical Model 4M main body was cast without the outer velocity-booster rings that surround the fuel-discharge nozzles in the center of each primary. Airflow testing shows that these units contain a maximum capacity of roughly 828 cfm, or an increase of more than 50 cfm over a comparable Model 4M.

Developed for the 1971 455 H.O. and subsequently used in 400- and 455-ci manual transmission engines, the lack of booster rings degraded nozzle signal, and that negatively affected off-idle and low-speed emissions. The design lasted just one year as federal emissions regulations tightened for 1972. Because of limited availability, and the

A unique Rochester Quadrajet carburetor was developed for the 1971 455 H.O. Independent testing shows a maximum airflow capacity of 828 cfm. This unique casting was also used on 400 and 455 manual transmission applications that year also. These high-flow castings lasted only one year and are quite valuable.

The 1971 455 H.O. Quadrajet (Continued)

fact that they were used on some of the most-desirable 1971 model-year vehicles, such castings were produced in relatively low volume and are highly sought after by restoration enthusiasts today.

The performance advantages associated with increased airflow makes this carburetor sought after by performance enthusiasts. Independent dyno and drag strip testing shows that this casting is capable of producing as much as 10 additional horsepower over a comparable 750 cfm Model 4M. Numbers to look for when searching are 7041263, 7041267, 7041268, 7041270, and 7041273. Expect to spend anywhere from several hundred to several thousand dollars depending upon the application. ∎

Removing the outer booster ring in the velocity stack of a conventional Model 4M Quadrajet (left) increased airflow, and this change was used for the 1971 455 H.O. casting (right). The booster wasn't only simply eliminated, the center booster ring surrounding the center discharge nozzle was lengthened to promote maximum nozzle signal. The overall result was airflow improvement of more than 50 cfm over the standard casting.

Pontiac began using the Quadrajet in 1966 on its 6-cylinder Sprint engines, and for its performance V-8s in 1967. But the Carter AFB 4-barrel remained the specified unit for certain 1967 applications. The Quadrajet was used exclusively in 1968 on all 4-barrel Pontiac applications and though the casting saw minor changes over the years, the Model 4M remained Pontiac's only 4-barrel through 1974.

The Model 4M that Pontiac used contains a primary diameter of 13/32 inch, and they're generally referred to by their assumed airflow rating of 750 cfm. Independent airflow testing reveals that this value is actually pretty close. With the secondary air valve adjusted to the maximum flow position, these castings are capable of flowing as much as 775 cfm.

Rochester took a couple of different approaches toward increasing the airflow capacity of its Model 4M during the early 1970s. Pontiac worked closely with Rochester to develop a unique casting that lacks the outer ring of the booster cluster in the primary bore for specific 1971 applications. The 1973–1974 Super

The Rochester Quadrajet was introduced in 1967 as a Tri-Power replacement. It replaced the AFB in low-performance 1968 applications as well and became Pontiac's only production 4-barrel carburetor. The design promotes maximum street manners while operating on the primary circuit and strong full-throttle performance when the large secondary barrels open. It saw minor modifications over the years and was used by Pontiac through the end of V-8 production 1981.

Duty 455 uses a Quadrajet with a revised main body, which includes a primary diameter increase of 1/4 inch to a new total of 17/32 inches. The latter unit is often referred to as an 800-cfm casting, and independent airflow testing shows that its total capacity is just a bit more than 810 cfm.

A modified version of the 4M, designated Model M4M, was introduced for the 1975 model year. Not only did the redesigned unit contain several internal enhancements to improve engine efficiency, the main body of every Pontiac V-8 (from 301 to 455, depending upon the model year) featured the 17/32-inch-diameter primary, like the Super Duty's Model 4M casting. Scorned by many as smog-era carburetors with very lean fuel metering, the casting changed very little for the remainder of the 1970s, and it makes for an excellent performance unit once it is modified correctly.

The Quadrajet saw some significant design changes during the 1980 model year as computer control command was introduced. Desig-nated E4M, many of the mechanical internals were replaced by electronic components, offering more precise control over the fuel curve, reducing emissions, and improving long-term consistency. However, the E4M requires an electronic module for normal operation.

Exhaust System

An exhaust system is designed to carry hot engine exhaust away from a vehicle while muffling the pressure waves (sound) at the same time. The very best exhaust system is one that effectively reduces engine noise without reducing engine performance. Noise-level regulations, overall exhaust tone, space constraints, and cost are also major factors that manufacturers must consider when designing complete exhaust systems for production vehicles, and performance is sometimes compromised in order to meet those goals.

The frame design of the 1955 Pontiac forced the use of a single exhaust system. Dual exhaust pipes were a popular upgrade with performance enthusiasts, however. In true hot rodder fashion, hobbyists devised several ways of adding a second pipe in search of a slight power increase.

A factory-installed dual-exhaust package was made available when a modified frame was introduced in 1956, which boosted the factory horsepower rating by about 10. Dual exhaust was then used on every regular production performance Pontiac through 1974, at which point a single exhaust catalyst was introduced.

Manifolds

Most regular-production Pontiac engines used log-style cast-iron exhaust manifolds. This design simply gathers the gas exiting the cylinder head in a central chamber, sends it through a common collector into 2- or 2.25-inch tubing, and then to a muffler. Many variations of this type were used over the years, and they are generally considered the most restrictive from a performance perspective.

Pontiac realized early on that separating and merging certain exhaust manifold runners and increasing their length improved

Common log-type exhaust manifolds are intended to do little more than gather exhaust gas and route it toward the muffler. Pontiac produced a wide variety of examples over the years for different chassis applications. While not the best choice for a high-performance rebuild, they are sufficient for mild-to-moderate performance applications. Used examples are relatively inexpensive, but be sure any replacement fits your particular Pontiac.

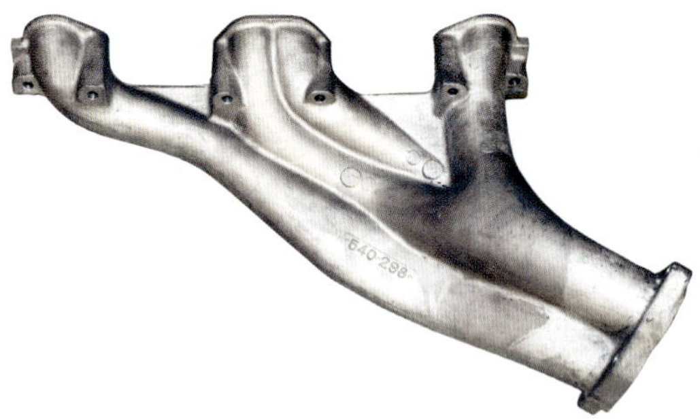

Pontiac's cast header was developed to maximize exhaust efficiency of the early Super Duty engines. It featured a bolt-on collector that could be uncapped to bypass the exhaust system. The most common unit was constructed of cast iron, but a cast-aluminum version, like this reproduction from Ram Air Restoration Enterprises, was available for certain applications. The Super Duty castings offer tube header-like performance.

engine efficiency, which translated into better high-speed performance. The first long-branch manifold was introduced in 1958, and the first full-length cast header was introduced for the Super Duty package a year later. These units remain among the best performance exhaust manifolds ever produced by an auto manufacturer.

The long-branch exhaust manifold was revised slightly for 1967 to accommodate the new Firebird chassis. Still featuring individual exhaust runners, it was used in all high-performance Firebird applications and was available in both D-port and round-port configurations.

A compact high-flow exhaust manifold was created for the 1967 Ram Air GTO. It was then used on various A-Body applications through 1972 and certain Firebirds from 1970 to 1974. Retaining four separate runners and a single collector, the Ram Air unit contained shorter runners, which are internally separated. The lack of runner length affects performance slightly, when compared to the long branch, but it remains a significant improvement over the standard log-type unit.

Pontiac used high-flow exhaust manifolds to improve the efficiency and usable power of its high-performance engines. Along with the other GM divisions, Pontiac also used specifically designed mufflers to produce optimal vehicle performance while providing its signature sound. This was achieved by using unique internal designs for each vehicle and sometimes even on certain applications.

Mufflers

Most Pontiac mufflers reduce sound pressure levels and eliminate undesirable droning through a combination of flow path management, frequency attenuation chambers, and pulse absorbing cavities. Original Pontiac mufflers generally flow 55 to 70 percent of a straight pipe, while those destined for high-performance applications typically utilized larger-diameter internal tubes and may flow slightly more.

Oldberg Manufacturing Company provided many of the mufflers used on various 1964 to 1973 Pontiac models. Pontiac's mufflers typically featured circular, extruded holes instead of linear perforations, which produced the trademark Pontiac sound. Pontiac's dual transverse mufflers maintained significant separation between the left and right sides of the exhaust flow after the two streams met in a blending chamber located in the center of the muffler. This gave the Firebird its unique sound.

Some mufflers, such as those used with the Super Duty 421 engine, were a straight-through design. Since these engines were limited-production units intended for sanctioned racing, maximum flow was more of a concern than sound quality or muffling ability. In some cases, multiple suppliers provided replacement mufflers stamped with the same GM part number. But they were not internally identical to the production units that were actually installed on the vehicle during assembly, subsequently affecting sound.

The "Ram Air" exhaust manifold was introduced in 1967 for the 400 H.O. and the tight confines of the A-Body chassis. Featuring four runners that are separated internally, its use expanded to the Firebird line in 1970. Available in both D-port and round-port configurations, they generally perform as well as any shorty-style aftermarket header.

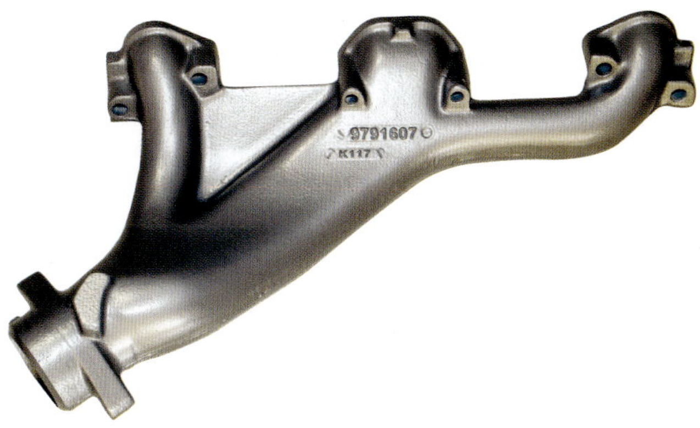

The "long-branch" exhaust manifold was an adaptation of the original Super Duty casting, which was developed to improve performance of certain first-gen Firebirds. Its use also included certain full-size vehicles with high-performance engines. On average, the long-branch manifold has a 7- to 10- hp advantage over a comparable Ram-Air type.

AFTERMARKET PARTS

A complete Pontiac engine can make an excellent usable core, but many of those now available may not be large enough or contain the best components to produce the desired amount of horsepower. While the aftermarket has heavily supported many other makes for several years, the number of choices for Pontiac hobbyists had been quite limited. But that isn't the case any longer. Virtually any component possibly required when rebuilding a Pontiac V-8 is being produced in some form, and often the choices are an easy way to increase output.

Block

The stock Pontiac block is quite adequate for most high-performance rebuilds. It accepts an overbore of up to 0.060 inch in most instances and possibly more after sonic testing to measure thickness. Boring routinely adds 5 to 12 ci depending upon the engine, and that can allow it to produce slightly more power while still operating reliably. Though complete block failure is rare, the stock block does not tolerate certain instances of grossly increasing displacement or greatly increasing performance level beyond its design capability. New blocks that contain additional material in critical areas, such as the deck surface, cylinder walls, lifter gallery, main saddles, and oil pan rail, are available for hobbyists looking to go to the next performance level.

Two separate companies currently produce unique aftermarket Pontiac blocks that are commonly used when building engines that displace 505 to 535 ci or more. K&M Performance produces the MR-1, which is available in cast iron or cast aluminum. The IA-II block is produced by AllPontiac.com and is also available in iron or

In today's world, any hobbyist can rebuild a Pontiac engine entirely from aftermarket components. This 535-inch engine was assembled with an IA-II block, a forged stroker assembly, a roller camshaft, Edelbrock cylinder heads and intake manifold, Holley 4-barrel carburetor, FlowKooler water pump, March serpentine belt drive, Doug's headers, and an MSD ignition system. It fits and installs just as an original Pontiac V-8.

Pontiac used 4-bolt main caps in its performance engines. Billet Speedworks, formerly Pro-Gram Engineering, produces a complete line of top-quality main caps for hobbyists who wish to add them to their engine. The Billet Speedworks 4-bolt cap is much beefier when compared to an original Pontiac 2-bolt unit. The block's main journals must be machined any time new main caps are installed.

aluminum. Either is sold by a number of Pontiac vendors. The blocks contain external dimensions similar to an original Pontiac unit but are generally thicker throughout and feature standard splayed 4-bolt main caps. The blocks are delivered fully machined and accept most original Pontiac hardware. The basic iron offerings start at several thousand dollars and a number of options are available.

Crankshaft

Pontiac's cast-iron crankshaft is a durable unit. Rarely does failure occur from fatigue during common operation. Secondary factors like vibration, detonation, or lubrication issues are more likely the root cause of a failure. The journal surfaces can generally be renewed with proper machining, but there are certain instances in which an original Pontiac crankshaft simply isn't reusable. While locating and using a suitable core is certainly possible, a few companies produce new Pontiac V-8 crankshafts that are readily available from most Pontiac vendors.

There are two types of new Pontiac crankshafts presently available. Using world-market material and overseas labor, several companies source a common cast crankshaft, which is finished to proprietary specifications. The overall quality and finish of the cast units was once questionable but has improved in recent years. Modern cast units are suitable for stock-type rebuilds and possibly even some high-performance rebuilds producing 500 hp or slightly more. With a relatively low cost of about $300 (or less), and a wide array of journal and stroke dimensions available, aftermarket cast-iron crankshafts are an acceptable solution to salvaging an original.

The second type of aftermarket Pontiac crankshaft is constructed of forged steel. These units generally cost a few hundred dollars more than their cast counterparts but are considerably stronger and a better choice for high-performance rebuilds producing more than about 550 hp and up to about 1,400 hp. A steel forging is mandatory in any maximum-performance effort, however. Though the number of journal and stroke configuration choices has been limited in the past, there seems to be a wider array available today, and the cost has become much more reasonable. Those who have direct experience the aftermarket forgings report excellent results.

Pistons and Rings

Cast-aluminum pistons were used in nearly all production Pontiac engines from the start of production until the end. High-quality stock-replacement cast pistons are produced by a few different manufacturers, such as Sealed Power and Keith Black Silv-O-Lite, and are readily available from a number of mail-order vendors at a very reasonable cost. As of 2019, a cast piston set costs around $300. Keith Black also offers a cast-hypereutectic piston, which is a modern silicon-aluminum alloy used to cast certain pistons. It is considered a step better than conventional aluminum and adds about $125 to the set cost. While either type of cast piston can provide an owner with a long

A few different companies offer new cast crankshafts that are essentially a direct replacement for an unusable original. It seems the most popular unit is from Eagle Specialty Products, but your favorite Pontiac vendor may have other suitable options. Forged steel replacements are also available for high-performance applications.

TRW Automotive forged-aluminum pistons have been a popular choice in performance rebuilds since the 1960s. Sealed Power now offers TRW's complete line of Power-forged pistons, which includes direct-replacement 400 and 455 pistons available in popular oversizes. The modern Sealed Power unit (left) is very similar to the cast-aluminum design originally developed by Pontiac (right). The black coating on the Sealed Power unit is a moly-graphite material that is screen printed and baked onto the piston skirt. It acts as a sacrificial barrier to prevent cylinder wall scuffing at start-up.

service life, it seems as if premature failure can occur if the pistons are not installed exactly as the manufacturer suggests and the engine operating conditions are anything but ideal.

Keith Black (KB) offers high-quality cast-hypereutectic and forged-aluminum pistons, which are direct fit for Pontiac applications. While the cast pistons are popular for budget rebuilds, forged pistons are a better choice for high-performance rebuilds where output exceeds about 350 hp. Available for the 400 and 455 in popular oversizes, KB pistons can be had with a flat-top head or with a slight dish to reduce compression. KB also offers one of the only direct-replacement 428 pistons available today. They are available in the same oversizes as others but with a 10-cc dish only.

When building a Pontiac V-8 and stock-replacement-type forged pistons are not compatible, Ross Racing Pistons offers an excellent aluminum forging that can be custom made to fit a specific application. Your machinist or favorite Pontiac vendor can help you determine the exact specifications that are required for your application.

Forged-aluminum pistons are far more forgiving. Most Pontiac vendors can supply you with a high-quality forging at a reasonable price. While manufacturers such as Ross or Diamond produce custom pistons that fit a specific application, Sealed Power, Keith Black, Probe, and JE Pistons are just a few of the companies that produce off-the-shelf forgings that are a direct fit for the Pontiac V-8, which start out around $400 per set. If your rebuild uses a stock-stroke crankshaft and stock-length connecting rods, then stock-replacement forgings are an excellent choice. Custom pistons are required when using a long-stroke crankshaft or aftermarket connecting rods.

Working in conjunction with the pistons, piston rings are designed to keep compression and combustion pressures from passing around the piston and into the crankcase while lubricating the cylinder walls. Piston rings are commonly constructed of many different materials, such as iron and stainless steel, and are usually moly coated. Depending upon the application, ring sets can come pre-gapped for a certain size of bore with overlapping ends for custom gapping and those designed to be completely file fit. Piston rings come in various thicknesses. Thicker ring packs tend to seal better, while thinner ring packs tend produce less drag at high RPM, which can translate into more performance. There are distinct advantages to the various types of piston rings available and your machinist or Pontiac vendor can suggest the set and type that works best with your application, whether it's for high-performance street, street/strip, or race.

Piston rings are an important part of any rebuild. A number of companies produce quality offerings, but Total Seal is an industry leader. The type of piston ring and amount of end gap your rebuild requires depends mostly upon the piston being used and the intended application and operating range. Total Seal produces a number of high-quality piston rings from entry-level ductile moly to high-end diamond-coated rings for most applications.

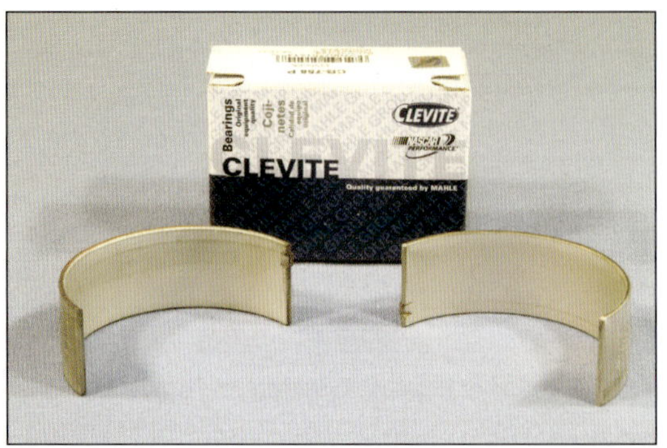

Mahle Clevite has been producing engine bearings for many years and the company remains one of the most popular bearing manufacturers today. Clevite offers a few different bearing levels with characteristics that differ with the intended loads that each may see. It produces connecting rod bearings for Pontiac applications that are undersized up to 0.040 inch in 0.010-inch increments. Main journal bearings are available in an undersize up to 0.030 inch.

Connecting Rods

A connecting rod is among the engine's most stressed components. In constant motion, it is designed to endure compressive loads while changing direction several times each second without fatiguing. The severe operating conditions make reusing high-mileage cast-iron units a questionable endeavor, especially if engine output or maximum engine speed is significantly increased. Original cast rods can be reused in stock-type rebuilds if your machinist finds them to be crack free and in good reusable condition. While some hobbyists have taken extra steps to increase strength, such as beam polishing and shot peening, I think the cost of modern forged replacements is a much better investment.

Though Pontiac used cast rods in most of its passenger car engines and failure during normal operating was quite rare, its specialized high-performance engines received heat-treated steel forgings. The originals were expensive and difficult to find and remain so today. For years, only a small number of Pontiac-spec forged rods were available on the aftermarket, and they too were once very costly. Modern forgings, however, make upgrading to a forged-steel connecting rod a much more sensible option during any rebuild.

RPM International offers an entry-level connecting rod for Pontiac V-8 engines constructed of forged 5140-steel. The stock-style RPM rod, an I-beam design with dimensions identical to a standard Pontiac unit, is an affordable choice for any application where a cast-iron original is being considered. The unit is marketed under various names, available from most major Pontiac vendors for under $300, features 7/16-inch American Racing Products (ARP) bolts, and is suitable up to roughly 500 hp. I selected these rods for the 400 rebuild featured in this book.

Eagle Specialty Products (or ESP) has been producing forged-steel H-beam connecting rods with stock Pontiac dimensions for years. In response to consumer inquiry, ESP recently developed a forged 5140-steel I-beam connecting rod for Pontiac V-8s. It includes stock dimensions, press-fit wrist pins, 7/16-inch ARP bolts, and precise machining that leads to excellent consistency. It can be considered a high-quality option for Pontiac V-8s that use stock-length connecting rods and produce up to 500 hp. ESP's 5140-steel forging generally retails for less than $400.

Upgrading to 4340-steel forging is a worthwhile investment for any engine, especially if you're planning an engine rebuild that generates more than 500 hp and up to about 800. A 4340-alloy steel rod is chosen for its desirable endurance qualities, and a number of companies offer such connecting rods specifically for Pontiac V-8s. Along with RPM International, Scat Enterprises and ESP are other companies that produce 4340-steel rods for Pontiac applications.

It's likely that the raw forgings may come from the same overseas supplier, but the cost of similar rods can vary between $300 and $500 per set. The price difference generally reflects of the number or types of finishing steps performed. So, it may be worthwhile to purchase a more expensive set of connecting rod if your budget allows, especially when considering that there are no negatives associated with a connecting rod that's too strong for a particular application. Other connecting rods constructed of billet-steel or aluminum are required for specialized applications where the specific strength and/or lightweight characteristics are required to withstand output or RPM. These units are available from manufacturers such as Carrillo Industries, Crower Cams, and Oliver Racing Parts, and can be quite costly.

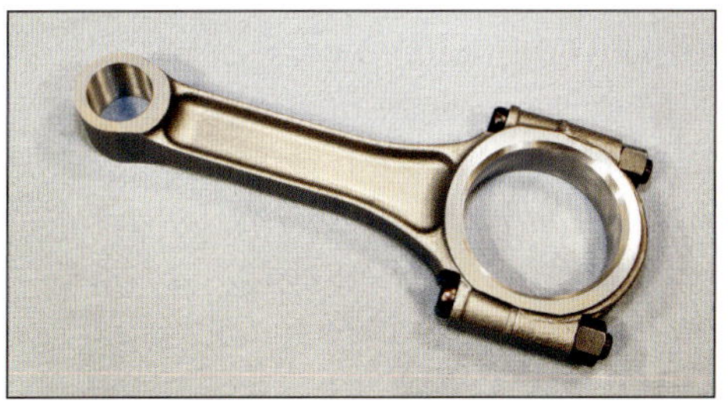

Forged connecting rods were once very expensive and the choices available in Pontiac specifications were extremely limited. RPM International has developed a stock-replacement forged rod constructed of 5140-steel for the Pontiac V-8. Most Pontiac vendors offer these rods under various names, and the cost is about the same as reconditioning a set of cast originals. Many hobbyists reported excellent results in engines producing less than 500 hp.

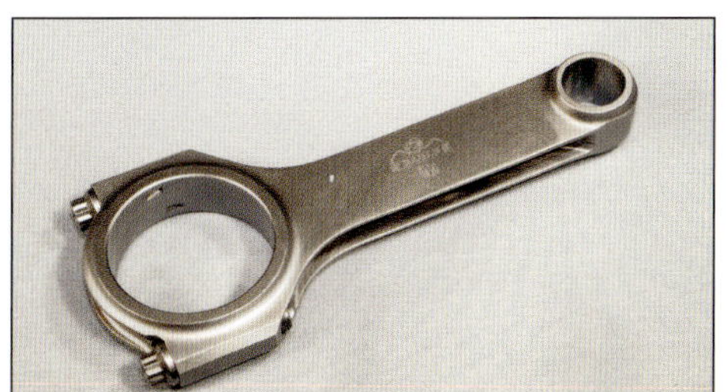

Eagle Specialty Products (ESP) was among the first manufacturers to offer a relatively affordable forged steel connecting rod for Pontiac engines. Constructed of 4340-steel and finished to ESP specifications, it is an excellent choice for high-performance rebuilds, especially when output exceeds 500 hp. ESP also offers a forged 5140-steel connecting rod as an affordable solution for builds up to 500 hp.

What's the Difference Between Pressed and Floating Piston Wrist Pins?

An engine's pistons are fastened to the connecting rods by a length of high-strength tubular steel known as a wrist pin. Most production Pontiac engines from 1958 forward used a pressed wrist pin design. Pontiac used a floating wrist pin design from 1955 to 1957, and it is common when using aftermarket pistons or high-RPM applications today.

A pressed wrist pin setup relies on an interference fit between the wrist pin and connecting rod. During assembly, the piston wrist pin bore, or "small end of the rod" as it's known, is heated, which causes the metal to expand, and the piston wrist pin is inserted into the rod opening. After the rod cools naturally and the material around the wrist pin contracts, the pin remains stationary on the rod while the piston pivots on it, providing quiet, consistent operation.

A floating pin design requires a bushed rod, which is essentially the same connecting rod used in pressed-pin applications, but the wrist pin bore is enlarged and a bronze bushing is installed. The wrist pin is then secured to the connecting rod by retaining clips on each end of the piston. This design allows the piston and pin to "float" on the connecting rod, dissipating the total compressive load.

The wrist pin retention method that's best for your application largely depends upon the pistons and connecting rods you choose to run. Some stock-type replacement pistons lack the retaining ring groove, which requires the use of pressed pins. High-end performance pistons, however, almost always include the ring groove. Some connecting rods are only available for one type. For a street-driven Pontiac V-8, one type isn't necessarily better than the other. Just be sure the wrist pin retention methods of the components you choose are compatible. ■

Specific connecting rod preparation is required for the type of wrist pin being used. Original and aftermarket connecting rods intended for pressed wrist pins (left) require a specific amount of clearance between the wrist pin bore and wrist pin diameter. Aftermarket rods intended for floating wrist pins are fitted with a bronze bushing (right), which is generally left undersized from the manufacturer. The machinist should hone to the piston manufacturer's suggested specification.

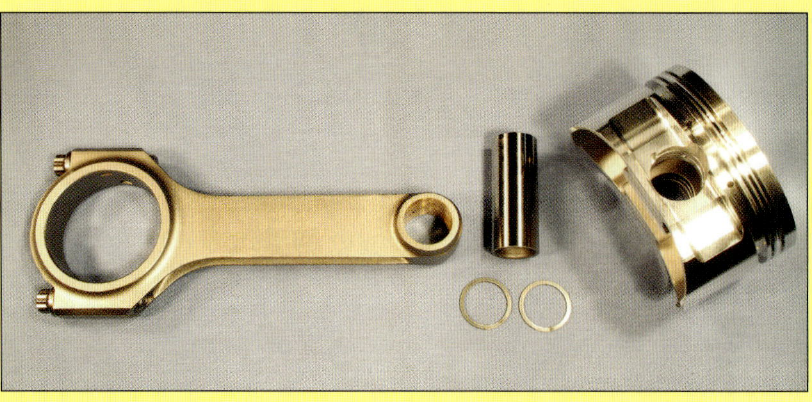

Most aftermarket connecting rods are designed to accept floating wrist pins, and that requires aftermarket pistons with a pin-locking clip groove on each end of the wrist pin bore. A complete assembly, like this, is commonly included in aftermarket stroker kits. After honing, assembly consists of first lubricating the bronze bushing with 30-weight oil. The wrist pin is then inserted into the piston and connecting rod, and the clips are installed into the piston grooves with a specific tool.

Stroker Kits

Adding engine displacement is an easy way to increase output, and the most common method when rebuilding a Pontiac V-8 has simply been enlarging bore diameter. Lengthening the crankshaft stroke is another popular method, but the process is quite involved if you're using an original Pontiac crankshaft. It requires resizing the crankshaft's rod journals from the stock Pontiac diameter of 2.25 to 2.2 inches, a measurement more closely associated with big-block Chevy engines. The rod journal is then offset-machined in the process, which relocates the axis and allows stroke to be lengthened by 0.040 inch or slightly more, adding another 6 to 8 ci of total displacement.

With the somewhat recent availability of aftermarket Pontiac crankshafts with a wide array of journal and stroke dimensions, many vendors brought to market complete rotating assembly kits that include a new crankshaft, forged-steel connecting rods, forged-aluminum pistons, and the required rings and bearings. The crankshaft usually features a stroke length of 4.21 to 4.25 inches and 2.2-inch rod journals. It is combined with 6.8-inch connecting rods, which are also normally associated with big-block Chevy engines. Complete stroker kits make it much more practical and affordable to build a stroker engine and increase the displacement and power output of most Pontiac V-8s.

Stroker Kit Choices

Stroker kits are an easy way to significantly increase the displacement and output of 350 and 400 engines. A standard Pontiac 400 block that's been bored 0.060 inch, for instance, can displace as much as 467 ci by simply adding an aftermarket crankshaft with a 4.25-inch stroke, which otherwise drops in easily with little modification. A 455 can be made as large as 474 ci using a similar combination. The added stroke in either instance allows the engine to produce more torque in a usable RPM range (at a reasonable cost) with minimal effort.

Most Pontiac vendors offer complete stroker kits that include a long-stroke crankshaft, forged connecting rods and pistons, and new bearings and piston rings. Companies, such as Butler Performance and Kauffman Racing Equipment (KRE), offer complete entry-level kits that start out at less than $1,400, and include a cast crank and forged 5140-steel connecting rods. Options, such as custom forged pistons, a forged-steel crankshaft, and forged 4340-steel connecting rods, can add several hundred dollars to that cost.

In past years, owners had to select the right combination of top-end components to make a lesser-displacement engine run as well as a larger engine. Stroker kits remain the quickest and most affordable way of increasing the output of virtually any Pontiac V-8. There really aren't any negative side effects associated with lengthening engine stroke in a street-driven car. The resultant torque increase generally makes it more pleasurable to drive at a low speed and spins the tires much easier! ■

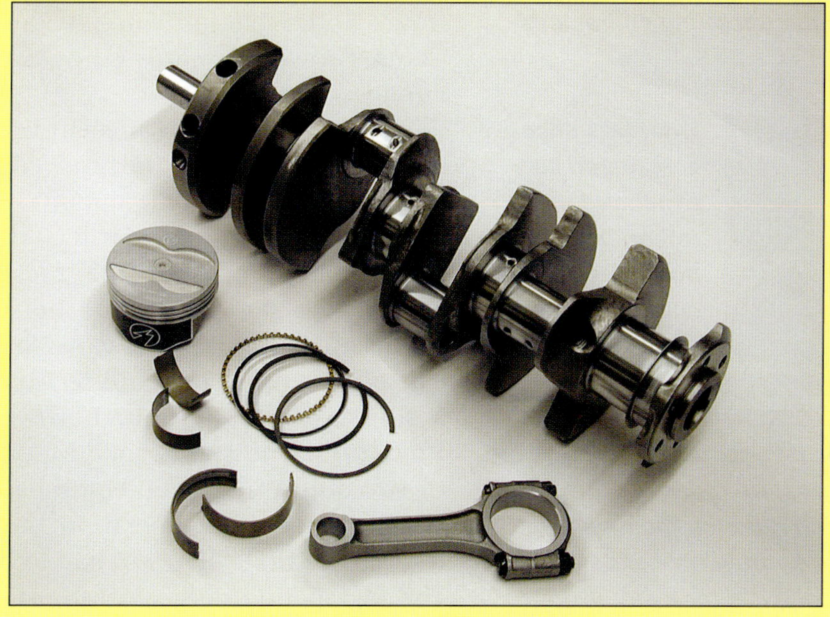

Complete rotating assembly kits that include a new crankshaft, forged connecting rods, forged pistons, and rings and bearings are quite popular. Budget kits generally include stock-replacement-type components, but a number of upgrades are available. The stroker kits include a long-stroke crankshaft and are an easy way to reliably increase displacement and output at a very reasonable cost. (Photo Courtesy Butler Performance)

Valvetrain

The valvetrain is comprised of many components and the camshaft is at the heart of it all. There are four major types used in modern high-performance engine rebuilds and general terms are used to describe them. Hydraulic flat-tappet and roller camshafts use tappets, or "lifters" as they're more commonly known, that rely on pressurized engine oil to continually adjust an internal plunger, which ensures that the valvetrain components remain in constant contact for quiet operation. Manual-lash flat-tappet and roller camshafts, which are often referred to as "mechanical" or "solid" units, require that valve lash be set manually.

Flat-Tappet Cams

A hydraulic flat-tappet camshaft operates quietly and consistently and requires very little maintenance. The sheer number of available grinds from most camshaft manufacturers makes them a popular choice. They remain an excellent choice for any Pontiac engine regardless of the intended application. Any flat-tappet camshaft requires careful break-in to prevent premature lobe and/or lifter failure and engine oil with sufficient anti-wear additives to protect the contact surfaces during normal use.

Along with several aftermarket flat-tappet camshafts, Melling also offers high-quality replicas of Pontiac's 068, 744, and 041 grinds in exact specifications. Other companies such as Comp Cams and Crower offer a complete line of flat-tappet cams for all types of applications.

At high engine speed, certain hydraulic lifters don't have sufficient time to bleed down, and that can cause the valves to float. That is the only real negative associated with hydraulic flat-tappet cams. Engine speed in excess of 6,000 rpm is quite possible if high-quality lifters are used. I highly suggest American-made lifters and prefer purchasing from Butler Performance, Comp Cams, Crower, Howards Cams, and Lunati.

A solid flat-tappet camshaft uses a lifter with a fixed pushrod cup. Beyond the suggested amount of valve lash, the lifter transfers the entire lobe profile to the rocker arm, which can add several horsepower at high RPM. The valve lash can make a solid cam noisier than a similar hydraulic unit, however. Vintage lock nuts were good for one or two adjustments and could back off during normal operation, and that meant that valve lash had to be checked periodically and adjusted as needed.

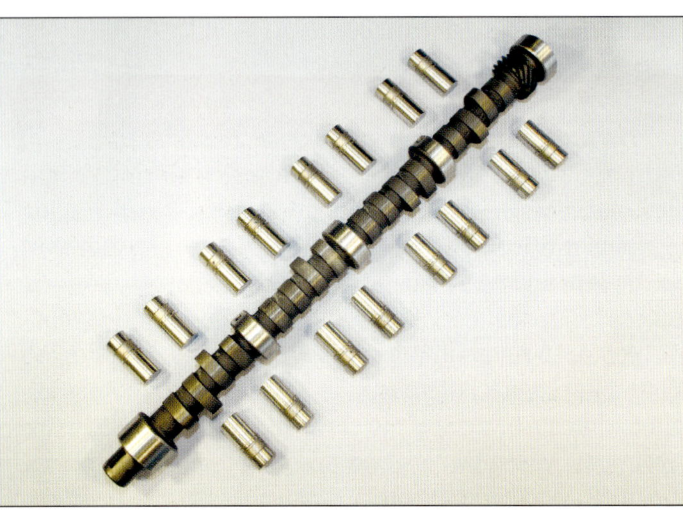

Pontiac always used flat-tappet camshafts in its engines. Melling reproduces several of Pontiac's popular hydraulic camshafts, such as the 068, 744, and 041. Most aftermarket camshaft manufacturers offer a number of different mechanical and hydraulic grinds. Usually a 0.050-inch intake duration between 200 and 225 degrees and valve lift less than 0.500 inch produces the best total performance and reliability for a street-driven Pontiac V-8. Your machinist or Pontiac vendor can help you select a grind that best complements the operating characteristics of your engine.

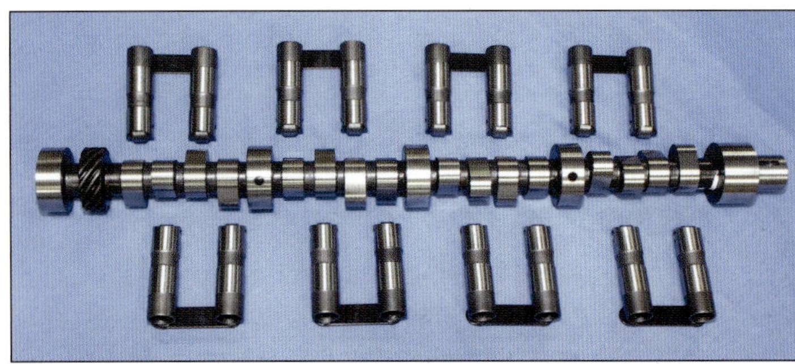

What was once considered very expensive and rather exotic is now relatively commonplace in modern performance rebuilds. Hydraulic roller camshafts are used in all production engines for passenger cars today and are a popular upgrade with Pontiac hobbyists. The aggressive roller lobe profile allows the engine to tolerate slightly more 0.050-inch duration than a similar flat-tappet without compromising street manners. A hydraulic roller cam with 220 to 240 degrees of 0.050-inch intake duration is typical for a street-driven Pontiac V-8.

Modern rocker arm studs with flat tops and positive locking nuts have essentially eliminated the need for continual valve lash adjustments, but many believe that regular valve lash maintenance is still required. That reputation tends to limit the popularity of solid flat-tappet cams for street applications today. When combined with ARP rocker studs and lock nuts, solid flat-tappet cams are quite reliable and can be checked annually but should require no adjustment. In fact, if any lash adjustment is required, it may actually indicate abnormal valvetrain wear that should immediately be inspected for.

Roller Cams

Hydraulic roller camshafts have become quite popular in recent years. Instead of a flat-tappet lifter that rides on the lobe, a specific lifter fitted with a roller wheel is used to reduce friction, and that allows for a camshaft with a more aggressive lobe profile. When compared to a flat-tappet camshaft with similar 0.050-inch duration specs, with a hydraulic roller, the valve stays seated longer, improving idle quality and vacuum and then opens at a quicker rate with extended dwell at max lobe lift. Both factors give a hydraulic roller camshaft a

slight performance edge when compared to a similar flat-tappet. The only real shortcoming to a hydraulic roller is component cost. Off-the-shelf and custom hydraulic roller camshafts are available from Comp Cams, Crower, Howards Cams, and Lunati. Technicians at those companies or your preferred Pontiac vendor can spec one for your application.

At one time, the relatively heavy roller lifters and the valve springs required to control them at high engine speed caused the lifters to bleed down uncontrollably. That led to a poor performance, which gave hydraulic roller cams a negative reputation early on. As hydraulic roller lifter technology improves, so does the quality of roller lifters for the Pontiac V-8. Lifters from companies such as Comp Cams, Crower, Howards Cams, and Lunati can operate reliably up to 6,000 rpm and possibly more.

The most popular type of camshaft for serious performance applications is a solid roller. Like a solid flat-tappet, the roller wheel on the lifter follows the lobe and there's no hydraulic pressure to compromise valve action. The friction reduction allows for a much more aggressive lobe profile, which opens and closes the valves at a much quicker rate

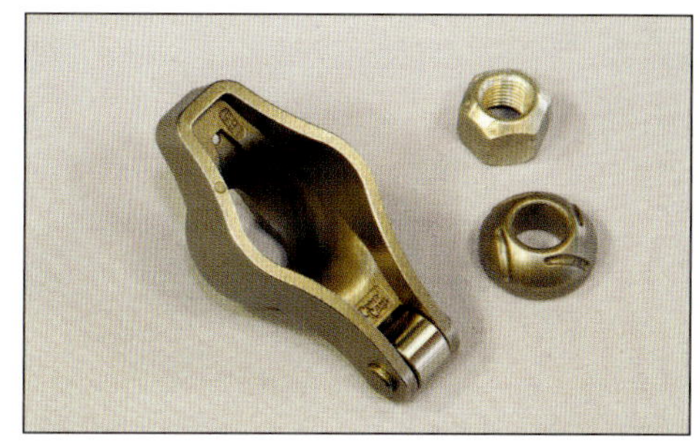

New rocker arms should be part of any performance rebuild if the budget allows. Units with a roller tip can combat against the side loading that causes premature valve guide wear. Comp Cams's high-quality roller tip rockers are available in 1.52:1 and 1.65:1 ratios. They are an excellent choice when upgrading from the stock stamped-steel rockers with a flat-tappet camshaft.

and can increase performance. But the valve springs and components required to control that action make a solid roller cam unpractical for street-driven applications.

Rocker Arms

An engine sees camshaft duration and lift at the valve. The lifter transfers camshaft lobe lift to the rocker arm, where it is converted into valve lift. Gross valve lift is easily calculated by simply multiplying lobe lift by the rocker arm ratio. Pontiac's stock ball-stud rocker arm features a 1.5:1 ratio, and when used together with a typical Pontiac cam with 0.271 inch of lobe lift, gross lift at the valve calculates to approximately 0.407 inch.

While stock-replacement rocker arms are readily available from a local parts store or mail-order vendors, modern roller-tip rockers—such as those from Comp Cams—install like the stock units but include a roller tip to lessen the side loading, which causes valve guide wear. Many companies offer full roller rocker arms

The major advantage that roller cams offer over flat-tappet grinds is friction reduction. Roller lifters feature a hardened steel wheel that can follow a much more aggressive lobe profile when compared to a similar flat-tappet (right). Roller cams can allow the valve to open and close at a much quicker rate while providing more dwell area under the curve (left).

In addition to its roller tip, full roller rocker arms include a roller trunnion, which reduces the friction and valve loading associated with ball-stud-type units. Premium examples, such as this 1.6:1-ratio, cast-alloy unit from Crower, generally provide a more consistent ratio, which can translate into smoother and more consistent engine operation. Though cheaper examples may seem attractive, I suggest spending the extra money for higher-quality units from popular manufacturers.

that use a cast-alloy or stainless-steel body and combine a roller tip and roller trunnion to further reduce friction. At the speed that most street-driven Pontiac engines operate, there is likely no measurable performance difference in any rocker type. While full roller rockers arms can be used with flat-tappet or roller camshafts alike, I recommend limiting roller-tip rocker arms to flat-tappet only.

High-Ratio Rocker Arms

A popular modification that often increases performance is the use of high-ratio rocker arms. Not only does a high-ratio rocker arm increase gross valve lift, it can simulate the effects of added duration as the valves open and close at a quicker rate. Pontiac used 1.65:1 rocker arms on its R/A-IV to increase gross valve lift from 0.470 inch to roughly 0.520 inch. While it may seem easier to simply select a cam that provides the desired amount of lift with 1.5:1 rockers, higher-ratio

rockers are actually less stressful on the block's lifter bores because less lobe lift causes less lifter travel.

To achieve a higher ratio, a rocker arm's pushrod cup is moved closer to its fulcrum. That can change the angle of the pushrod's path, causing it to contact the pushrod hole that's machined into the cylinder head. In most instances, the pushrod guide hole can be elongated by using a grinder to gain sufficient clearance. This task must be performed while the cylinder heads are removed from the engine.

Valve Springs

An engine's valve springs are designed to control valve motion. The valve spring compresses when the valve opens and must keep the valve firmly on its seat when it relaxes. Most Pontiac engines originally used a dual cylindrical spring package. Most aftermarket dual-spring packages include an inner and outer spring and an internal damper, which is placed between the springs to minimize coil surge. Springs of this type are available in a wide array of pressure ratings from many manufacturers. They are an excellent choice for street-driven Pontiacs with either flat-tappet or hydraulic roller cams. Most cam companies can suggest the type that works best with a particular grind.

A conical valve spring, or "beehive" spring as it's often called, features a cylindrically shaped body that tapers as it reaches the top. The shape considerably increases the spring rate and reduces the amount of moving mass within the spring, also allowing for the use of a smaller-diameter retainer. The uniquely shaped spring offers increased spring load but reduces the friction generated from added valvetrain mass and component deflection. Though conical springs are quite popular in modern production engines and are an excellent choice for specialized applications, they are not generally required for street-driven Pontiacs.

Cylinder Heads

Measured airflow of an unmodified Pontiac D-port cylinder head with 2.11-inch intake valves peaks at approximately 210 cfm at 28 inches of pressure. That amount of airflow should easily support 350 to 400 hp on a larger engine. While that output level may satisfy many owners, there are others seeking to significantly boost performance. That often requires an airflow increase, and that once meant spending hours grinding material from the cylinder head intake and exhaust ports.

When porting cylinder heads, the intent is to improve overall

Valve springs are often overlooked, but they play a critical role in the performance of an engine. They control valve action while not fatiguing from harmonics created from normal operation. Pontiac engines used a dual-spring package, and it remains very popular during rebuilds. A conical valve spring with a beehive-like shape can effectively control valve action while reducing valvetrain mass (left). It can be used in certain conditions where an aftermarket dual-spring package (right) cannot.

airflow without making the intake port too large, which can negatively affect throttle response and low-speed performance. It entails removing material from areas that restrict airflow while leaving material in areas that otherwise have little effect. A flow bench can be used to measure airflow, or the cylinder heads can be installed on the engine and the performance recorded on the drag strip or engine dyno.

There are now more sensible options than porting your own cylinder heads. Builders such as Butler Performance and KRE offer hand-porting services. SD Performance has created a computerized porting program that can increase the intake airflow of a basic cast-iron D-port head to as much as 280 cfm. Additionally, modern aftermarket aluminum castings with the capacity to flow substantially more air than an unmodified original are readily available from a few different sources. Any of these high-quality offerings are available in ready-to-run condition for $2,000 (or less) and should provide plenty of performance for almost any street-driven Pontiac.

SD Performance has developed proprietary CNC programs for nearly any cast-iron cylinder head that Pontiac produced. The basic package delivers 250 cfm of peak intake airflow and an exhaust-port flow that's at least 75 percent of that amount. In addition to the beautiful port work, the castings are fully machined and contain top-quality hardware, including 2.11/1.77-inch valves and valve springs matched for the type of camshaft being used. With a relatively small intake port volume of 165 cc, SD Performance's CNC-ported heads can produce up to 500 hp while maintaining good port velocity, which maximizes low-speed street manners.

KRE recognized the need for a modern D-port cylinder head for high-horsepower applications. It developed and released its own aluminum casting, which is now available from a number of vendors. Intake port volume is relatively small at 185 cc, which is intended to enhance low-lift airflow, but the casting peaks at approximately 260 cfm in as-cast form. The KRE casting includes 2.11/1.66-inch stainless steel valves and high-quality valve springs. A fast-burn combustion chamber maximizes combustion efficiency. The KRE D-port head has proven itself as an excellent value for anyone looking for an alternative to reusing a stock casting or to increase performance.

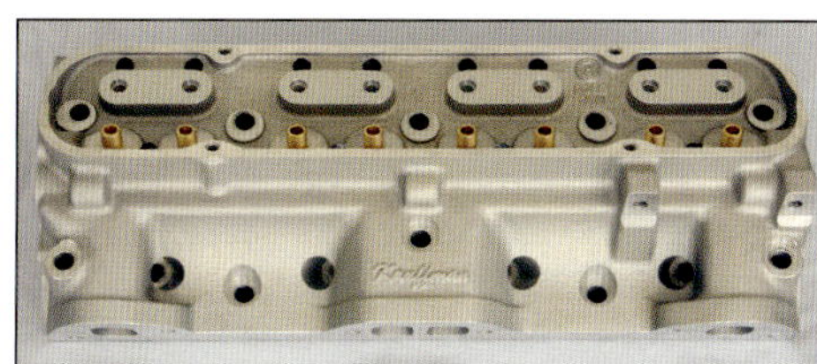

Cast-aluminum cylinder heads are quite popular. Kauffman Racing Equipment (KRE) produces a high-flow D-port aluminum casting. It can be used as a modern replacement in any application in which a modified cast-iron D-port is being considered. Boasting 260-cfm of airflow and moderately sized intake ports to maintain good low-speed street manners, the KRE D-port installs easily onto any Pontiac V-8 block and accepts all original Pontiac hardware. It also features a fast burn–shaped combustion chamber to improve operational efficiency.

During the 1990s, Edelbrock created a high-quality cast-aluminum cylinder head for the Pontiac V-8 based on the popular Ram Air IV design. Its Performer RPM round port–type casting is available in two variations: the original wedge-shaped combustion chamber and a fully CNC machined combustion chamber with fast-burn shape for improved combustion efficiency. Either version is available with 72- or 87-cc combustion chamber volumes. Both feature an intake port volume of 215 cc and are capable of flowing 280 cfm in as-cast form. Requiring the use of round-port exhaust manifolds or tubular headers, the Edelbrock round port includes 2.11/1.66-inch valves and valve spring options for flat-tappet or hydraulic roller camshafts rated to 0.575-inch lift. The Edelbrock round port is an excellent performance value when compared to original round-port cylinder heads.

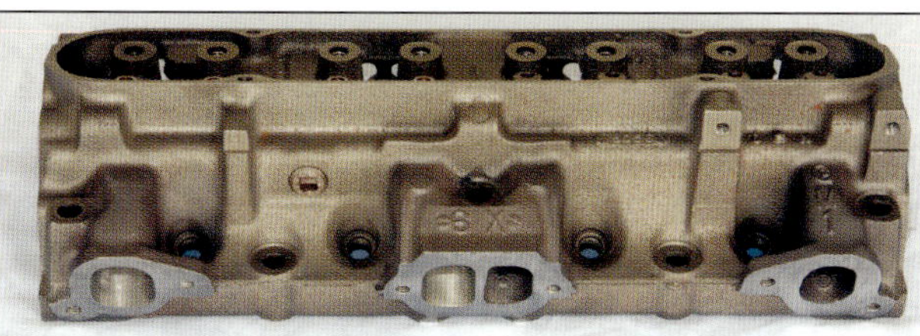

SD Performance can take a traditional Pontiac cylinder head and significantly increase its airflow capacity to 250 cfm or more by using its CNC mill. While not all engines need ported cylinder heads to run well, additional airflow is required for significant performance increases, and SD Performance can easily handle that task for you.

Edelbrock's cast-aluminum cylinder head is likely the most popular aftermarket casting on the market today. The large intake ports are capable of flowing at least 280 cfm in as-cast form, and the exhaust port has a round-type shape, which accepts conventional round-port exhaust manifolds or headers. In addition to high-performance applications in which generous amounts of airflow are required, the Edelbrock casting can be considered as a modern replacement to Pontiac's desirable round-port castings.

Edelbrock also offers its Performer D-port casting for Pontiac V-8s. Featuring 2.11/1.66-inch valves and a reduced intake port volume of 204 cc to improve throttle response when used on 389- and 400-inch applications, peak intake airflow measures around 270 cfm. Its combustion chambers displace 65, 72, or 87 cc, and the fast-burn shape promotes more efficiency than the open-chamber design found on the original Performer RPM casting. Included are flat-tappet or hydraulic roller–spec valve springs for gross lift measuring 0.575-inch. The Performer D-port is an excellent alternative to reusing original cast-iron D-port cylinder heads, particularly where increased performance is desired.

Intake Manifold

Many aftermarket companies have produced intake manifolds for the Pontiac V-8 for years. Some of those that produced popular offerings include Doug Nash, Edelbrock, Holley, and Offenhauser. While other modern companies may produce intake manifolds for specific cylinder heads or highly modified applications, Edelbrock has mass produced a wide array of intake manifolds for the Pontiac V-8 longer than any other.

Edelbrock presently offers at least four different cast-aluminum intake manifolds for the Pontiac V-8. While the others are single-plane designs that require an aftermarket carburetor, the dual-plane Performer and Performer RPM series castings are quite possibly the most popular aftermarket choices available today. The Performer intake manifold is considered a direct replacement

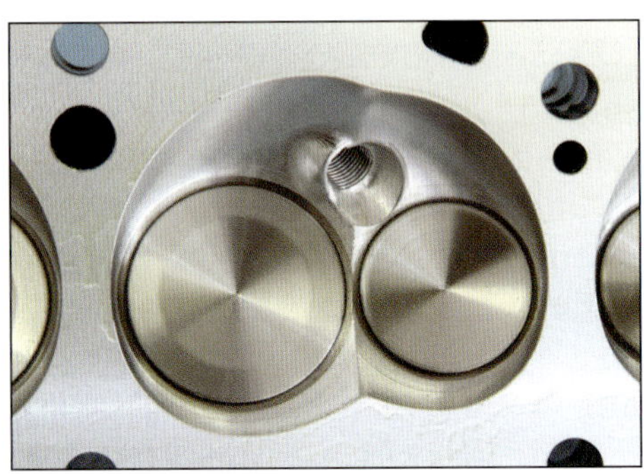

When Edelbrock originally introduced its round-port Performer RPM cylinder head, it contained an open-type combustion chamber. That casting is still available. Its Performer D-port includes a fast burn–shaped combustion chamber to maximize efficiency. That same technology was also incorporated into the round-port casting that Edelbrock markets as its Performer RPM CNC casting.

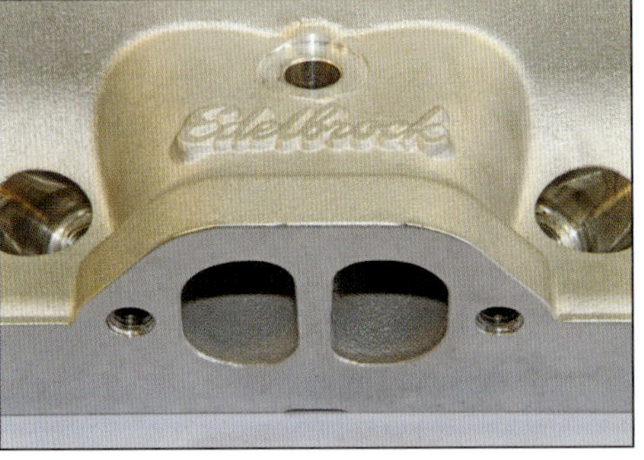

Since its introduction, the Edelbrock Performer D-port has been a popular cylinder head with performance-minded hobbyist. Its intake ports are slightly smaller than Edelbrock's round-port casting to promote mixture velocity for good low-speed street manners with smaller-displacement engines. As a result, peak intake airflow measures around 270 cfm in as-cast form.

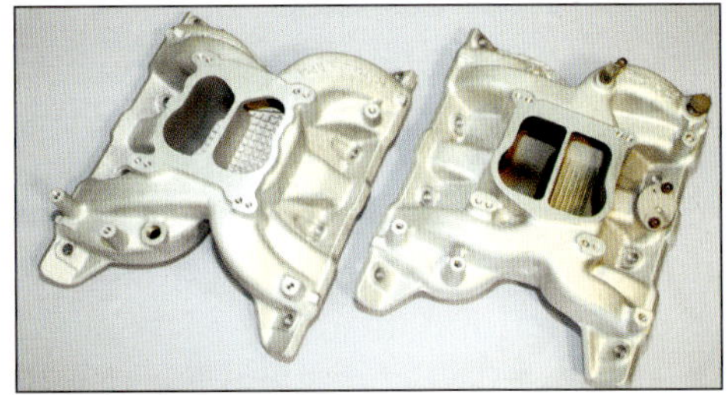

The original Pontiac intake manifold is an excellent dual-plane unit, but its cast-iron construction makes it relatively heavy. Edelbrock offers two distinct cast-aluminum manifolds that can be used as stock-type replacements. The Performer series manifold fits and functions much like the stock piece (right). The Performer RPM series manifold fits similarly but is more than 1 inch taller than stock and is designed to extend the effective powerband by several hundred RPM (left). The owners have removed the coolant crossovers on these units.

that installs and operates similarly to the factory cast-iron unit in most applications. With the ability to accept OEM emissions equipment, it remains 50-state legal. The main benefit the Performer offers over the stock piece is the weight savings of about 25 pounds.

The Edelbrock Performer RPM intake manifold is a unique dual-plane casting that's designed to improve high-RPM operation without grossly compromising throttle response and low-speed street manners. Though the Performer RPM isn't as efficient at low speed as the Performer, its relatively deep plenum and long, smoothly contoured runners extend its operating range by several hundred RPM. The deep plenum raises the carburetor flange more than 1 inch over a stock Pontiac unit, however, and that may present hood clearance issues in certain models.

Tri-Power induction remains quite popular with Pontiac hobbyists. Finding an original 1965–1966 cast-iron intake manifold for use with later-model cylinder headers or aftermarket aluminum offerings can be somewhat difficult and costly. This cast-aluminum unit is a high-quality reproduction of the 1966 Pontiac Tri-Power manifold, which includes the larger center carburetor. It is sold through a few different sources including Performance Years.

Carburetor

The Rochester 2- and 4-barrel carburetors have been out of regular production since the 1980s, but many remain in good, usable condition. It seems that a Tri-Power setup or single Quadrajet are the carburetors of choice for Pontiac hobbyists. With proper modifications, either can support significant amounts of horsepower. While basic Rochester rebuild kits and certain replacement components can be sourced from local parts stores, only a few companies currently support Rochester carburetor restoration and calibration components.

The Holley 4-barrel carburetor has been around for decades and it was the factory-issued unit on several high-performance Chevrolet applications during the 1960s and early 1970s. The only Pontiac engine to ever specify a Holley 4-barrel was the tunnel-port Ram Air V, but it was never a factory-installed engine on any production vehicle. Several complete engines were assembled

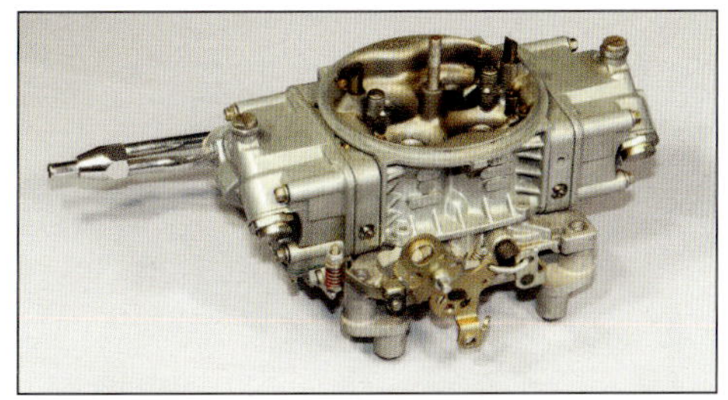

The Holley 4-barrel carburetor remains a popular choice for maximum-performance applications. Depending upon flow capacity, it can be a suitable choice for street use too. Fuel economy tends to suffer when compared to a properly calibrated Quadrajet, however. The Holley's square-bore bolt pattern requires an aftermarket intake manifold or a specific adapter plate to fit a stock manifold.

and sold through dealership parts departments and Holley produced a limited number of 4-barrels for it.

Over the years, a wide variety of new Holley 4-barrel carburetors with airflow ratings ranging from 650 to 1,000 cfm or more have been available through the aftermarket. With rebuild and calibration components readily available from most local parts stores or speed shops, the relatively easy tuneability makes Holley carburetors a popular choice for high-performance applications. The square-bore design does not allow for use on any regular-production Pontiac intake manifold, however. An aftermarket intake manifold with a square-bore bolt pattern, such as the Edelbrock Performer or Performer RPM, is required.

Fuel Pump

The AC division of General Motors produced most of the mechanical fuel pumps found on Pontiac V-8s. Most were application specific and included different

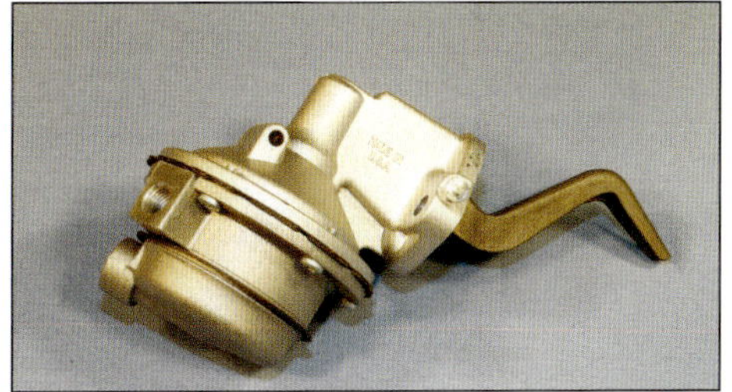

Stock Pontiac fuel pumps are adequate for stock-type rebuilds. Finding the factory high-volume units used in certain performance applications can be a bit difficult, however. Carter offers a high-quality mechanical fuel pump (number-M6907) that provides more fuel volume and pressure when compared to a stock replacement unit for high-performance applications at a reasonable cost.

fuel line routings, canister sizes, and flow volume and pressure ratings. ACDelco, Airtex-ASC, and Carter Fuel Systems presently produce stock replacement fuel pumps, and it's possible that they may be capable of delivering an adequate fuel supply for stock-type applications. Significantly increasing engine output might require an aftermarket fuel pump that can supply a greater amount of fuel volume with slightly higher pressure.

Upgrading to an aftermarket electric fuel pump may be the most popular option when an engine's fuel demand requires additional capacity, but it generally requires significantly modifying the existing fuel lines and adding the appropriate wiring to power its electric motor. Carter, Holley, and RobbMc Performance offer popular aftermarket mechanical fuel pumps for Pontiac applications that provide increased fuel capacity while installing relatively easily.

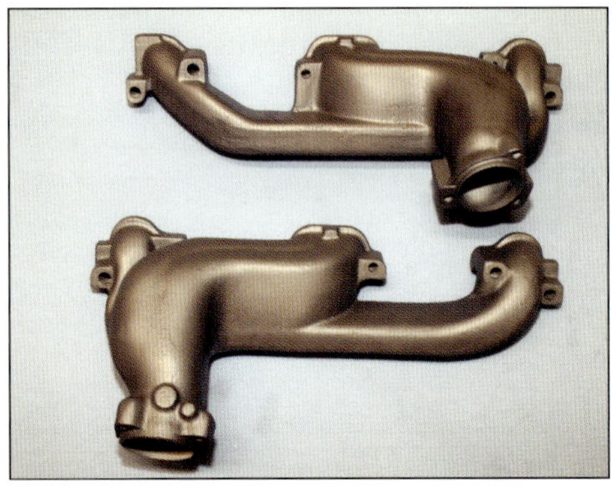

Ram Air Restoration Enterprises (RARE) reproduces Pontiac's most popular high-performance round-port and D-port exhaust manifolds. Using high-quality iron and proven casting and finishing techniques, RARE's manifolds are second to none. The list of available manifolds includes the Ram-Air style (shown), long-branch, and early Super Duty.

Exhaust Manifold

When Pontiac developed its high-performance engine packages, it usually included a unique exhaust manifold aimed at improving exhaust flow. The castings were highly coveted for years because they performed almost as well as tubular headers and were guaranteed to fit the intended Pontiac's chassis without any clearance issues. These were once worth several hundred to thousands of dollars, depending upon condition.

The originals were cast in gray iron, however, and finding a pair that isn't warped or cracked can be a very difficult task today. Fortunately for Pontiac hobbyists, a few different companies are casting exact reproductions of a few of Pontiac high-flow exhaust manifolds. The offerings from Ram Air Restoration Enterprises (RARE) are among the best available. They include SD-421 cast headers in iron or aluminum, and long-branch and Ram Air–style manifolds in round-port or D-port versions.

RARE's manifolds are cast in the same process as Pontiac's, but

In addition to its near-exact reproductions for restoration applications, RARE has the capacity to increase the collector diameter of its Ram Air and long-branch exhaust manifolds to improve airflow and performance. The Ram Air unit on the left measures 2.45 inches in diameter and is considerably larger than the original casting at right.

RARE uses ductile-65 iron, which is extremely strong and durable. After casting, the ports are cut on a CNC mill to ensure proper configuration and perfect port alignment, while the internal runners and collector area are cleaned up by hand. To further improve airflow, RARE can enlarge the collector, which increases airflow 12 to 20 percent over stock and lessens the transition when running larger exhaust pipes. RARE manifolds include a lifetime warranty and can be considered an excellent alternative to tube headers for a street-driven application.

Gaskets and Fasteners

A gasket's job is to simply seal engine components and prevent outward leaks. Whether it's keeping coolant within its system or oil from seeping outward, there are a number of task-specific seals and gaskets

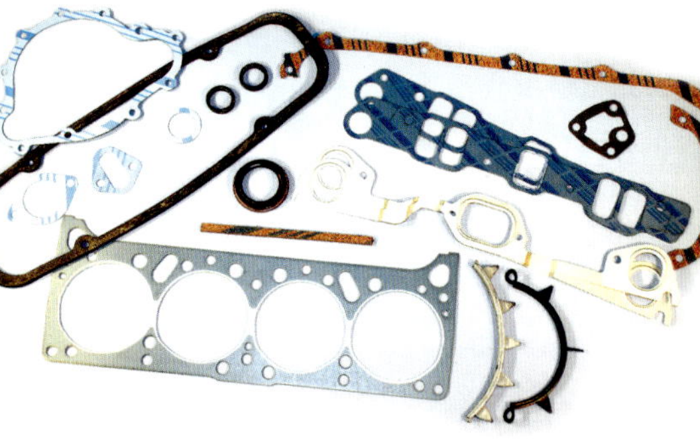

The Fel-Pro division of Federal Mogul produces high-quality gaskets that are a very popular choice with machine shops and engine builders. A complete gasket kit for Pontiac engines contains all of the necessary gaskets required during a complete rebuild. Most gasket sets for a specific component are available separately and can be sourced from your machine shop or local parts stores and be to you within a day or two.

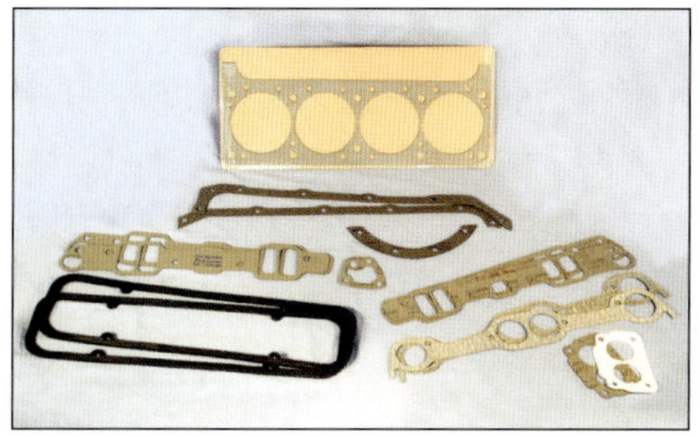

Tin Indian Performance offers its own line of high-quality gaskets and solid lip-type rear main seal for Pontiac engines. In addition to gaskets, the company has a wide variety of engine parts, including many of the small components that most others don't stock.

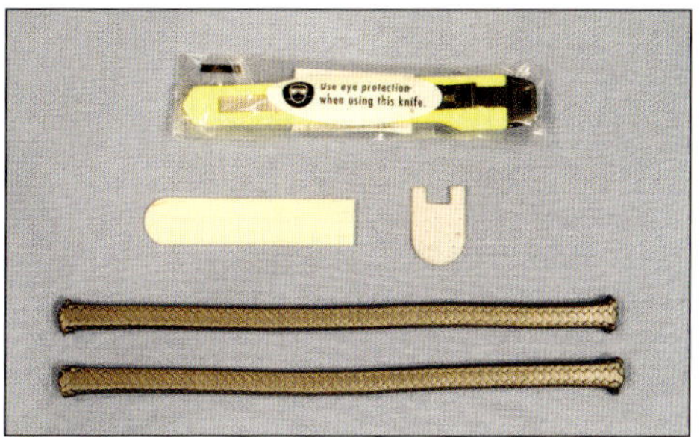

Pontiac's rope seal was originally very effective. Its effectiveness was compromised when the material was switched from asbestos to fiberglass. Best Gasket Company offers graphite rope–type rear main seal kits for Pontiac applications. Installation and function is much the same as the original Pontiac unit.

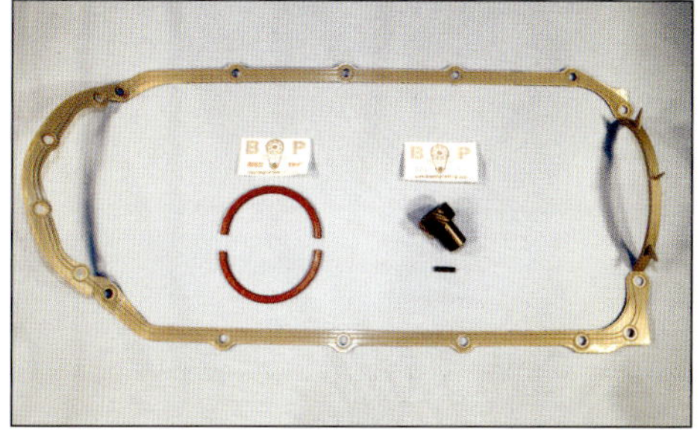

Most modern engines use a solid lip–type rear main seal to control oil. BOP Engineering created this unit constructed of Viton several years ago. It is quite effective when installed per the instructions. Though uncommon, the rear main seal groove machined into the block sometimes isn't concentric with the crankshaft. In these instances, the effectiveness of the BOP rear main seal can be compromised. BOP also offers a one-piece oil pan gasket and a composite distributor gear intended for roller camshafts.

found within an engine. There are a few different companies producing top-quality gasket sets for Pontiac engines today. Many machine shops and engine builders often use the popular Fel-Pro gasket sets. Fel-Pro gaskets are designed to fit well and provide a long service life.

A rear main seal prevents pressurized oil from escaping through the rear main journal. Modern engines generally use a rubber lip seal, but Pontiac used a braided rope seal containing asbestos. The rope seal was packed into a groove that was machined into the block and rear main cap. If installed correctly, it was quite effective and rarely leaked. The asbestos was eventually replaced with a fiberglass material because of government legislation, and it made installation difficult and leaks common.

Best Gasket Company offers a stock-type rope seal constructed of braided graphite strands. It fits and installs just as Pontiac's original seal and is an excellent solution. BOP Engineering developed a direct-replacement lip-type seal specifically for the Pontiac V-8. It is constructed of Viton, popular with hobbyists, and

I've successfully used it in my own engines. BOP has recently developed a one-piece lip-seal that many owners report excellent results with. Confer with your Pontiac vendor about which seal may work best for your application.

A fastener's clamping force can be compromised if reused a number of times, and even the most capable fastener can be ruined the moment

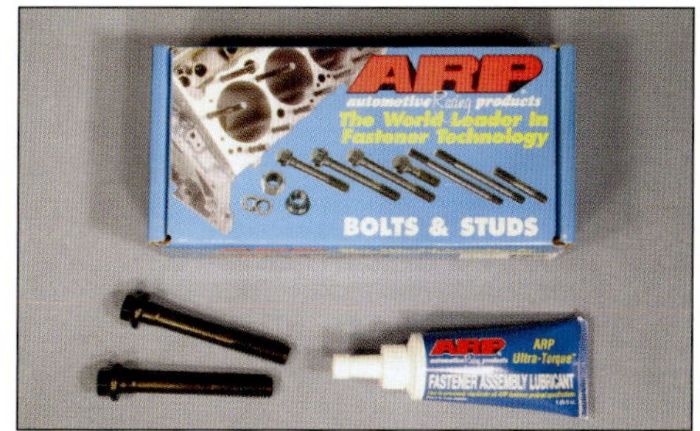

Automotive Racing Products (ARP) produces some of the best engine fasteners on the market. Cylinder head bolts, rocker arm studs, connecting rod bolts, and flywheel bolts are just a few of popular fasteners readily available for Pontiac applications. ARP also produces its own moly-based thread lubricant, which is suggested for assembly.

too much torque is applied. ARP is an industry-leading fastener manufacturer. It produces a complete line of high-quality, bolts, nuts, and studs, and offers many part numbers specific to Pontiac applications. ARP is the best choice when new fasteners are needed for any portion of a project.

An engine's valley pan and windage tray commonly need replacing during a rebuild because of severe corrosion or fatigue cracks. These Tomahawk units from Butler Performance are an excellent alternative to reusing originals. The valley pan is designed to clear roller lifters and the windage tray is thicker to resist fatigue.

MACHINING AND PREASSEMBLY

With a sound plan firmly in place, it's time to take your disassembled engine to the machine shop. It's best to make a single trip to deliver everything so your machinist can inspect it all at one time. Be prepared to discuss any irregularities you discovered during disassembly. It may point to an underlying issue that can be addressed during the rebuild.

When assembling any engine, its intended output and operating range must be within the realistic realm of possibility. While any Pontiac can perform suitably in stock form, modifying the original pieces or purchasing aftermarket components is often required to achieve significant performance increases. Each new component must be carefully selected to ensure that its operating characteristics complement the others. Haphazardly combining parts could otherwise produce an engine that only runs well in a limited RPM range or one that could self-destruct at high RPM.

The owner of our project 1967 400 being rebuilt wanted his engine to produce at least 360 hp. He based that number on the original rating of the 400 H.O. offered that year. Before spending dollar one on the project, I clarified several factors with him. This 400 in his 1967 GTO was original, and he didn't want to compromise originality in any way. That meant reusing the original block, cylinder heads, intake manifold, and carburetor if possible. And we depended on the machine shop to determine whether any of it was reusable or if we had to begin searching for replacements.

Machining

At this point, you have completely disassembled the engine and selected a reputable machine shop, so the rebuild portion of the project is ready to begin. I feel that it's best to take the entire engine to the machinist for complete inspection, even those parts that he might not otherwise touch. His experienced and discerning eye may notice something that you overlooked or didn't have proper equipment to detect.

I make it a habit to tag or mark any component I take with me to the machine shop so each can be quickly identified. I also suggest making a detailed list of the components that are being left behind so you can be sure each component is accounted for when that portion of project is complete.

The owner and I agreed to have Willard Auto Machine (WAM) in Omaha, Nebraska, perform the 400 rebuild. Many consider WAM one of the area's top engine building shops. WAM not only has the capability to fully machine any engine component in-house, its Land & Sea Dynomite engine dyno has been used to measure the output of the many Pontiac engines that owner Chuck

Willard has rebuilt over the years. I was completely confident in Chuck's ability to properly rebuild the 400. I asked that I be regularly updated of its progress and immediately notified of any irregularities, and he obliged.

Inspection

A complete engine rebuild begins with a deep cleaning of each component. That can include a thorough washing, acid bath, non-abrasive media blasting, or a relatively new process known as ultrasonic cleaning, which uses high-frequency sounds waves and a soapy mixture to clean components. The goal is to remove all traces of grease and grime from all of the engine components, which makes performing the visual inspection and any machining much easier. Under no circumstances should abrasive media, such as steel, sand, or glass, be used to clean any component. Minute particles can imbed into the component pores and/or cracks and crevices, making it impossible to completely remove. The media can dislodge during normal engine operation much later, causing serious internal damage.

Once each piece is completely clean, a quality machine shop inspects each component for any crack that could affect integrity. That process generally includes a magnetic particle inspection or pressure testing. When searching for external cracks, a component is dusted with small metallic particles, which tend to gather in cracks and become visible when the component is magnetized. Pressurized air can reveal any internal oil or coolant leaks. Your machinist can advise whether a component is salvageable if any cracks are detected.

Block Preparation

The block is the foundation of any engine. Its internal and external tolerances must be exact; otherwise, any component bolted to it may not function properly. In addition to thoroughly cleaning every coolant and oil passage to remove all traces or sludge or trapped grit, complete block machining should include boring and honing the cylinders, machining the cylinder head deck surface, and boring or honing

the main journals. The cam tunnel can also be checked if any usual bearing wear was found during disassembly. In our instance, the cam tunnel was straight. WAM determined that the abnormal wear was likely due to improperly installed cam bearings.

If the cylinders show little taper, it's possible that honing can restore the cylinder wall finish and promote maximum seal by using the existing pistons with new rings or replacement pistons of the same dimension. Most often, however, the cylinders

1 Wash Components

Before any machining is performed, Willard Auto Machine (WAM) thoroughly cleaned each component of the engine to remove any sludge and contaminants that might inhibit proper inspection and machining. The process can be performed in a number of ways. This includes solvent washing, non-abrasive media blasting, and ultrasonic cleaning. Any of these methods work quite well. What's available to you may depend upon the area you live. Local laws in some portions of the country may restrict the types of chemicals or methods that can be used.

2 Bore Block

After carefully inspecting the block for cracks and measuring cylinder wall thickness to verify that no less than 0.125-inch remains after machining, the block is sonic tested. Sound waves are blasted into the material and the reflectivity is calculated into thickness. The cylinders are then bored to a dimension that provides optimal cylinder ring seal. For Pontiacs, this usually starts at 0.030 inch and can increase up to as much as 0.060 inch, if thickness testing allows. This 400 had already been bored 0.030 inch. WAM removes only 0.010 more taking the bore diameter to a total of 4.16 inches. A steel torque plate should be used during boring and honing. It replicates the effects that the cylinder heads have on the cylinders when bolted to the block.

need to be enlarged to repair worn or damaged walls. An overbore of 0.030 to 0.060 inch is common during Pontiac V-8 rebuilds, but it's recommended that wall thickness be sonically checked to ensure it's not less than about 0.125 inch after machining for a street-driven Pontiac. New pistons and corresponding rings are required any time the bore is enlarged. Final honing to achieve the recommended amount of piston-to-cylinder-wall clearance should only be performed after the new pistons arrive.

Pontiac engines generally have good main cap alignment and rarely require any additional machining beyond a basic line hone. Any time new main caps are installed, the block should be line bored or honed, which ensures that the main journals are absolutely straight. Absolute precision is required during the process. The machinist should also use a small stone or file to deburr the main saddle and cap parting lines to remove any sharp edges that could prevent the bearings from being installed properly, or insert material behind it during bearing installation.

Crankshaft Preparation

Many modern machine shops do not have the proper equipment to machine crankshafts simply because of the rather high cost and limited usage. You shouldn't immediately assume that your chosen shop is inferior if it doesn't have such equipment, however. A quality machine shop can arrange to have your crankshaft sent to a reputable shop that specializes in servicing crankshafts.

If your rebuild includes an aftermarket crankshaft, it shouldn't require any additional machin-

3 Purchase New Pistons

After determining how much material must be removed from the block's cylinder walls, WAM sourced the correct-sized pistons and corresponding rings. The bore of this 400 was increased by 0.040 inch. Sealed Power is one company that offers a high-quality forged-aluminum piston that's ready-made for 0.040-plus 400 applications (number-L2262F040). The company's recommended moly-coated piston ring set was used to complement the pistons.

4 Measure Piston Diameter

When purchasing pistons and rings, the set often includes the exact piston dimensions and suggested piston-to-cylinder wall clearance and ring end gap. Even so, WAM still physically measured each piston diameter with an outside micrometer positioned about 2.5 inches downward from the head to ensure complete accuracy. In this instance, Sealed Power recommends 0.002 to 0.003 inch of clearance for its forged pistons.

5 Hone Block

When boring a block, the machinist usually stops 0.005 to 0.010 inch short of the final bore dimension. That's then followed by the honing process, which removes small amounts of material and allows the machinist to finely tailor the bore diameter to the precise amount of piston-to-cylinder wall clearance. The process also leaves behind a distinct crosshatch appearance that's required for maximum ring seal and lubrication.

6 Machine Block Deck

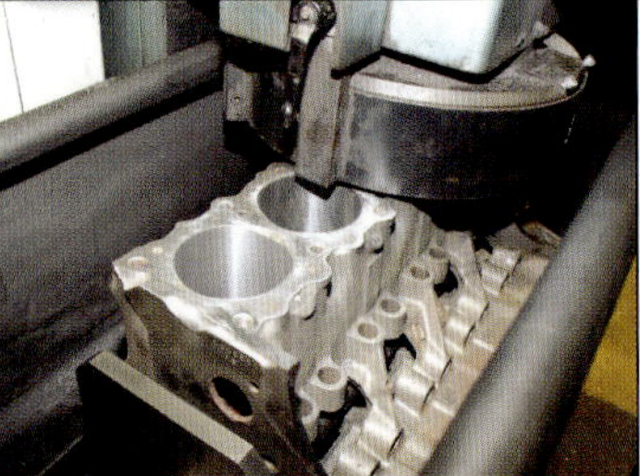

A block's deck surfaces are often distorted from years of use, especially if the engine was subject to significant overheating. A precision straight edge and feeler gauge is used to determine any areas that may not be straight. Optimal straightness can be achieved by lightly milling the deck surface on a horizontal mill. Compression height, as measured from the centerline of the crankshaft to the deck surface, should measure around 10.22 to 10.24 inches, depending on the pistons and connecting rods being used.

ing, but your machinist should still verify that its rod and main journals measure correctly, and that it's balanced properly. Your machinist can determine if your original Pontiac crankshaft is reusable and assess the condition of its journals if you plan to reuse it. If they are in relatively good shape, micropolishing may be all that's needed to renew the surfaces.

Journal machining is typically required and that generally consists of undersizing the journals, which is usually in 0.010-inch increments. The main journals of a Pontiac crankshaft can be undersized as much as 0.030 inch without compromising integrity. The rod journals can be undersized as much as 0.15 inch to the big-block Chevy journal diameter of 2.2 inches without issue. No additional surface hardening treatments, such as nitride or chroming, are required when building a street engine.

Occasionally, an original crankshaft can be bent. Straightening it is a delicate process that involves setting the crankshaft in a jig and carefully driving the counterweights in the required direction to ensure the main journals are straight. But it doesn't guarantee any result. A replacement crankshaft may be required if the original cannot be sufficiently adjusted.

Connecting Rod Preparation

Pontiac's cast ArmaSteel connecting rod has gained a negative reputation over the years. Many hobbyists believe that it immediately self-destructs much above 5,000 rpm. In reality, Pontiac's cast rod is quite durable and has been used successfully in engines that turn 6,000 rpm or slightly

7   Line Hone Main Journals

To ensure that the main journals are perfectly straight and that the crankshaft isn't subject to any undue stress, the main caps are installed and the block is line honed on a Sunnen line hone machine. This procedure removes a slight amount of material from the cap and block and can move the crankshaft centerline a bit closer to the camshaft. If the main journals require a considerable amount of machining, a slight amount of material can be removed from the mounting flange of the main caps and the assembly is line bored, which can be performed without moving the crankshaft centerline any closer to the camshaft. Ask your machinist if the parting lines were deburred and how much material was removed during the line-hone process. A shorter timing chain may be required in certain circumstances.

8   Grind Crankshaft Journals

The stock Pontiac crankshaft is quite durable. It did not need its journals hardened from the factory to improve strength like some other makes, so no additional hardening is required during a rebuild. A significant amount of material can be removed from its rod and main journals without greatly affecting durability. The most apparent limiting factor is the immediate availability of undersized bearings for Pontiac journals, which is as much as 0.030 inch in most instances. If either journal surface requires excessive undersizing, it may be best to source a replacement crankshaft.

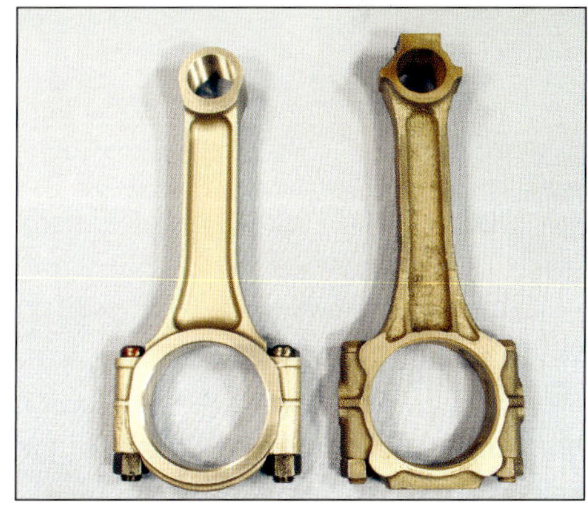

The stock cast Pontiac connecting rod (right) is sufficient for any street-driven application. Each rod should be magnetic particle inspected for cracks, measured and machined, and new fasteners added. For the cost of reconditioning an original set, I feel it's worthwhile to invest in a set of forged 5140-steel rods like that produced by RPM Industries (left). The RPM offering features dimensions identical to Pontiac's original rod and can be considered a modern replacement for any application where originals are being considered. The RPM rods are available from most Pontiac vendors for less than $300.

more. I don't suggest reusing original cast rods for a high-performance rebuild, mostly because affordable forged-steel options are readily available. But I am not suggesting that the original rods cannot be used when they are prepared properly.

If original cast rods are part of any rebuild, the machinist should carefully magnetic-particle inspect the rod body and cap for cracks. Any rod that even looks as if it has any area that could evolve into a crack should be replaced with another without exception. The rods should be checked for straightness, and modern high-quality 3/8-inch fasteners, such as PN 190-6001 from ARP, are highly recommended. These require 50 ft-lbs of torque using ARP's moly-based thread lubricant. The ARP fasteners replace the Pontiac originals, which otherwise require 43 ft-lbs using 30-weight oil. The crankshaft end of the rod should be resized. That includes removing a bit of material from the cap and body parting lines and machining the bore to return it to proper dimension. The parting lines should be deburred for optimal bearing installation.

9. Measure Connecting Rod Crankshaft Bore

After placing each RPM rod into a soft-jawed vise and tightening the nuts of the ARP fasteners to 75 ft-lbs, WAM checks the crankshaft bore (or large end) of each new forged-steel connecting rod to ensure that the opening is perfectly round. A slight amount of variance is corrected by removing material from the parting line of the rod cap, reinstalling the cap, and honing the bore to the proper specification. The parting line should be deburred after machining to prevent bearing damage during installation.

10. Hone Connecting Rod and Piston for Wrist Pin

The wrist pin bore (or small end) of each connecting rod and the corresponding hole on the piston is honed to 0.001 inch to accommodate the press-fit wrist pin. The honing process ensures a precise amount of clearance between the connecting rod and wrist pin. The piston wrist pin bore is about 0.0005 inch larger than the pin, which allows the piston to pivot freely on the wrist pin once the engine comes up to normal operating temperature.

There are two main types of aftermarket forged rods available for Pontiac V-8 engines: I-beam and H-beam. The debate over which type is better largely depends upon the intended application, but it's generally stated that an H-beam rod is more resistant to bending when compared to an I-beam rod. In reality, either should be quite sufficient for most street-driven Pontiac V-8s.

Even though it may seem that aftermarket connecting rods should arrive in ready-to-run condition, it's highly advisable that the machinist measure the entire set to verify that each is within the stated tolerances. It's not uncommon to find one or several needing its crankshaft bore honed slightly. Whether running original cast rods or aftermarket forged units, the piston wrist pin bores usually have to be honed to achieve proper clearance for the wrist pin that's included with the new piston.

I routinely consider all connecting rod options when choosing a connecting rod for an engine. Because most street-driven Pontiac engines, like this 400, do not usually turn more than 5,500 rpm or generate much more than 400 hp, a set of stock-length 5140-steel forgings from RPM International were more than sufficient for a build of this level, and the cost is quite reasonable. These are the rods I chose for this particular rebuild, but Eagle Specialty Products 5140-steel rods would have been equally acceptable.

Balancing

Component balancing should be part of any rebuild, no matter how basic. The process consists of weight matching the entire reciprocating assembly. This includes the pistons,

11 Balance Connecting Rods and Pistons

Balancing the reciprocating assembly ensures smooth, consistent engine operation and should be part of any rebuild. A precision scale is used to measure the weight of each piston, pin, and connecting rod individually. Material is then removed from designated areas of the pistons and rods until the heaviest pieces weigh nearly the same as the lightest. When weighing connecting rods, better shops use a specific hanger like this, which allows the operator to accurately measure both ends of the rod for exact balance.

12 Balance Crankshaft

A series of bobweights are fastened to the crankshaft rod journals, which replicates the effects of the rotating and reciprocating masses. The crankshaft is spun at low speed and a strobe light tells the operator exactly where weight should be added or removed from the factory counterweights. WAM generally gets the crankshaft very close before adding the timing chain gear, harmonic balancer, and flywheel or flexplate, and then finishes the process. The flywheel or flexplate the engine is balanced with should be the one that's used in the vehicle. So, if a replacement is required, it should be purchased by this portion of the rebuild. It ensures that the entire reciprocating assembly is fully balanced. You should have your machine shop perform this function, so your engine operates at maximum efficiency.

13 Chamfer Oil Holes

The technician waits to polish the crankshaft journals until the unit is fully balanced, which is intended to remove any marring that could occur when the bobweights are installed to the rod journals during the balancing process. Before beginning, he or she chamfers the oil holes to improve bearing lubrication on a round grinding stone—a step many machine shops do not perform.

connecting rods, and crankshaft. The harmonic balancer and flywheel or flexplate are also included in certain applications. Balancing minimizes engine vibrations through a certain RPM and serves to maximize performance while increasing engine life, particularly of the main bearings.

Crankshaft Polishing

The crankshaft machining process generally leaves behind a rough journal surface that can quickly destroy a new bearing. After all machining and balancing is complete, the crankshaft is installed onto a special lathe, where it is rotated at relatively low speed while the operator uses a belt polisher to polish the freshly machined journals, removing all minute rough edges and burrs. The result is a super-smooth journal surface, which should provide optimal lubrication and long bearing life.

Intake Manifold Selection

An intake manifold is designed to operate within a specific RPM range on a given engine combination. Plenum volume, cross-sectional runner area, and overall runner length are factors that help a manifold achieve optimal performance for the intended application. Though any manifold operates on any engine at any practical engine speed, performance ultimately suffers as engine speed varies outside the manifold's intended operating range. There are two major groups of 4-barrel intake manifolds: single-plane and dual-plane, and the operational characteristic of either is somewhat specific.

Single-plane castings generally favor higher-horsepower combinations that operate at high engine

14 Crankshaft Polishing

The crankshaft polishing process is rather straightforward. The crankshaft is mounted into a special lathe, and it's spun at a low speed while the journals are polished with specific polishing bands of varied coarseness. The end result is super-smooth main and rod journals that should provide thousands of miles of reliable operation.

15 Valve Guides

As a valve guide wears over the course of many thousands of miles or normal operation, it tends to lose its ability to properly locate the valve and prevent oil from passing by. A common repair is to hone the cast-iron guides and install thin-wall bronze liners. Another common repair that seems to be much more permanent includes machining the existing cast-iron guide and installing an entirely new guide constructed of cast-iron or bronze. When using cast-iron cylinder heads, 0.0015-inch intake and 0.0020-inch exhaust of valve stem clearance should be sufficient.

have an open plenum design, in which each of the eight runners pulls from the entire carburetor to improve high-speed cylinder fill. A direct trade-off, however, is less carburetor signal at idle and low-engine speed, which tends to negatively affect throttle response, low-speed performance, and overall economy.

Dual-plane manifolds are designed to develop maximum average power over a broad RPM range. They consist of a split plenum in which four cylinders pull from one half of the carburetor and the remaining four pull from the other half. The design increases the speed of the air passing through the carburetor, which tends to improve fuel atomization, making dual-plane manifolds very efficient at low- and mid-RPM ranges. However, this design can adversely affect high-speed operation because only half of the carburetor is available to supply air to each cylinder.

The best intake manifold for any application depends upon engine displacement, cylinder-head flow, camshaft duration, and the intended purpose and operating range of the engine. The stock Pontiac intake manifold was developed to produce maximum usable torque, and this

16 Hardened Exhaust Seats

When lead was removed from gasoline in the early 1970s, premature exhaust seat failure was fairly common. Consequently, Pontiac began hardening its cylinder head exhaust valve seats in 1972, but the process only hardened the material at the surface and immediately beneath it. It was generally removed after two valve jobs. Hardened exhaust valve seats are required on engines that are driven daily or run hard. The process of adding hardened seats is relatively simple. The seat is cut to a specific dimension and a hardened seat is coated with liquid sealer and driven into place. After allowing sufficient time to cure, the new valve seat is permanently located and ready to have the valve seat cut in.

17 Determine the Correct-Sized Bearings

While it may seem that all engine bearings are created equal, the thickness of various bearings can differ among the manufacturers and the different types offered. Unless you provide your machinist with a specific brand or set of connecting rod and main journal bearings, he or she undoubtedly has a brand and type in mind while machining your components. The specific thickness is calculated into the clearance measurements and using other bearings can affect the result. It may be best to let your machinist supply you with his or her preferred brand of bearings for your rebuild. Just the same, a different brand of bearing can sometimes be used if slightly more or less clearance is required.

design remains an excellent choice for most street-driven applications. It should sustain 5,500 rpm (or slightly more) on any 350 or 400, while that may be a few hundred RPM less on larger engines. I felt that the 400's original cast-iron intake manifold was the best choice for its intended operating parameters.

Cylinder Head Preparation

An engine inhales and exhales through the cylinder head intake and exhaust ports. The overall condition of the valves and seats can have a dramatic effect on total airflow. Worn or leaky valve guides or seals can allow the engine to pull oil into its cylinders. Weak valve springs can cause the valves to bounce, which can cause any number of operating issues. Excessive bolt torque, running excessively hot, and heating and cooling cycles in general can distort any of the cylinder head surfaces.

Proper machining of original Pontiac heads should include a quality valve job and quite possibly new valve seats if the existing units have been cut too many times or damage is detected. The valve guides found on original Pontiac cylinder heads were constructed of cast iron and are essentially an integral part of the casting. When repair is required, knurling was popular in the past, but it's not recommended in any instance today. A thin-wall bronze liner is a popular method of repairing worn guides, but machining the cylinder head to accept a new guide is generally the best solution.

Some companies offer new valve guides constructed of cast iron, but manganese-bronze is a more popular alloy. According to SI Valves, an industry leader, bronze generally wears less under load when compared to iron, and its porous nature allows it to retain oil, which tends to better lubricate the valve stem. Bronze requires slightly more valve stem clearance when compared to

When performing a valve job, multiple seat angles can improve airflow at all lift points, but especially at low- and mid-lift ranges. The multiple seat angles tend to smooth-out the transition from the port into the chamber. A multi-angle valve job used to require that the operator make three or more separate cuts into a valve seat with specially designed cutting stones, and the task required precise accuracy, otherwise airflow could suffer some degree. Modern cutting tips can cut any number of multiple seat angles at one time, which has significantly improved the quality and efficiency of a typical valve job. A talented machinist carefully measures the depth of each valve seat to check consistency and ensure that the valves are all in the same location in relation. The valves should also be marked with some type of dye or marking compound and test fit in the head and rotated to determine the location that the seat angles contact on another and that the pattern is concentric.

If sourcing new valves during a rebuild, the seat angle may not need to be modified, but used valves almost always need to be refaced. The process includes locking the valve into a variable mandrel, which spins it against a grinding stone at high speed. The process also allows the machinist to verify that the valve stem is straight and that the valve isn't bent in any way.

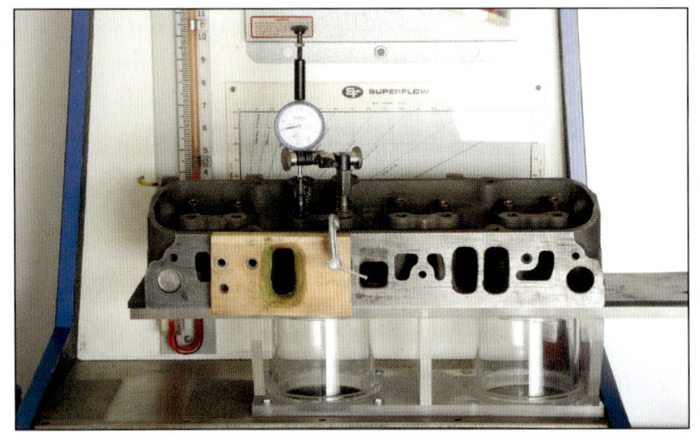

A flow bench is an excellent tool used by professionals to measure the static airflow capacity of cylinder heads, intake manifolds, and carburetors. I own and operate a SuperFlow number-SF-110, which is quite sufficient for comparing airflow for my own projects. The intake and exhaust ports of the 400's 670 cylinder heads peaked at 212 and 165 cfm at 28 inches of pressure, respectively. The capacity falls right in line with other D-port castings with 2.11/1.77-inch valves that I've measured and should be capable of sustaining 400 hp.

cast iron, however, since it expands quicker than iron when exposed to the heat generated during normal operation. Using the valve stem clearance specifications found in the Pontiac service manual along with bronze guides can significantly limit valve travel, causing it to "stick" in the guide.

Exhaust valve seat wear became a concern in the early 1970s when most tetraethyl lead was removed from gasoline. The lead acted as a high-temperature lubricant that protected the valve seat against significant wear caused by the exhaust valve during normal operation. Internal testing at Pontiac showed that significant valve seat wear was common, especially in engines that regularly operated under heavy loads, such as high-performance race applications or those vehicles equipped with trailer packages.

Machining the cylinder head to accept a hardened-steel exhaust valve seat, which is far less susceptible to wear, is considered a permanent solution. But it wasn't cost effective for manufacturers from a production standpoint. Pontiac developed a process known as "induction harden-

ing," which consists of electronically heating an exhaust seat and then immediately quenching it. It artificially hardens the iron to a depth of 0.050 to 0.100 inch, which combats seat wear. Pontiac began using the process on all its cylinder heads from 1972 forward, but the induction-hardened material was generally cut away after two valve jobs.

Using hardened exhaust seats should be a consideration when performing a valve job on any Pontiac cylinder head. Installation is relatively easy, and the process is one that any quality machine shop should be equipped to perform.

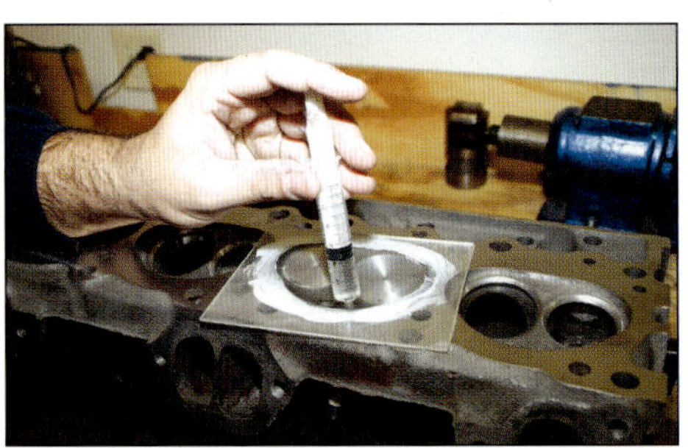

Measuring combustion chamber volume is an accurate way to determine compression ratio. Most shops have precision equipment available, but I have found that I can replicate those results by using graduated syringes sourced from an animal feed supply store, a thick piece of clear plastic with two holes drilled into it, and rubbing alcohol. I mount a cylinder head onto a cylinder head stand, level it out, apply a thin coat of white grease around the chamber, lay the plastic piece in place, and then insert a measured amount of fluid into the chamber through one hole while trapped air bleeds out of the other. I carefully record the amount of volume the chamber displaces. These 670 castings measured exactly 75 cc after the chambers were relieved.

Hardened exhaust seats can increase service life and extend the effects that a multiple-angle valve job offers. Because fuel lubricates the intake valve seat, it is not subjected to such wear. Intake valve seats may be required to restore valvetrain geometry if a cylinder head has had several valve jobs over the years.

Pontiac revised most of its cylinder heads for the 1967 model year. The number-670 casting found on the 400 being rebuilt is among the best D-port Pontiac ever produced. Using my SuperFlow SF-110 flow bench, I found that the intake ports of these particular castings peak at 212 cfm at 28 inches of pressure at just under 0.500-inch valve lift. I've learned over the years that most D-port castings with 2.11-inch valves flow similarly and that the available amount of airflow is more than enough to support 400 hp with the right combination of components.

Compression Ratio

During the compression stroke, the tighter the fuel/air mixture is compressed within a cylinder, the more intense the combustion. Each point of compression added to a

---

street-driven Pontiac V-8 can result in an increase of some 8 to 12 hp and ft-lbs of torque at every RPM point. In fact, a compression ratio increase does not produce any negative attributes so long as sufficient-octane fuel is available. But insufficient octane for a given compression ratio can lead to an engine that self-destructs from detonation.

The fuel octane ratings most commonly available at service station pumps are now 89 and 91. The maximum compression ratio I recommend for safe operation of a Pontiac V-8 with cast-iron cylinder heads on 91-octane fuel is 9.5:1. Some hobbyists are willing to push that to 10:1 or slightly more, which can result in an additional 5 to 10 hp and ft-lbs of torque, but it can require closely monitoring an engine's fuel and

The cylinder head is installed in a surfacing mill and a minimal amount of material is removed from the deck surface to ensure it's completely flat for maximum cylinder seal. The process also reduces combustion chamber volume, and that's something that must be considered when rebuilding a high-compression engine that operates on pump fuel. When dealing with Pontiacs, it's generally accepted that each 0.005-inch removed from the cylinder head deck surface reduces combustion chamber volume by 1 cc. It's highly recommended to physically measure chamber volume before and after any machining.

timing curves and always listening intently for detonation. If you plan to use 89 octane, I recommend limiting compression to 9:1. While a machine shop may use more precise equipment, a simple graduated syringe can be used to determine approximate chamber volume and resultant compression ratio, using the calculator found on the Performance Trends Engine Analyzer program.

Engines that use aftermarket aluminum cylinder heads can tolerate an additional 0.500 to 0.750 point of compression for typical operation on a given fuel octane. The ability to run a higher compression ratio with aluminum castings doesn't directly equate to a power increase. Aluminum dissipates heat quicker than cast iron, so slightly more compression is required to overcome the thermal loss, allowing an engine to produce the same amount of power as a similar engine fitted with similar-flowing cast-iron cylinder heads. I recommend limiting compression to 10.25:1 when using aluminum castings and 91-octane fuel.

When originality is less of a concern, simply selecting a similar D-port cylinder head with the desired amount of chamber volume may be the easiest way to set the compression ratio. A common modification to decrease combustion chamber volume is to mill the cylinder head deck flange, which effectively reduces volume and raises compression. If more combustion chamber volume is required, a popular method is to remove material in areas of the combustion chamber that do not affect quench. Pistons with a significant dish can also be used to reduce the compression ratio.

After consulting with a number of reputable Pontiac engine builders, I planned for a compression ratio of 10:1 to maintain peak performance from this 400. The closed-combustion-chamber 670 casting measured at 72 cc and would produce slightly more compression than I wanted. KRE is one company that has developed a method of modifying 670 combustion chambers to increase volume and improve flame propagation. The owner sent these castings to KRE where chamber volume was increased to 75 cc.

Camshaft Selection

Choosing a camshaft may seem as easy as opening a manufacturer's catalog and selecting a grind that contains the same approximate operating range as the engine you're building. However, you can't always rely on the catalog suggestions to be accurate. While the information may be usable as a guideline to loosely interpret the operating differences between two or more grinds, the actual powerband is often less relevant when considering a camshaft for a Pontiac.

Any camshaft can be physically installed into any Pontiac V-8 from 287 to 455, but there are consequences. For instance, the operating range of a 287 using a specific camshaft may be several hundred RPM different if it were used in a 455. Also, the cylinder head airflow, exhaust system efficiency, transmission type, rear axle gearing, and the way the car is to be used are all factors that must be considered when selecting a camshaft for any engine.

When comparing camshafts, duration at 0.050-inch lifter rise may be the most accurate way to predict how similar units might affect performance. Generally, a camshaft with more duration tends to favor higher-RPM operation than one with less

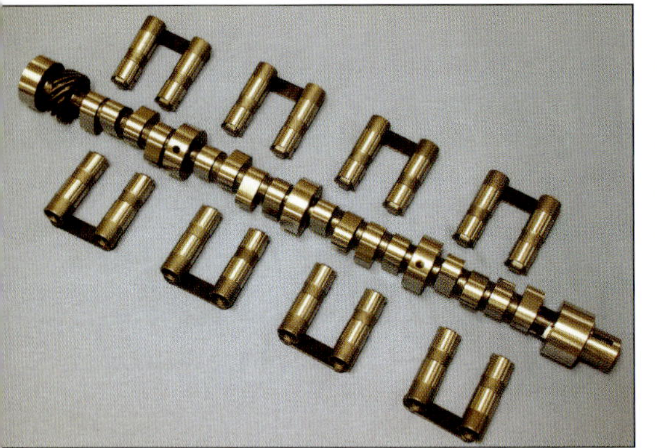

Hydraulic roller camshafts are quite popular for street-driven cars and the cost to step up to one is much more reasonable during a rebuild, which included a new camshaft, lifter set, and valve springs anyway. Kauffman Racing Equipment supplied this custom-ground hydraulic roller from Comp Cams, which features 218/224 degrees of 0.050-inch duration, a lobe-separation angle of 112 degrees, an intake centerline of 108 degrees, and nearly 0.500-inch valve lift when combined with 1.5:1-ratio rockers. It should be ideal for the 400, which spends much of its time operating at low RPM.

duration. A camshaft with a wider lobe separation angle (LSA) tends to provide better idle quality while spreading the power over a wider range when compared to a similar grind with less LSA. A moderate amount of valve lift is desirable for performance, but the valve lift should not exceed the airflow capacity of the cylinder heads or lift range of the valve springs.

Flat-tappet camshafts are cheap, readily available, and generally install into a Pontiac V-8 without any modifications. While flat-tappet cams perform well and remain an excellent value, the hobby has seen a distinct trend toward hydraulic roller camshafts for street-driven applications.

Not only does the roller action reduce friction and allow for a more aggressive lobe profile, initial break-in isn't required and there's no real chance of lobe and/or lifter failure that's been commonly associated with the reformulation of modern-spec oil. Converting an existing engine from a flat-tappet to a hydraulic roller cam can cost several hundred dollars, but the cost is much more affordable if a new cam is needed during a rebuild.

When considering a camshaft for this 400, I wanted a grind that provided strong full-throttle response. It also had to idle well to accommodate the additional load from the air conditioning compressor and produce plenty of low-speed torque because the relatively high rear-axle gearing meant the 400 would be around 2,000 rpm while cruising on the highway. From past experience with similar combinations, I knew the chosen hydraulic flat-tappet or roller cam needed no more than about 220 degrees of intake duration at 0.050 inch and an LSA of 112 to 114 degrees to produce a smoother idle.

I consulted with many top-name Pontiac builders to find a cam that best suited this 400's needs. Each stated that, if the budget allowed, a hydraulic roller was a wise choice. All agreed that, because of our limitations, 0.050-inch intake duration of 220 degrees (or less) and a wider LSA best suited the 400's intended operating parameters. We couldn't locate a hydraulic roller camshaft containing the exact specifications we wanted, however, so Comp Cams produced for us a custom-spec hydraulic roller camshaft with 218/224 degrees of 0.050-inch duration, an LSA of 112 degrees, and an intake centerline of 108 degrees. Valve lift was limited to 0.500 inch to complement the airflow capacity of the cylinder heads.

Preassembly

With machining complete, engine assembly is nearly ready to begin. You have to decide whether you want to handle the task yourself or let the machine shop assemble all or a portion of the engine for you. I have had WAM completely assemble engines for me as well as simply machine the components while I handle the complete assembly myself. Each time, I've found their measurements to be exact, which makes home assembly much less stressful, but that doesn't mean that I don't check their work by using a thorough preassembly process.

Once machining is complete, you must claim all of an engine's components and each returned component should be checked against the list you made during drop-off to ensure that everything is accounted for. Plan to intently discuss the entire machining process with your machinist and specifically ask if any irregularities were found. He or she should also provide a detailed list of the critical clearance specifications that were recorded during machining and the appropriate piston rings and bearing sets suggested for use. You may be able to use other bearings, but thickness can vary slightly among the types and available brands.

The amount of component clearance you record during the preassembly process should mirror that supplied by the machinist for every component involved. I highly recommend measuring two and sometimes three times to ensure repeatable accuracy. Any significant variance should immediately be brought to your machinist's attention. It may involve returning certain components to the shop for verification, and he or she should be willing to assist.

My preassembly process consists of many steps. It's performed in a clean and dry environment and each component is handled carefully. The machined surfaces and bearing coatings are delicate and can scratch easily, and any error can require additional machining or purchasing new pieces. I'm confident that if you find clearance specifications similar to those supplied by the machinist, you have an engine that's machined properly and should provide you with many miles of issue-free operation after proper final assembly.

Block Preassembly

1 Wash the Block

Though the machine shop should have cleaned all of the components after the machining process, preassembly begins by thoroughly washing the block and crankshaft with hot, soapy water to remove any trace debris that could dislodge and damage the engine bearings. Scrub every passage with an appropriately sized wire brush and force pressurized water into every opening or crevice. I prefer to let the components air-dry and then blow compressed air throughout the entire piece to remove any trapped water. Each bolt hole is chased with a lubricated tap to clean the threads. Use lint-free towels and a high-power cleaner that leaves behind no residue to clean all the contact surfaces. If the components have to be stored any length of time, the freshly machined surfaces must be sprayed down with a water-displacing lubricant for protection.

Special Tool, Precision Measurement

2 Measure Piston-to-Cylinder Wall Clearance

A specific amount of piston-to-cylinder wall clearance is required during assembly to maintain consistent operation once the different metals expand as the engine reaches normal operating temperature. Too little clearance can score the piston skirt and cylinder wall; too much clearance can cause excessive noise known as "piston slap," and oil consumption or blowby is often the result. Piston-to-cylinder wall clearance is determined by subtracting the piston diameter from the bore diameter. The exact amount of clearance varies with the type of piston being used—cast-alloy pistons differ from forgings. Each piston manufacturer provides a suggested clearance tolerance for its pistons, and the manufacturer or machinist can provide you with that. Using a dial bore gauge to measure all eight cylinders and an outside micrometer to measure each piston, speak directly to your machinist if any of your measurements fall outside of the suggested clearance tolerance.

3 Measure Piston Ring Gap

The piston ring pack being used in the 400 is a moly-coated set designed specifically for the Sealed Power pistons and a bore diameter of 4.16 inches. These rings come pre-gapped, and the top and second rings have different gaps. Each ring must be checked to be sure its gap measures within the manufacturer's suggested tolerance. To measure the gap, a ring is installed into a cylinder and a squaring tool is used to properly locate the piston ring down into the cylinder. A piston can also be used. Gap is measured by placing a feeler gauge between the ring ends. If the gap measures within the manufacturer's suggested tolerances, then the ring's position is noted, so it can be reunited with that cylinder during assembly. That process continues until each cylinder and piston ring is accounted for. The ring ends can be carefully filed if slightly more clearance is needed, but it's best to simply replace any ring that requires more than a reasonable amount of filing. Cast-alloy pistons may require a different gap than forged-aluminum pistons. If using pistons and rings from different suppliers, then contact the piston and ring manufacturers to verify the piston ring gap spec is compatible with that particular combination.

4 Arrange Pistons and Rods

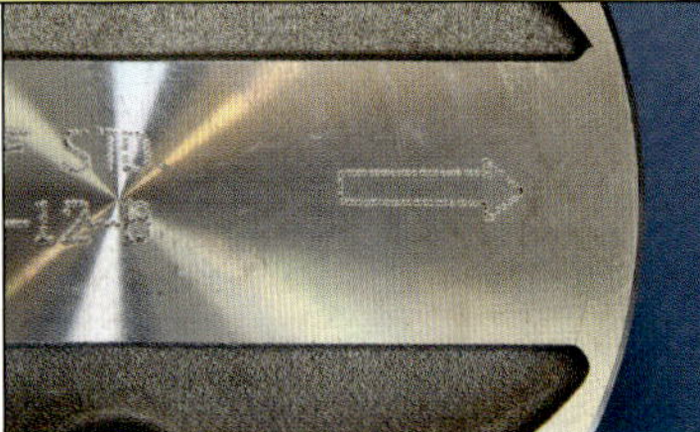

The connecting rod must be properly orientated with the piston before the piston wrist pins are installed. Connecting rods are chamfered on one side and flat on the other. The chamfered side corresponds with the rod journal fillet on the crankshaft. Stock-type pistons with an offset wrist pin are marked with a notch or symbol indicating which end should face toward the front of the engine. Some aftermarket pistons have specific valve clearance notches that must correspond with the intake and exhaust valve positions. Your machinist can assist if you have any question with that. When assembling the piston and connecting rod assembly, the piston arrow should face forward, while the chamfers should face the counterweight. The chamfer on connecting rods designated for cylinder numbers-2, -4, -6, and -8 faces toward the front of the engine, while the chamfer on numbers-1, -3, -5, and -7 faces the flywheel. An easy way to differentiate proper rod orientation is to use the bearing notches. They should always face toward the camshaft during proper installation.

5 Measure Connecting Rod Side Clearance

Your machinist may have noted the intended cylinder position for each respective connecting rod during the machining process. If reusing connecting rods, you must verify the method the machinist used, so you do not confuse any indicators he or she may have added with any you might have made during disassembly. Measure the diameter of each pair of connecting rods to verify the amount of side clearance once installed. Using a dial caliper, the rods are held tightly together with the chamfered side of each rod facing outward. They should be rotated slightly so the wrist pin bores are not touching and then the measurement is recorded. The caliper is also used to measure the diameter of the intended connecting rod journal on the crankshaft. The difference equates to the amount of connecting rod side clearance. It should be very close to the number specified by the connecting rod manufacturer and that noted by your machinist.

     HOW TO REBUILD PONTIAC V-8s

6 Install Wrist Pins

On pressed–wrist pin applications, the wrist pin needs to be pressed through the wrist pin bore of the connecting rod. Most shops have a specific heater that's capable of heating the small end of the rod to roughly 400°F. It should have a fixture that holds the piston and prevents the wrist pin from being driven in too far. The task can also be performed by using a large press or a handheld propane torch. However, improper technique can gall the surfaces. And a connecting rod's integrity can be severely compromised if the rod is excessively or improperly overheated. If the machinist hasn't denoted a connecting rod's cylinder orientation during machining, a permanent marker can be used to write on each piston head the respective position of the piston and connecting rod assembly.

7 Measure Main Bearing Clearance

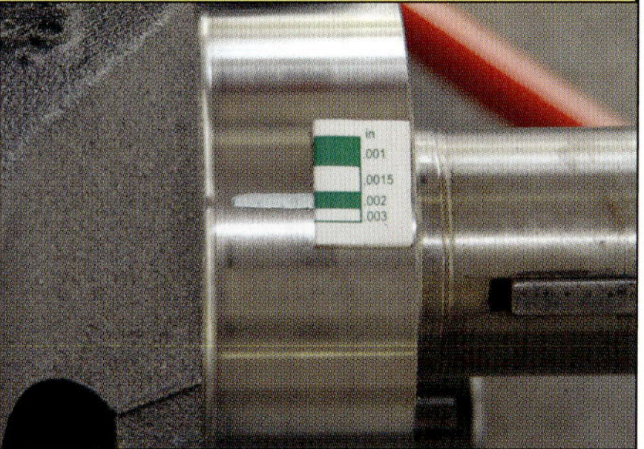

An outside micrometer can be used to measure each crankshaft main-journal diameter and determine main bearing clearance. A dial-bore gauge is used to measure the diameter of each main journal with the bearings and main cap installed. Subtracting the values determines the amount of bearing clearance at each respective main journal. It can also be determined with Plastigauge. That process consists of wiping clean the bearing surface of each main journal saddle and main cap, installing the bearings into the block and main caps, and setting the crankshaft into place. A length of Plastigauge is set onto the crankshaft journal and the main caps are installed. Gentle tapping with a hammer may be required to get the main caps to fully seat on the alignment dowels, but any twisting or turning of the crankshaft ruins the effort. It unlikely that your machinist removed the main cap alignment dowels during machining. If any are missing, you should contact the shop and ask for replacements. Otherwise Pioneer replacement dowels (number-PG-225) can be sourced from a local parts store. Stock Pontiac bolt threads are coated with 30-weight oil, and the front four are tightened from front to rear starting with the number-3 cap working outward using a 3/4-inch socket to a maximum of 100 ft-lbs in 20 ft-lb increments. Working from the center cap outward prevents crankshaft distortion in case that the block's main saddles and/or crankshaft weren't machined perfectly straight. The bolts for the rear main cap are torqued to a maximum of 120 ft-lbs with a 15/16-inch socket and a similar sequence. When using aftermarket fasteners, refer to the manufacturer's lubrication and torque specs. The strip of Plastigauge crushes as the bolts are tightened. After the bolts and main caps are removed, comparing the Plastigauge width against the wrapper reveals the amount of bearing clearance at each main journal. The same procedure is repeated for the remaining four main journals. The numbers should all be very close and around 0.002 to 0.0035 inch, depending upon the engine. If any variance is detected from the machinist's recommended specs for the main bearing clearance, you need to start the Plastigauge process over and verify the measurements. Consult your machinist if the variance persists.

8 Rotate Crankshaft and Inspect for Block Clearance

After very carefully removing the Plastigauge residue from the crankshaft journal surface and bearings, using extreme caution to not damage the machined surfaces or bearing coatings, remove the crankshaft and carefully set it aside. Make sure the crank and bearings are free from any debris and apply a liberal coating of assembly lube on the main saddle bearings. Reinstall the crankshaft, apply assembly lube onto the main journal surfaces, and reinstall the main bearings caps. Before torquing the main caps, use a large screwdriver or pry bar placed between a cap and crankshaft counterweight to gently thrust the crank forward and then rearward to center the thrust bearing. The main cap bolts should again be torqued to the amounts and procedure outlined in step 7. The crankshaft should rotate very easily, using your fingertips and light pressure. Rotate it several times, closely inspecting for any area where its counterweights could contact the block. It should be no less than 0.250 inch in any direction. Consult with your machinist if the crankshaft exhibits any rotational difficulty or detectable block contact.

9 Measure Thrust Clearance

Also commonly referred to as "crankshaft endplay," a slight amount of front-to-rear crankshaft movement is required for normal operation. It is easiest to measure it with a dial-indicator that is perfectly aligned with the crankshaft centerline. Using a large screwdriver, the crankshaft is pried rearward and the dial indicator is reset to zero. The crankshaft is then pried forward and the amount of forward thrust is displayed on the dial indicator. Factory specs call for 0.003 to 0.009 inch. This 400 crankshaft measures 0.007 inch.

10 Measure Connecting Rod Bearing Clearance

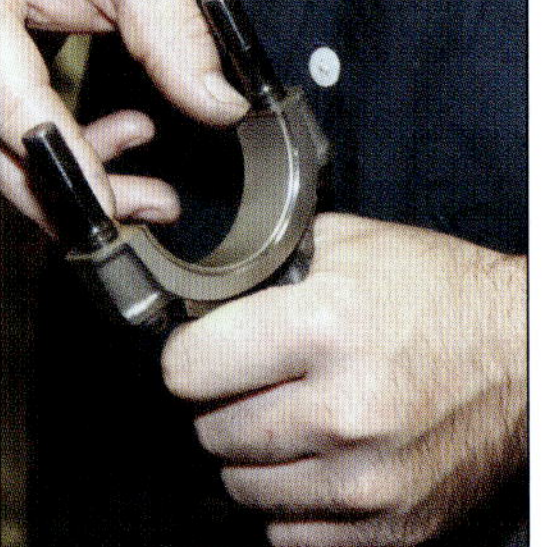
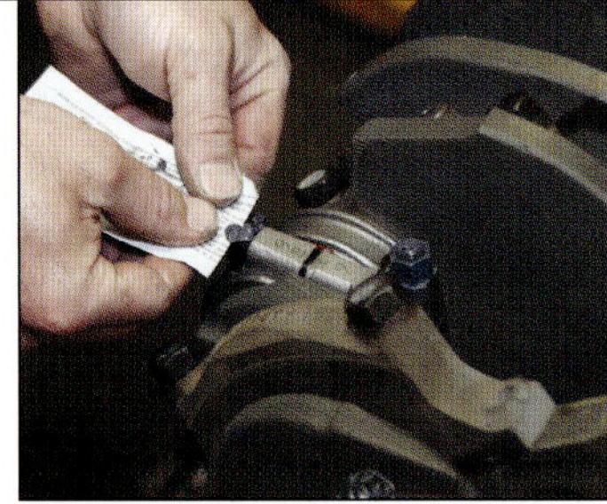

Connecting rod bearing clearance can be more difficult to measure than main bearing clearance. An outside micrometer can also be used to measure the crankshaft journal dimension, and a dial-bore gauge is used to measure the crankshaft bore of each connecting rod with the bearings installed and the fasteners tightened to the manufacturer's recommended torque spec. The connecting rods can be locked into a soft-jawed vise to properly torque the cap nuts. It is sometimes more convenient to use Plastigauge to determine the approximate amount of bearing clearance, but any crankshaft movement or rotating can severely skew the result. By installing an opposing pair of connecting rods intended for the crankshaft rod journal, bearing clearance is checked one journal at a time. Using a soft-jaw vise, the connecting rod cap nuts are removed, the bearing surface is wiped clean, a bearing is

10 Measure Connecting Rod Bearing Clearance *CONTINUED*

carefully installed, and the piston-and-connecting rod assembly is inserted into its designated cylinder. Extreme caution is used to prevent marring any of the machined surfaces. The bearing surface of the cap is wiped clean, a bearing is carefully installed, and a length of Plastigauge is laid onto the crankshaft journal surface. The rod cap is installed, and the nuts are tightened finger-tight. The corresponding connecting rod assembly is inserted into the opposing cylinder in a similar manner. Stock cast connecting rod bolts are torqued to a total of 43 ft-lbs in about 15-ft-lb increments using 30-weight oil to lubricate the threads. ARP's 3/8-inch replacements require 50 ft-lbs with moly-based lube. If using aftermarket connecting rods as we are in this 400, refer to the manufacturer's recommending torque specification and lubricant. The Plastigauge crushes evenly as the bolts are tightened. When applying torque, the nuts must be tightened and loosened in a manner that absolutely prevents the crankshaft from rotating. I have found wrenching to or from the front or rear of the engine provides the best results. After removing the nuts and connecting rod caps, connecting rod bearing clearance is determined by comparing the width of the Plastigauge to the measurements on its wrapper. The amount of clearance should be somewhere between 0.0015 and 0.0025, depending upon the application. The process is repeated until bearing clearance is measured for all eight connecting rods. The Plastigauge process must be repeated if much variance is found. Immediately consult with your machinist if your rod bearing clearances vary from his or her suggestions.

Precision Measurements

11 Verify Connecting Rod Side Clearance

After the rod bearing clearance has been recorded for an opposing pair of connecting rods on a crankshaft rod journal and the Plastigauge residue has been removed from the journal and bearings, the bearing is lubricated, the aftermarket connecting rod caps can be reinstalled, and the nuts again tightened to the proper torque specification for the fastener and/or connecting rod being used. The connecting rods can be spread apart and a feeler gauge inserted between them to verify that the amount of connecting rod side clearance calculated earlier is accurate. Your machinist can advise if any variance is found. Also rotate the engine several times with each pair of opposing connecting rods installed to closely check for any area where the connecting rod body or cap may contact the block or opposing piston. It's generally not an issue when using original or stock replacement components, but clearance should be verified any time aftermarket rotating assembly pieces are used.

Precision Measurements

12 Measure Deck Height

When speaking of deck height during an engine rebuild, it refers to the amount of clearance between the block deck surface and the piston head. Ideally the piston head and block deck are on the same plane, which is generally referred to as "zero deck," but usually the piston sits a few thousandths below the deck surface. To determine deck height, while measuring side clearance and the number-1 piston is installed, rotate the block so it is top-side up, and rotate the crankshaft so the number-1 piston is at TDC. Using a precision straightedge and a feeler gauge, place the straightedge across the deck surface and measure the clearance between it and the straightedge.

Cylinder Head Preassembly

1 Install Piston Rings

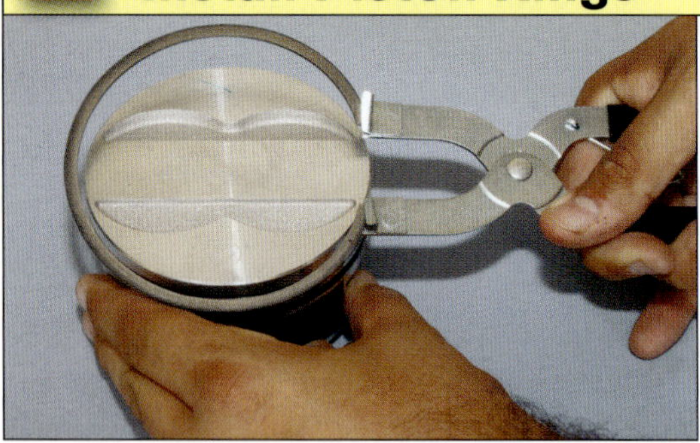

When installing piston rings, some hobbyists choose to install them by walking a ring around the piston and into the groove. That can sometimes permanently distort the ring or cause it to lose tension. I much prefer to use this special tool, which evenly spreads the ring at the gap and makes installation much less risky. It's available from a number of sources. Some piston rings are beveled or tapered and require specific installation. Follow the manufacturer's suggestions for proper orientation during install.

2 Verify Valve Guide Clearance

Measuring valve stem clearance requires a valve guide dial-bore indicator, and it's a task-specific tool that's impractical for hobbyists to purchase. An easier method is to liberally coat a valve stem with 30-weight oil and slowly insert it into its respective valve guide. The valve is rotated while using an in-and-out motion to fully lubricate the new guide. After several seconds of this action to allow for sufficient lubrication, the valve should move in and out with relative ease. It is then held slightly open and shifted in every direction to verify that the guide is completely tight and that no unwanted movement is present.

3 Measure Valve Spring Install Height

Manufacturers rate valve springs at specific amounts of pressure at certain coil heights. A camshaft manufacturer will recommend the amount of open and closed spring pressure that's required for a specific cam, and that can depend upon the type. The cam company, your favorite Pontiac vendor, or your machinist can provide you with a set of valve springs that best fits your needs, and your machinist can verify valve spring pressure and coil bind point by using a specific compressor. Your machinist should prepare your cylinder heads for a specific valve spring "install height," which is required to maintain the recommended amount of closed pressure and coil clearance at peak valve lift. Installation height is checked by using a valve, a valve retainer, the locks you plan to use, and a valve spring micrometer. Your machinist can machine the spring pocket if slightly more height is required or supply you with valve spring shims if less height is required.

4 Install Valve Seals

Pontiac originally used rubber O-rings and metal spring shields for oil control, but modern positive valve seals are a much better option. Your machinist can machine the top of your valve guides to accept the type of valve seal you chose to run. In this instance, the valve seal simply presses onto the top of the valve guide. Once a valve is inserted into the guide and through the seal, however, the valve should not be removed without a special sleeve that covers the valve stem tip. The tip can contain sharp edges that can tear the seal, compromising its oil control ability. Your machinist can supply you with this small sleeve.

Special Tool, Precision Measurement

5 Measure Retainer-to-Seal Clearance

Using a camshaft with relatively high valve lift can cause the retainer to contact the valve seal during operation, and that can create any number of operating issues. The amount of clearance can be determined by using a valve, a valve retainer, and locks you plan to use, and combining them with a test spring. Insert the valve into the guide and assemble the test spring, retainer, and locks. Manually forcing the retainer into the seal while recording the travel with a dial indicator reveals the amount of available clearance. It should be no less than 0.075 inch after subtracting peak valve lift.

Special Tool

6 Install Valve Springs

Your cylinder heads should still be clean from the thorough washing the machine shop performed after the machining process. If not, they can be thoroughly washed with soap and water, and the excess water blown away with compressed air. If all your measurements check out satisfactorily, you can install the new valve springs and valvetrain hardware with a valve spring compressor.

7 Install Freeze Plugs

After designating a driver- and passenger-side head, the coolant jacket plugs can be installed. If your machinist didn't supply you with a set, a Dorman or Melling set can be sourced from a local parts store. The opening in the cylinder head is coated with high-temperature liquid sealer, which flows out once the engine reaches normal operating temperature. Drive the plug into the opening with an appropriately sized socket. Install a plug into the rear opening on the intake manifold flange on the driver-side head. A heater core nipple is installed into the rear opening of the intake flange on the passenger's side. A new heater core nipple is available from most Pontiac vendors at a reasonable cost. The completed cylinder heads can be set aside until needed during engine assembly.

Final Assembly

Final assembly is the most important step of any rebuild. The assembly process often varies slightly from person to person. There's no issue with that as long as the technique produces an engine that operates consistently and reliably for long periods of time.

Depending upon the year, your Pontiac V-8 may contain unique components that must be installed in a specific manner or require a specific technique. I highly recommend referring to a Pontiac Service Manual for your year of engine, so you can learn the rebuild techniques that may be specific to your engine. I also recommend consulting with the manufacturers or a Pontiac vendor for proper installation information and torque specifications for any aftermarket components being used.

A careful, methodical approach is the safest way to be sure that your engine rebuild is successful. Plan to check and recheck your work often, and don't be afraid to call the experts if you have questions along the way.

Key Areas

There are a few areas of every rebuild that I feel are very important. Many of the tools listed in chapter 2 can each determine a successful rebuild versus one that can end in failure. In addition, but rarely considered by those less experienced, cleanliness, assembly lubricants, and sealers should be considered a critical part of every rebuild. Many hobbyists are unfamiliar with how important each is and how to properly use them.

Cleanliness

An engine consists of many precisely machined and polished surfaces. The components operate at very close tolerances with a thin film of lubrication between them to reduce friction. Any dirt or debris within the engine can compromise that lubrication film, causing irreparable damage to the components that you likely spent a healthy sum having machined or purchasing new. Any damage could require additional

Any time the rebuild process stops for more than a few minutes, the engine should be covered with a large plastic bag specifically designed for that purpose. It's intended to protect the vulnerable engine from contaminants such as water, metallic particles, or dirt and dust that may be floating about your shop or garage. If your machinist didn't give you one, you can also use almost any heavy-duty plastic bag that's large enough to completely cover the engine.

machining or polishing, or even buying a new replacement.

I cannot stress enough that every precaution to prevent any type of contamination must be taken during the assembly portion of any rebuild. If there is any question about the cleanliness of any engine component, even if it's new and fresh out of the package, it's best to blow it out with compressed air, thoroughly wash it with hot soapy water, or wipe it down with residue-free solvent and a lint-free cloth. You can never be too safe!

The engine assembly room or area of professional engine building shops is usually very clean and organized and free from any substance or contaminant that could compromise a rebuild. Your garage or shop shouldn't be much different. The area should be extremely clean—free of any dust or dirt that could be kicked up while walking around. The bench surface should be very clean. I sometimes lay down several layers of clean newspaper if I detect any visible contaminants on the bench surface. The tools required for assembly are also thoroughly cleaned with residue-free solvent and a lint-free cloth.

Assembly Lubricants

High-quality assembly lubricant is very thick and protects delicate surfaces with tight tolerances, such as the bearing and journal and a rear main seal, during assembly and initial start-up. Heavier engine oil, such as a 30W break-in variety, is used to lubricate certain contact surfaces, including cylinder walls and piston rings.

Engine oil is also used to lubricate bolt threads. A couple drops directly onto the threads and under the bolt head is all that's required for proper installation. Too much oil can produce an improper torque reading or worse, cause the bolt to hydraulic lock, possibly splitting the bolt hole while tightening the fastener to the suggested amount of torque.

If you're using aftermarket fasteners like those from ARP, a specific thread lubricant may be required. ARP offers a moly-based paste that it recommends when tightening its fasteners. While 30W oil can also be used, a different amount of torque may be required. Check with your fastener manufacturer for more information on suggested lubricant and torque specifications.

Use a roll of lint-free paper towels dampened with a common water-displacement lubricant (such as WD-40) to wipe down the cylinder walls. The walls are only clean when you find no trace of dirt or debris on a clean towel. Be sure that your hands are clean too! Any contaminants on your hands could transfer to the cylinder walls.

If the cleanliness of any engine component is questionable, it should be washed again with soapy water. Use a soft bristle brush to scrub the block's cylinder walls and crankshaft after the preassembly process, and rinse everything thoroughly with clean water. You can also use residue-free solvents and lint-free cloths to wipe contact surfaces just prior to assembly. You can never be too clean when building any engine!

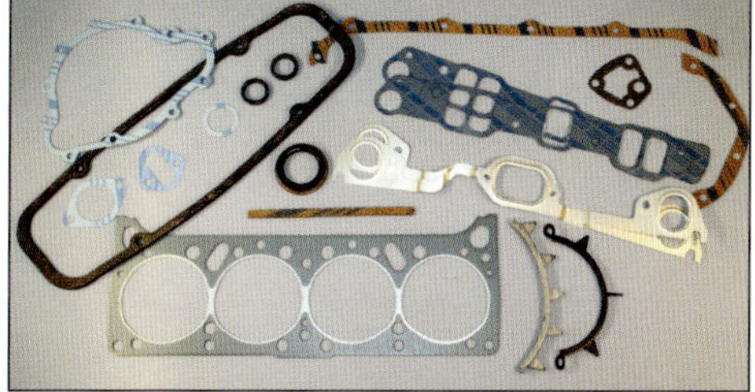

A Fel-Pro number-2806 Gasket Kit contains virtually every gasket required to completely assemble a typical Pontiac engine. These are readily available from your favorite Pontiac vendor or mail-order retailer; your machinist may be able to provide you with the same kit at a competitive price. The basic kit is designed for D-port engines, so if you are rebuilding an engine with round-port cylinder heads, then you must separately purchase specific intake and exhaust manifolds.

Sealers

I've had excellent success with Permatex-brand Ultra Black RTV silicone sealer. I suggest using it sparingly, however. Some hobbyists tend to use heavy applications to prevent leaks. I am more inclined to let the gasket do its job and use a very light coat of sealer to simply hold the gasket in place or fill in pits or pores in the contact surfaces. It is readily available at your auto parts store, and your machinist can recommend one of a number of other high-quality brands and types available.

Thread lock compound seals the bolts into threads and prevents them from vibrating loose. There are different "colors" available and the largest difference seems to be the method of removal. Red is very popular, but bolt removal requires a combination of heat and hand tools. Blue thread lock is the best choice for engine rebuilds since it is service-removable, which means that bolts are easily removed with hand tools for quick disassembly. I routinely use blue thread lock for certain bolts during engine rebuilds. A small drop is all that's required to lubricate the threads and prevent a bolt from loosening.

Short-Block Preparation

Professional Mechanic Tip

1 Dress Camshaft Bearings

The five bearings used to support the camshaft of a Pontiac V-8 are identical. Each has a more pronounced bevel on one end for easier installation. The beveled end points toward the rear of the engine and is intended to prevent galling while being driven into place. Use a file or small knife to "dress" the opposite end before installation. It removes any sharp edges that can score the camshaft journal.

Special Tool

2 Install Camshaft Bearings

Use a camshaft bearing installation tool to install the bearings in the block. Working from the front of the block, install the rear journal first. Drive each bearing into place without any lubrication. The bearing's oil hole must be perfectly aligned with the feedhole located in the main saddle, otherwise oil starvation can occur. It's generally not feasible to purchase a camshaft bearing installation tool for a single rebuild. It may be best to let your machinist perform the task for you.

Precision Measurement, Important!  

3 Install Rear Cam Plug

The block contains a machined step just rearward of the last cam bearing that's intended to keep the rear plug from being driven in too far. Coat a steel plug with liquid sealer and drive it into place with an appropriately sized socket. The lip of the steel plug should be recessed approximately 0.300 inch below the surface. Driving the rear plug in too far can cause the cam to contact it during typical operation, sending metallic filings throughout your engine!

4 Test Fit Camshaft

Install the camshaft to verify that the cam bearings are properly aligned and that sufficient rear cam-plug clearance exists. Lightly lubricate the camshaft journals with 30-weight oil and insert the camshaft into the cam tunnel. Make sure the camshaft is supported and the cam lobes don't make harsh contact with the bearings because damage could result. The cam should rotate easily by hand with little effort and without any binding. Push the cam rearward and if its snout is recessed from the front surface of the block by any amount, then sufficient rear cam plug clearance is present. The cam is carefully removed to prevent damaging the new bearings and set aside for installation a bit later.

5 Install Block Freeze Plugs

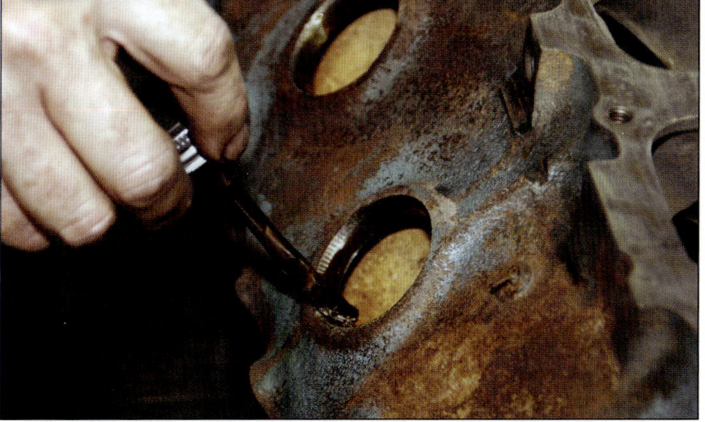 

Your machinist can supply you with a complete steel plug kit that includes every coolant and threaded-oil plug required for complete assembly. Otherwise, complete plugs kits from Dorman or Melling are available at most local auto parts stores. Installation is very straightforward. Coat the block opening with high-quality liquid sealer. Using an appropriately sized socket, drive a steel plug into place until it is flush with the block. A bearing driver can also be used.

6 Install Oil Gallery Plugs

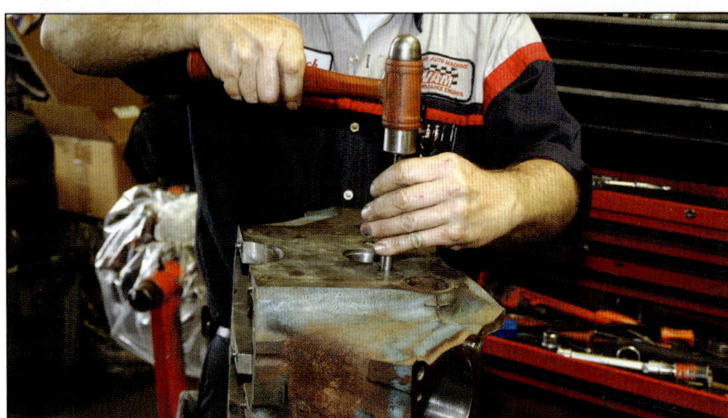

A series of pressed and threaded pipe plugs seal the oil gallery front and rear. Coat the threaded plugs with liquid Teflon sealer and install them very tightly with a proper-sized hex-head socket. Coat the pressed plugs up front with a liquid sealer and drive them into place with an appropriately sized drift. The plug lip should be about 1/8 inch below the surface, and the material around them is staked for optimal retention. A popular modification in high-performance applications is to tap the front oil gallery holes and install threaded plugs instead of pressed plugs, which prevents them from pushing out under high oil pressure conditions. It's generally not required for stock-type rebuilds, however.

Professional Mechanic Tip, Important!

7 Don't Forget the Hidden Oil Plug!

A threaded pipe plug seals the passenger-side oil gallery. It installs from the rear of the block and is hidden under a pressed plug. It's one that novice Pontiac builders often omit and it results in extremely low oil pressure. Fixing the issue requires a complete engine removal and partial disassembly, so you don't want to forget to install the plug! A common modification is drilling a 0.030-inch hole into the hidden plug, which your machinist can perform for you on a lathe. It provides the camshaft and distributor gears with a constant jet of pressurized oil to reduce wear, especially when using a steel roller cam. The plug threads are coated with liquid Teflon sealer and tightened like the others with an appropriately sized hex-head or square-head socket and a 3/8-inch drive ratchet. The pressed plug that covers it is simply driven into place with a small socket.

Rotating Assembly Installation Preparation

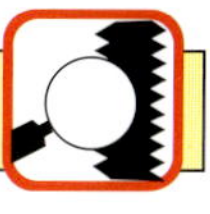

Critical Inspection

1 Install Connecting Rod Bearings

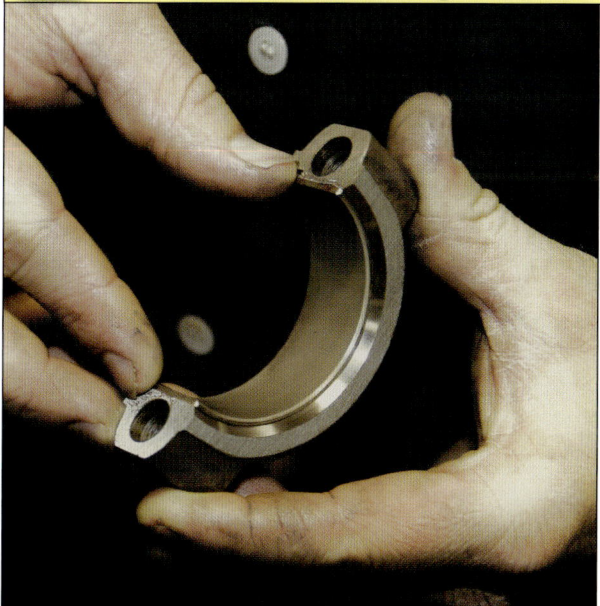

The connecting rod bearings should still be clean and in excellent condition even after the preassembly checks. Wipe the connecting rod body and cap saddles completely clean of oil and debris along with the backs of the bearing shell. Even the smallest particles can compromise the bearing's ability to carry its intended load, possibly leading to premature failure. There is usually no specific upper or lower rod bearing. Some brands or types may be different, however. Refer to the bearing instructions or consult with your machinist for verification. Without any lubrication, carefully press the bearings into place with extra attention to bearing tang alignment. They should fit snug in the rod and cap.

2 Lubricate Connecting Rod Bearings

Both connecting rod bearing halves receive a generous amount of assembly lubricant on the journal surface. Assembly lube is thick enough that it should remain in place for several minutes without running or dripping.

3 Organize Short-Block Parts

Just before short-block assembly begins, I set out all of the associated components to be sure that everything is accounted for and that the main caps and piston-and-rod assemblies are arranged in an order that corresponds with cylinder location. I also install protective caps onto the connecting rod bolts, which cover the bolt threads, to protect the freshly machined block and crankshaft surfaces from scratches during piston installation. Available from your machinist or mail-order retailer, you can also cut your own from length of 1/2-inch-diameter rubber hose. I also had the machine shop thoroughly clean all of the engine's nuts and bolts. I organized them for easy accessibility too.

Rear Main Seal Installation

1 Insert Rear Seal

With the engine back on an engine stand, install the rear main seal. There are a number of suitable rear main seal options available on the aftermarket. The GraphTite seal from Best Gasket Company installs and functions much like an original asbestos rope seal. One half of the new rope seal is laid over the seal groove that's machined into the block, while the other half is laid over the corresponding groove in the rear main cap.

2 Pack the Seal

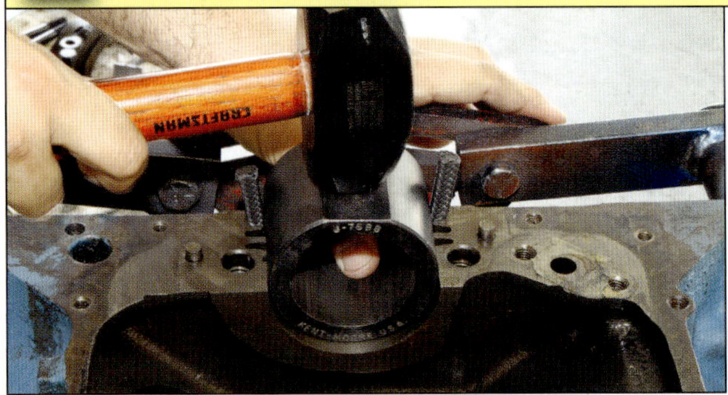

A number of tools can be used to pack a rope rear main seal into the groove. Those include a large socket, a length of steel pipe, or even a wooden rolling pin. Tightly pack the seal to a depth that replicates the approximate crankshaft diameter and into the anti-rotation holes that are drilled into the seal groove. I purchased a special tool that Kent-Moore produced a number of years ago. It was developed for Pontiac dealers and used by service department technicians for this very task.

3 Install RTV Sealer

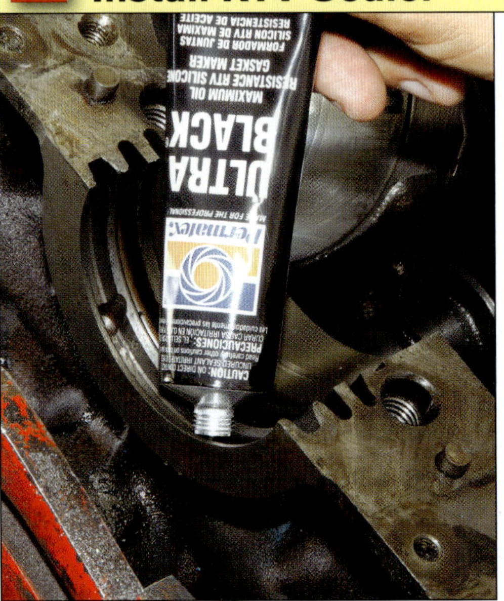

The newly formed rope seal halves are removed from the rear main seal groove in the block and main cap. Be sure to keep each orientated correctly. Apply a thin bead of RTV sealer onto the rope or into the grooves. A very small amount is needed. It serves only to prevent the rope seal from rotating at initial start-up.

4 Reinstall Formed Rope Seal

Each half of the formed rope seal is reinstalled into its respective groove and repacked. It isn't uncommon to find a small amount of RTV sealer seeping around the seal while repacking it. Wipe it away with a clean towel.

5 Cut Rope Seal

Best Gasket Company's GraphTite rope seal kit includes a blade, a wooden finger guard, and a spacing template. Trim the excess ends of the rope seal in the block and main cap. The rope should cut cleanly and without any frayed edges. The spacer leaves the rope seal protruding about 0.015 inch above the block surface, and it's pressed flush by hand. When the main cap is installed, the rope ends compress slightly providing a positive seal.

6 Apply RTV Sealer

The rope rear main seal installation is complete. Liberally coat it with assembly lube when installing the main bearings and lubricate the crankshaft just before setting it in place, which prevents damage during initial start-up. Apply a very thin layer of RTV or anerobic sealer to the block and main cap mating surfaces that surround the rope seal during main cap installation to seal any pores that could lead to potential leaks. However, no sealer is applied directly to the rope ends.

Short-Block Assembly

1 Install Oil Dipstick Tube

The oil dipstick tube located in the block is typically removed during machining. The original can be reinstalled if the machinist was able to salvage it. A replacement can otherwise be purchased from your favorite Pontiac vendor. Slide the tapered end of the dipstick tube though the opening in the block. Drive it through the block with a brass drift until it is completely flush with the block interior surface. Then rotate the block 180 degrees for camshaft installation.

2 Install Camshaft Keyway

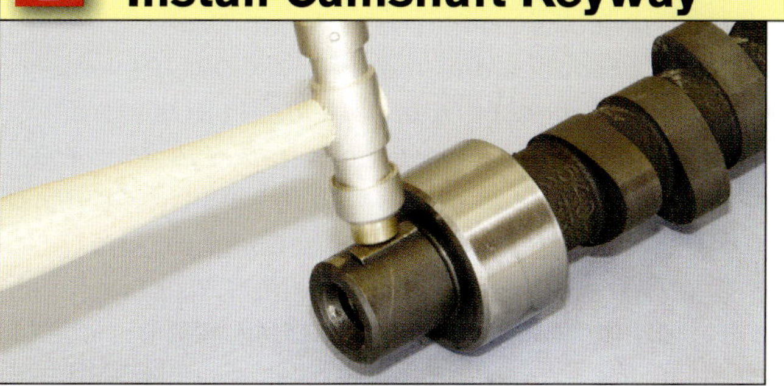

If your machinist didn't supply you with a new 3/16- x 3/4-inch camshaft keyway, one is available from Dura-Bond (number-AK-002-P), which can be sourced from a local parts store. Place the camshaft on a solid surface and install the keyway into the groove located in the front snout. Some hobbyists use a large pair of pliers or a vise to squeeze the key into place. I prefer gently tapping it in with a small brass hammer. No matter the method, use caution to prevent damage to the cam journal surface.

3 Install Camshaft

Lubricate the camshaft bearing journals with 30W oil, and liberally coat the distributor gear with assembly lube. Cover the lobes with the camshaft manufacturer's recommended lubricant, which is specifically designed for break-in. In this instance, Comp Cams recommends simple assembly lube for its hydraulic roller unit, but a flat-tappet camshaft may require a thicker substance or paste, which the camshaft manufacturer should supply for you. Once the camshaft is installed, the engine is rotated 180 degrees for bottom-end assembly.

Critical Inspection

4 Install Main Bearings

Like the connecting rod bearings, the main bearings should still be in excellent condition after the preassembly process. Wipe the block and cap saddles clean of any oil and debris. Without lubrication, press the bearings into place and pay careful attention to bearing tang alignment. Depending upon the type of main bearings being used, there may be specific upper and lower halves. If there is a specific orientation, you need to be sure the main bearings are correctly installed in the proper position. Refer to bearing instructions, or consult with the bearing manufacturer or your machinist if there is any question. Remember, saddle and cap numbers-1, -2, and -3 use the same bearings. The thrust bearing is installed onto number-4. And the widest bearing is installed onto the rear main saddle and cap. The main saddle bearings surfaces and rear main seal are liberally coated in assembly lube.

5 Install Crankshaft

Be sure that the machinist installed a new 3/16 x 1 3/8-inch crankshaft keyway into the crank snout. If not, Dura-Bond produces one (number-AK-001-P), which is available from your local parts store. The crank keyway is installed in a manner identical to the camshaft keyway. Gently set the crankshaft onto the lubricated bearings in the main saddle. Apply a liberal coating of assembly lube directly to the exposed journal surfaces.

6 Install Main Caps

The main caps are set on their respective journals and gently pressed onto the alignment dowels by hand. The first four caps are numbered. The cap is correctly oriented if the crankshaft snout is to the left of cap number-1. If any cap requires slightly more persuasion, gently tap it with a soft hammer until the cap is firmly positioned on the dowels. Smear a dab of RTV sealer onto the mating surfaces of the main cap and block that surround the rear main seal when installing the main cap. The sealer fills in the micro-pores that might otherwise allow some oil seepage.

Torque Fasteners

7 Install Main Cap Bolts

The main cap bolt threads and just beneath the head are lubricated with 30W oil. When using original Pontiac fasteners, the bolts of the first four caps are tightened with a 3/4-inch socket. Use a 15/16-inch socket to tighten the rear main cap bolts. Start at the number-3 cap and work outward; tighten the bolts to 60 ft-lbs with a 1/2-inch-drive torque wrench. Each bolt is then tightened to 80 ft-lbs, and again to a total of 100 ft-lbs. Stock rear main cap bolts require one additional step and are tightened to 120 ft-lbs. Refer to the manufacturer's lubrication and torque specs if aftermarket fasteners are used. Rotate the crankshaft several times by hand to be sure that there isn't any binding or contact with the block and that the assembly lube is evenly dispersed across the bearing and journal surfaces. If the crank rotates smoothly, the main cap bolt settings are rechecked with the torque wrench to be sure that the main caps are installed properly. The block is then rotated so the left-hand bank of cylinders is parallel with the ground so the pistons can be installed.

Important!

8 Arrange Piston Rings

Liberally lubricate the cylinder walls with 30W oil, and rotate the crankshaft so the number-1 rod journal is at the bottom of its travel in relation to the block. Taking the piston-and-connecting rod assembly designated for the number-1 cylinder, lubricate its wrist pin with oil and insert it into the number-1 cylinder with one hand while supporting the connecting rod from beneath with the other. Piston installation stops just before the piston rings contact the block. The piston rings are rotated so the end gaps of each are about 90 degrees apart from the next to promote maximum cylinder seal. Exact gap orientation isn't overly critical since the rings move about during normal operation. The entire ring pack is well lubricated with 30W oil.

9   Compress Rings and Install Piston

Compress the piston rings with a piston ring compressor and drive the piston into the cylinder with a non-marring tool, such as the handle of a soft-faced hammer. Once the ring pack is well within the cylinder, set aside the piston ring compressor, and drive the piston completely into the block with one hand while supporting the connecting rod from underneath the block with the other hand. Continue gently driving the piston into the cylinder until the connecting rod bearing is firmly seated onto the crankshaft rod journal.

10   Install Connecting Rod Cap and Nuts

Remove the connecting rod bolt covers and install the connecting rod cap. The bearing should still be coated with assembly lube and the cap must be orientated correctly to prevent backward installation. Use the appropriate lubricant recommended to lubricate the rod bolt threads. Pontiac specified 30-weight oil for the original fasteners in its cast connecting rod. Aftermarket manufacturers may suggest something different such as the moly-based lube that RPM International suggests for the ARP bolts it uses. Use a 9/16-inch socket to firmly tighten the nuts before moving onto the next cylinder for piston install. It becomes harder to rotate the crankshaft as more connecting rods are attached to it. I thread a spare harmonic balancer bolt into the crankshaft snout and rotate the engine with a 15/16-inch wrench.

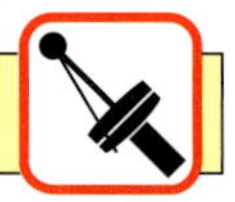

11   Tighten Connecting Rod Nuts

The same process outlined in the past three steps is used to install all the pistons on one cylinder bank. The block is then rotated so the remaining pistons can be installed in their corresponding cylinders. Once the eight piston-and-connecting rod assemblies are installed, rotate the block until it is upside down. Then use the appropriate-size socket for the rod nuts and a 3/8-inch-drive torque wrench to tighten the nuts to OEM or aftermarket recommended specifications, working from front to rear. Refer to the OEM torque specification chart on page 128, or the aftermarket manufacturer's specification sheet for the proper amount. Check with your machinist or connecting rod supplier for the appropriate torque specifications if any other connecting rod or fastener is used during your rebuild.

12 Install Lower Oil Dipstick Tube

Insert the lower oil dipstick tube into the intermediate tube in the block, and the windage tray retains it from underneath. Add a drop of blue thread lock to the threads of the four bolts securing the windage tray to the main caps. Install the bolts with a 1/2-inch socket and tighten them to 15 ft-lbs. Pontiac stopped installing windage trays on its engines during the 1970s. In these instances, the lower dipstick tube is retained by a welded tab that is bolted to the number-3 main cap. Install the bolts with the same tools and torque specifications. This is an excellent time to test fit the actual oil dipstick you plan to use to be sure it installs without binding. You may need to rotate the engine slightly, but simply insert the dipstick into the intermediate tube. If your Pontiac is equipped with air-conditioning, be sure the upper dipstick tube is also installed during the test fit.

Professional Mechanic Tip, Torque Fasteners

13 Thoroughly Clean Oil Pump

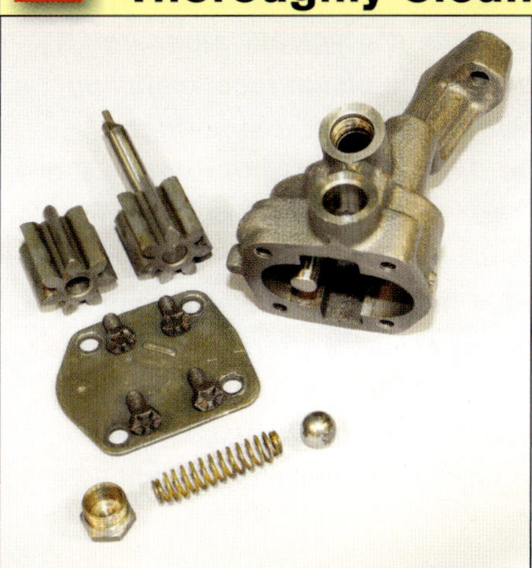

Pontiac used oil pumps that generate a maximum oil pressure of 40- or 60-psi in most of its production engines. The Melling M54DS oil pump may be the most popular choice for modern rebuilds, and that's what I am installing here. It's wise to remove the bolts that secure the bottom plate to the oil pump body with a 1/2-inch socket. Remove the nut securing the pressure regulator spring and check ball with a 13/16-inch socket. Closely inspect the unit to be sure that it is completely free from any metal burrs or debris. Pay close attention to the orientation of the dimples machined into the gears, so that they can be reinstalled correctly. Remove small burrs with a small file or stone. You should contact your machinist if you notice any significant irregularities, such as pits or machining errors. Otherwise, the bolts receive a drop of blue thread lock, and they and the pressure regulator nut are reinstalled and tightened to 15 ft-lbs.

Intake Centerline

Most new camshafts include a detailed specification card that contains such information as cam timing, valve lift, and a suggested intake centerline (ICL) installation point. Simply aligning the timing set dots during installation often positions the ICL at the manufacturer's suggested setting in relation to the crankshaft angle, providing satisfactory performance. However, taking the time to actually measure the camshaft with a camshaft degree kit can maximize performance.

A high-quality camshaft degree kit should include a crankshaft turning fixture, a graduated degree wheel, a wire pointer, a mechanical piston stop, a dial indicator to track lobe lift, and detailed instructions that outline the proper procedure to accurately degree a camshaft. The cost can be as much as a few hundred dollars, depending upon what's included in the kit. It is an invaluable resource to help find exactly where a camshaft is positioned, which is a critical element when tuning for maximum performance.

The idea is to verify that the valve events of a camshaft occur at the most opportune time for a given combination. An engine doesn't begin building cylinder pressure until the intake valve closes, and that point has a fixed relation to the position of a camshaft's ICL. Generally, the point selected by the camshaft manufacturer provides satisfactory performance. Advancing or retarding the ICL in relation to the crankshaft using a specific timing set or offset keyway changes the point at which the intake valve closes, and that can affect overall performance.

If you have access to a camshaft degree kit, it may be a worthwhile venture to verify that the ICL of the camshaft is installed at the suggested position when the timing set dots are properly aligned. If you find that the number varies from the information supplied by the camshaft manufacturer, plan to discuss it with your machinist, Pontiac vendor, or camshaft manufacturer to determine if there are any advantages to adjusting the ICL in your instance. ■

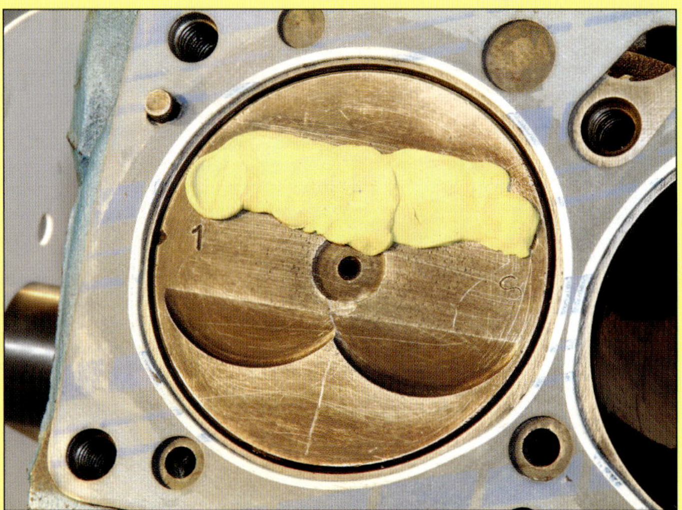

Piston-to-valve clearance is a critical measurement that should be verified during an engine rebuild. Too little clearance can cause the valves to contact the piston, leading to any number of operational concerns. Piston-to-valve issues occur when using stock or stock-type components during a rebuild. It's typically measured by placing modeling clay on the piston face, installing a cylinder head fitted with lightweight test springs, assembling a portion of the valvetrain, and rotating the engine several times. The valve compresses the modeling clay and the thickness recorded after disassembly is the amount of available piston-to-valve clearance. If your rebuild includes an aggressive aftermarket camshaft, pistons with small valve relief volume, or excessively milled cylinder heads, you should discuss the measuring and verifying piston-to-valve clearance with your machinist.

A camshaft degree kit contains all the necessary components to accurately degree a camshaft in relation to crankshaft angle. It allows the operator to measure each valve event and adjust certain parameters to maximize performance. A degree kit like this from Comp Cams is relatively easy to use and contains detailed instructions for proper use.

14 Install Oil Pump Pickup

Important!

Installing the oil pump pickup can be a bit challenging for first-timers. A slip-fit design secures it to the body. I generally place the pickup in my home freezer several hours before install, which causes the metal to contract slightly, making the install a bit easier. Drive the pickup into place by sliding a 3/4-inch open-end wrench against the embossed collar on the pickup tube and tap it in with a hammer. If using an original oil pan, align the pickup at the midway point between the slot that's created by the recess cast into the oil pump body and the bottom plate when it's fully seated. Consult with the oil pan manufacturer if using an aftermarket oil pan. Though rare, the oil pump pickup can fall out of the body, requiring major engine disassembly to repair. To prevent the pickup from falling out during normal operation, you can tack weld the body and pickup together. Your machinist can perform any portion of this step for you.

15 Install Oil Pump

Torque Fasteners

Drop into the block the intermediate shaft that drives the oil pump. Its pinch-tabs rest against the block's cast loop, and the opposite end engages the oil pump drive on the pump body. Align the oil pump gasket and oil pump with the holes in the block, place a drop of blue thread lock on the bolts, and tighten them to 30 ft-lbs with a 3/8-inch-drive torque wrench and a 9/16-inch socket.

16 Install Camshaft Thrust Plate

Rotate the engine 180 degrees, so it sits right side up and the camshaft thrust plate is installed. The plate limits the camshaft's forward travel, and it contains a machined groove on one side that supplies the timing chain with pressurized oil. Install the plate with the machined groove facing the camshaft. Place a drop of blue thread lock on the bolts. Use a 1/2-inch socket and a 3/8-inch drive torque wrench to tighten the bolts to 20 ft-lbs. A new thrust plate should be used if the camshaft contact surface of the original appears scored in any way.

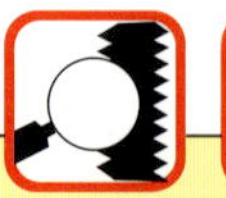

17 Install Timing Set

18 Verify Timing Dot Alignment

Install the timing set onto the camshaft and crankshaft snouts. Rotate the crankshaft so the number-1 piston is at Top Dead Center (TDC). Temporarily install the crankshaft gear onto the crankshaft snout to verify that its TDC timing dot is at the 12-o'clock position. Even with lubrication, the gear should fit tightly on the crankshaft keyway without any wobbling or free play. Temporarily install the camshaft gear onto the camshaft snout. It too should fit tightly on its keyway. Rotate the camshaft so its timing dot is at the 12-o'clock position and remove the gears. Some prying may be required. Install the timing set as a unit while maintaining proper timing dot alignment. I use a Sealed Power number-3112 roller set and soak the timing chain in 30W oil prior to installation.

Always position the TDC timing dot on the crankshaft gear at the 12-o'clock position during timing set installation. However, the camshaft gear timing dot can be installed at 6 or 12 o'clock. Either position has no effect on camshaft timing and positions the camshaft in same relation to the crankshaft. It does, however, affect ignition timing. When the timing dots are aligned at 12 o'clock, the engine is at the number-1 firing position. With the cam gear at 6 o'clock, the engine is placed at the number-6 firing position. Since the crank rotates twice as fast as the camshaft, either position can be used as long as the distributor is installed accordingly. I routinely rotate the crankshaft several times, stopping the cam gear at the 6-o'clock position just to verify that the timing dots are exactly aligned with that position too. The crankshaft is then rotated one more revolution so the cam gear returns to 12 o'clock for the remainder of engine assembly.

19 Install Fuel Pump Eccentric

The fuel pump eccentric is a two-piece design that consists of a fixed center and a floating outer bushing. A stamped tab fits into a corresponding hole on the cam gear.

Install the cam gear bolt, using a drop of blue thread sealer on the threads. Use a 3/4-inch socket and tighten it to 40 ft-lbs with a 1/2-inch-drive torque wrench. A helper may be required to keep the crankshaft from rotating. When finished with this step, I rotate the engine 180 degrees to perform the next steps.

20 Install Timing Cover

The machinist should have thoroughly cleaned the timing cover along with the other parts. Upon its return, closely inspect it for any pits or cracks that could affect its ability to properly seal the engine. Use a 5/16-18 tap to restore the fuel pump bolt threads. Gently drive the new front seal into place with a hammer. Many hobbyists use an excessive amount of RTV sealer around the coolant holes in an attempt to prevent leaks when installing the timing cover. Unless it or the block is pitted, I smear only enough to hold the new Fel-Pro gasket to the timing cover. Install the new Fel-Pro timing cover alignment sleeves into the bottom bolt holes of the timing cover, and fasten the unit to the engine with bolts and studs with nuts. If your studs were damaged during disassembly and your machinist didn't supply you with new ones, you can source new 4-inch-long studs from a local hardware store or industrial fastener supplier. Be sure the stud has 3/8-16 threads on one end and 3/8-24 on the other. You may need to refer to your disassembly photos to reference the year-specific locations and the number required. Thread the coarse-thread end of the stud (3/8-16) into the block until it bottoms out. Use a 9/16-inch socket to tighten the timing cover's nuts and bolts to 15 ft-lbs with a 3/8-inch-drive torque wrench.

21 Install Oil Pan Gasket

Apply a very light coating of RTV sealer onto the oil pan rail of the block and timing cover. Lay a new Fel-Pro oil pan gasket into place. The sealer is used only to keep the gaskets from moving around during oil pan installation. However, the joints where the gaskets meet receive a bead of RTV sealer to prevent leaks. Pontiac used at least three rear pan gasket designs over the years. The type required for your rebuild depends upon the engine and oil pan vintage. Fortunately, the Fel-Pro gasket kit contains the various types. In this instance, the five tabs are cut off the rubber seal, so it can be laid on the main cap and a bead of RTV sealer applied to each end to prevent leaks.

22 Install Oil Pan

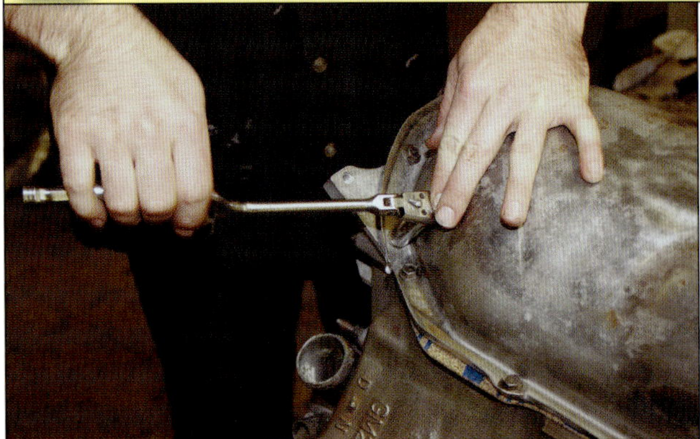

The oil pan is another component that the machinist should have thoroughly cleaned for you. Simply lay it onto the gaskets and use a total of 18 bolts to fasten it to the block and timing cover. A 7/16-inch socket and 3/8-inch-drive torque wrench is used to tighten most of the bolts to 12 ft-lbs. Some engines use two slightly longer bolts at each rear corner of the oil pan, which are accompanied by steel reinforcing straps. If present, these bolts are tightened to 20 ft-lbs when used with the straps. Reproductions are available if yours are missing. Tighten the oil pan drain plug to 22 ft-lbs with an 11/16-inch socket.

Long-Block Assembly

1 Install Cylinder Head Gaskets

Rotate the engine 180 degrees and prepare the deck surfaces for cylinder head gasket installation. Check to be sure the machinist reinstalled the four cylinder-head-alignment dowel pins in the deck surface. If not, a Dura-Bond replacement set (number-AD-927-P) can be sourced from a local auto parts store. They are easily tapped into place with a hammer. Using a lint-free cloth and residue-free solvent, wipe the machined surface clean of any contaminant that could impede the gasket's ability to properly seal the cylinders. The Fel-Pro head gasket requires no additional sealer and is installed dry. Pay close attention to its proper orientation; the correct side of the gasket faces up. Lay the gasket onto the block and press it onto the cylinder head alignment dowels.

2 Install Cylinder Heads

The cylinder heads should still be fully assembled from the preassembly process. The freeze plugs and coolant nipple installed during preassembly require that the cylinder heads be installed on a specific side. Orient the cylinder heads so the coolant nipple is on the passenger-side rear and a freeze plug is on the driver-side rear. A cylinder head is installed by lifting it over the block deck surface and carefully aligning it with the alignment dowels until it drops into place. Use caution to prevent pinching your fingers! Then thread a long head bolt (by hand) into the center hole to prevent the head from falling off until other cylinder head bolts can be installed.

3 Install Cylinder Head Bolts

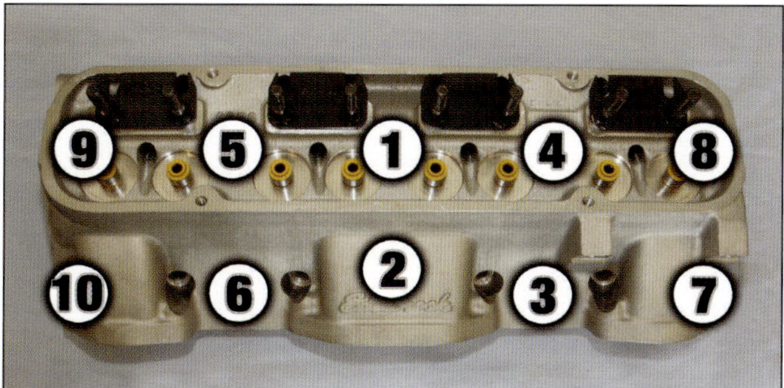

Pontiac used cylinder head bolts of various lengths on any given engine. Refer to your photos and/or disassembly notes to determine the proper locations. If there's any question about their orientation, set a cylinder head on its side and rearrange the bolts until an equal amount of threads protrude from the deck surface. Tighten the head bolts with a specific sequence that's intended to evenly load the cylinder head and crush the gasket. It starts at the center and spirals outward. If using original Pontiac bolts, lubricate the threads and beneath the head with 30W oil. Tighten the bolts to 60 ft-lbs with a 3/4-inch socket and a 1/2-inch-drive torque wrench. Tighten the bolts to 80 ft-lbs in that same pattern, and use a final torque setting of 100 ft-lbs. If aftermarket fasteners are being used, reference the manufacturer's recommended torque specification and thread lubricant. The cylinder head showing the torque sequence is mostly disassembled for photographic purposes. No thread sealer is required unless rebuilding a 301 (or 265 variant).

Elongating the Pushrod Guide Holes for High-Ratio Rockers

When designing its cylinder heads, Pontiac properly located the pushrod guide hole to allow for normal pushrod operation with 1.5:1 rocker arms. Moving the pushrod cup closer to the stud increases the rocker arm ratio, and that changes the pushrod angle in relation to the cylinder head and the path it travels during normal operation.

In most instances, rocker arm ratios greater than 1.5:1 can cause certain pushrods to rub the top of the guide hole, which is drilled into the cylinder head. To prevent any chance of interference, the top of each pushrod guide hole can be elongated with a grinding stone. The hole should be about one-third wider at the top and tapering downward until reaching about halfway. This modification must be performed when the cylinder heads are assembled. The castings must be thoroughly cleaned after. ■

In most instances, Pontiac's cylinder heads are designed to accommodate the normal pushrod travel associated with 1.5:1-ratio rocker arms. Increasing the rocker arm ratio can cause interference between certain pushrods and the guide hole, which is drilled into the cylinder head. Elongating the pushrod guide hole is the only solution for increasing pushrod clearance. Grinding at an angle downward about 1 inch can provide sufficient clearance for high-ratio rocker arms. All work should be performed while the cylinder heads are off the engine and disassembled.

4 Check Pushrod Length

Original Pontiac pushrods measure 5/16-inch wide and 9.13-inches long. As long as they are not bent, originals can often be reused in rebuilds that use stock-replacement flat-tappet camshafts but only if the block or cylinder heads haven't been milled excessively. Aggressive flat-tappet and roller camshafts almost always require special-length pushrods to maintain optimal valvetrain geometry. The components required to determine proper pushrod length are a pair of lifters and rocker studs, one rocker arm that will be used on the engine, and an adjustable pushrod. The pushrod is adjusted to a length that puts the rocker tip near the center of the valve stem while the lifter is positioned on the base lobe of the camshaft, so it doesn't roll off the edge of the valve stem at peak lift. After the proper length has been determined, measure the adjustable pushrod with a caliper. The required length in this instance is 8.55 inches. A diameter of 11/32 inch is recommended whenever possible to combat deflection.

5 Paint Engine

Waiting for the custom pushrods to arrive from Comp Cams proved the perfect opportunity to paint the engine and, specifically, the portions that are otherwise inaccessible when the engine is completely assembled. Pontiac Blue Metallic Paint (number 62200) from OEM Paints closely resembles the original shade of light-metallic-blue paint that Pontiac used from 1966 to 1970. OEM Paints uses a specific formulation when designing its complete line of quality engine paints that resist high-temperature discoloration. OEM's Pontiac engine colors are readily available in a spray can. The valley pan is set in place to prevent painting the lifter valley, and painter's tape is used to mask off any area that shouldn't be painted, particularly any of the machined flanges and the distributor hole.

6 Install Rocker Arms and Guide Plates

Original Pontiac guide plates are sufficient if stock-diameter pushrods are reused, but thicker aftermarket pushrods may require new guide plates. Replacement guide plates from Sealed Power are installed along with 7/16-inch rocker studs from ARP. The guide plates are sandwiched between the cylinder head and rocker studs. Tighten the rocker studs to 55 ft-lbs with an 11/16-inch socket and 1/2-inch-drive torque wrench.

7 | Install Lifters, Pushrods, and Rocker Arms

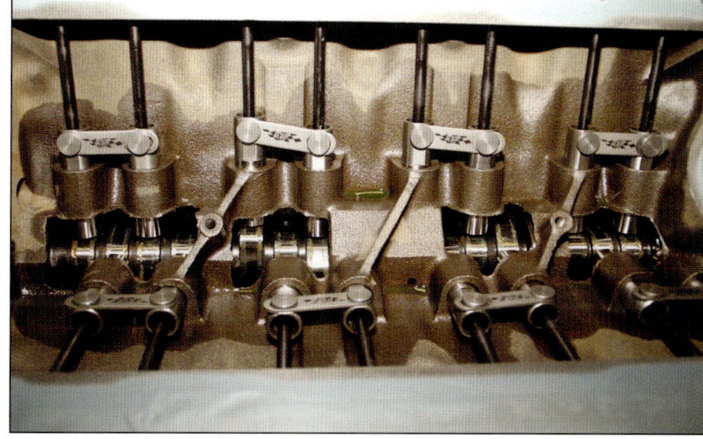

Thoroughly coat the camshaft lobes with the manufacturer's suggested break-in lubricant. Soak the lifters and rocker arms in 30W engine oil for several minutes. If a flat-tappet camshaft is used, coat the lifters' faces with camshaft break-in lubricant. Install the lifters into the lifter bores. They should easily slide into place. The new pushrods are set into place in the lifter cups. Apply a drop of assembly lube to the roller rocker pushrod cup, install the rocker arm onto the rocker stud, and thread the lock nut into place.

There's a Hole in My Head!

Beginning in 1972, Pontiac revised the exhaust crossover of its cylinder heads. The crossover opening gained a blind hole directly above it. The size of one corresponding crossover passage on the intake manifold was also revised accordingly.

I've yet to find a printed Pontiac source that details the reasoning for the addition of the blind hole above the crossover. Some say it was added to isolate engine oil from direct exhaust heat, reducing overall oil temperature and the chance of it cooking in that area. Others say it was a direct attempt at keeping owners from installing different intake manifolds, which may directly affect emissions.

No matter the reason, many hobbyists have grown very concerned upon finding a gaping hole after installing an intake manifold, fearing that a major leak exists. If the intake manifold is from 1972 or later, however, then the rectangular opening, which is located directly above the exhaust crossover passage on the intake manifold and cylinder head, should be considered common and no reason for concern.

However, combining cylinder heads from 1972 and later with a pre-1972 intake manifold, which has a larger passage on the right side, can lead to an exhaust leak. Solving the issue is as easy as filling the right-side blind hole with a high-temperature epoxy until it is flush with the intake manifold flange. Another acceptable solution is fashioning a steel shim and placing it over the hole during intake manifold gasket installation. Either method should effectively prevent potential exhaust leaks related to the crossover mismatch. ∎

With the 1972 model year, Pontiac added a blind hole above the exhaust crossover in its cylinder heads. By design, it remains uncovered by the gasket and intake manifold. The sight of a gaping hole causes concern for many hobbyists, but Pontiac placed the opening there on purpose and it is considered normal for any 1972-and-later engine. If using a pre-1972 intake manifold with later heads, an exhaust leak can develop over the right-side opening, which isn't covered or plugged.

8 Set Valve Lash

Production engines generally use a non-adjustable valvetrain. If your rebuild includes a stock-type camshaft, stamped steel rocker arms, and original rocker studs with a shouldered design, lubricate the rocker's pivot balls with assembly lube and lubricate the nuts with 30W oil. Tighten the nuts to 20 ft-lbs with a 5/8-inch socket and 3/8-inch-drive torque wrench. An adjustable valvetrain gives complete control over valve lash, and that can translate into extended high-RPM operation and a slight power increase. It is required when using an aggressive hydraulic, solid flat-tappet, or any roller cam. Set the lash on a solid camshaft with a feeler gauge placed between the rocker arm and valve stem. The amount of required lash can range from 0.010 to 0.030 inch, depending upon the camshaft and application. Any solid cam should be accompanied by recommended valve lash specifications from the manufacturer. The hydraulic lifter limits the amount of valve lash on a hydraulic camshaft. A quality set of roller rocker arms includes a positive lock nut (often referred to as a poly-lock), which has an internal screw that locks against the rocker stud to positively set valve lash. Aftermarket stamped steel rocker arms usually include a jam nut, which is serrated at the top and must be replaced after a few valve lash adjustments. The less a hydraulic lifter's plunger travels, the more it acts like a solid lifter, possibly increasing performance and extending engine RPM. Because the internal tolerances and operational characteristics of hydraulic lifters differ among the manufacturers, consult with your lifter supplier for the recommended amount of preload, but you are likely to end up between one-quarter to one turn past zero lash. To properly set lifter preload when using a hydraulic cam, rotate the pushrod with two fingers and slowly tighten the lock nut until drag on the pushrod can be felt. Watch the lifter plunger closely to be sure it hasn't compressed any. Using a 5/8-inch wrench, tighten the lock nut a third turn more, which preloads the lifter a minimal amount, minimizing valve lash and internal plunger travel. Insert a hex-head wrench into the internal locking screw, and tighten it and the nut against the rocker stud as a unit. The total amount of preload is about half a turn in this instance.

9 Install Valley Pan

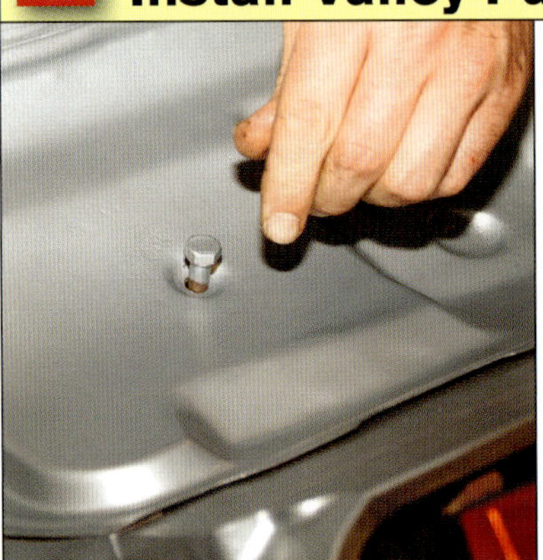

The valley pan is another component that the machinist should thoroughly clean for you. It is a two-piece design that's welded together and contains an internal baffle intended to prevent the engine from ingesting engine oil mist through the Positive Crankcase Ventilation (PCV) valve that is located within it. After years of use, sludge generally results from the continuous oil mist it is exposed to, which is difficult to remove. Absolutely no abrasives should ever be used to clean the valley pan. It's full of cracks and crevices that can hide small particles that can eventually fall into the engine or be drawn in by the PCV system. If your machinist cannot get the internals completely clean after soaking it in a hot tank and/or spray washing it, it may be wise to invest in a replacement. Glue the appropriate Fel-Pro gasket to the valley pan gasket rail with gasket adhesive. If the gasket rails are not bent, RTV sealer should not be required on the block. Once dry, the valley pan is tightened to 3.5 ft-lbs with a 7/16-inch socket. If using a roller camshaft, the valley pan must be test fit to verify that sufficient lifter clearance exists. To do this, apply assembly lube onto the highest point of the lifter bodies, install the valley pan, and rotate the engine several times. Remove the valley pan and check for any signs of lifter contact. Minor clearance is gained by dimpling the contact areas of the valley pan with a small hammer. Major clearance issues once required significant pan modifications, but a new valley designed to accommodate roller lifters may be the best option. The new Tomahawk valley pan from Pacific Performance Racing is a top-quality unit that appears, installs, and functions just like an original but provides sufficient clearance. It is an excellent choice whenever a replacement valley pan is required.

10 Install Water Pump

A new high-quality FlowKooler water pump was sourced for the rebuild. It is installed onto the timing cover but not before the internal divider plate, which properly directs and regulates coolant, is installed. The gasket surfaces of the timing cover and water pump (and divider plate in some instances) receive a thin coating of RTV sealer to fill in any pits or pores that could lead to coolant leaks. Depending upon the model year, the water pump is secured to timing cover with 9 to 11 bolts and possibly some nuts with studs. Tighten them with a 1/2-inch wrench to 15 ft-lbs. In later years, two sleeves with rubber seals are used to seal the timing cover and internal divider plate. The Fel-Pro gasket kit should contain the appropriate gaskets and new rubber seals.

Should I Block the Oil Filter Bypass?

Pontiac's oiling system is well designed and includes a bypass that's intended to prevent major failure by providing an alternate path for oil to circulate, should the filter ever plug during normal operation.

The bypass is located within the oil filter adapter, and it operates via the oil-pressure differential. If the pressure of the oil entering the filter is several pounds greater than the oil exiting the filter, the resultant backpressure collapses a spring, which allows a varying amount of unfiltered oil to circulate throughout the engine at that moment.

It's quite common to block the bypass orifice in the adapter during rebuilds, and the task is as simple as tapping threads into the soft housing and inserting an appropriately sized pipe plug. Hobbyists almost always state that no unfiltered oil should circulate through the engine at any time. While the concept is sound, many modern oil filters include an internal bypass, which essentially circulates unfiltered oil should a blockage occur.

So what should you do during your rebuild? Taking a cue from Pontiac, I see little reason to block the adapter's oil filter bypass in a street-driven application. Pontiac felt such a failsafe was important, and its presence undoubtedly saved a number of engines over the years. This was especially true in the days when oil change intervals of daily-driven Pontiacs were extended beyond a normal range, and high-quality multi-viscosity oil wasn't yet readily available.

I use high-quality oil and a good filter for my Pontiac and am committed to regular change intervals. I'm more

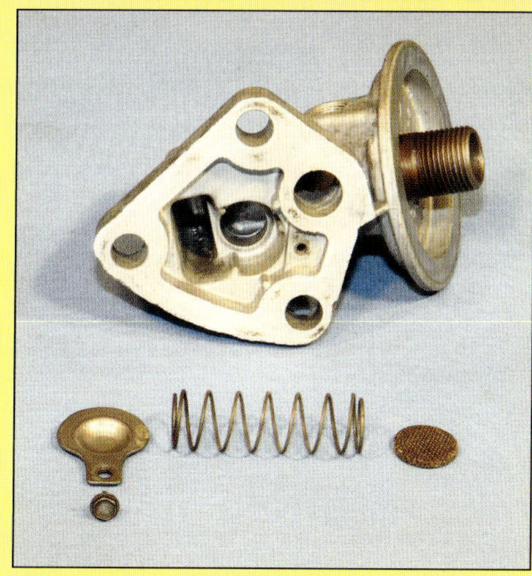

During any rebuild, I routinely disassemble the bypass assembly. I thoroughly clean the bypass valve and seat to remove any dirt or grit that may have accumulated in that area over the years and then simply reassemble it in an identical fashion. This ensures that the bypass is able to perform its intended task should filter failure occur anytime after a freshly rebuilt engine has been in service.

fearful of starving my engine's bearings of lubrication for even a moment than I am of unfiltered oil circulating throughout my engine.

I feel that if the filter is fulfilling its intended task right up to when the blockage occurs, the engine oil should be relatively free of any debris. Oil that bypasses the filter should then present less of a risk of major bearing damage than the catastrophic internal damage that would likely result if a filter blockage of any type (even for an instant) limits oil circulation. ■

11 Install Harmonic Balancer

A harmonic balancer is a key engine component that must function exactly as intended, which is to damp harmful frequencies that travel through the crankshaft. Any variance could cause catastrophic engine damage and any questionable original should be replaced. A number of new 1968-and-later replacements are available. Most Pontiac vendors can supply you with one if needed. Otherwise, any Pontiac harmonic balancer can be rebuilt by companies that specialize in this service. This 1967 unit was renewed a few years ago. The balancer should slide onto the crankshaft snout, fit snuggly on the crankshaft keyway, and not wobble in any way. A gear press can be used to persuade stubborn units, but a balancer should never be forced on nor should it be struck with a hammer. Install the balancer bolt with a 15/16-inch socket and tighten to 160 ft-lbs with a 1/2-inch-drive torque wrench. A long, hardened-steel 1/2-inch-20 stud can be threaded into a flywheel bolt hole on the flywheel register and locked against the engine stand to keep the engine from rotating so full torque can be applied to the balancer bolt. The balancer bolt must be tightened to the appropriate torque setting, otherwise significant engine damage could result. Once installed, rotate the engine so the balancer timing mark is aligned with the TDC mark on the timing cover. A helper can place a finger over the number-1 spark plug hole to verify that the engine is building compression as the piston travels toward the top. This ensures that the number-1 cylinder is on the compression stroke, which is required to properly install the distributor. The lower accessory pulley is also installed at this time, and if so, be sure to include the reinforcing ring, which serves to prevent the pulley bolts from tearing out under normal operation.

Bolt-On Components Installation

1 Install Intake Manifold

Lay a new Fel-Pro intake manifold gasket onto the intake manifold flange of each cylinder head. Use a couple of small dabs of RTV sealer to hold them in place. The rubber ring that seals the coolant crossover to the timing cover is also held in place with RTV sealer. To prevent leaks, I smear a small amount of sealer on the timing cover surface that contacts the intake manifold to seal any pits and pores. Set the manifold carefully into place. By hand, thread in the 10 intake manifold bolts, paying close attention to gasket alignment during install. You may need to refer to your notes to properly position certain bolts. With the bolts hand tight, install the long bolt that seals the timing cover and intake manifold. It draws the manifold forward as it is tightened to 15 ft-lbs with a 7/16-inch socket and 3/8-inch-drive torque wrench. The manifold bolts are then tightened to 40 ft-lbs with a 9/16-inch socket and a 3/8-inch torque wrench. Do this in a crisscross pattern, working from the center outward.

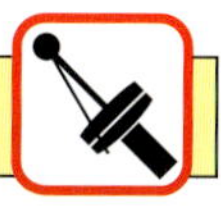

Torque Fasteners

2 Install Thermostat Housing

A new 180-degree thermostat is set into the coolant crossover. The intake manifold surface receives a light coating of RTV sealer to seal any pits that could cause leaks. The machinist surfaced the thermostat housing with a stationary belt sander. Set a new gasket in place and tighten the bolts and/or nuts to 30 ft-lbs with a 9/16-inch socket and 3/8-inch-drive torque wrench.

Torque Fasteners

3 Install Valve Covers

Original oil drippers may not fit when using aftermarket roller rocker arms. They can generally be omitted without compromising component longevity, if using roller rockers. Oil drippers were welded to the valve cover in later years, and some adjustment may be required with aftermarket rocker arms. If using the bolt-on style, fasten the oil drippers to the head bolt studs with a 9/16-inch socket to install the nuts, and tighten them to 30 ft-lbs with a 3/8-inch-drive torque wrench. Glue a new 1/8-inch thick Fel-Pro gasket to each valve cover with gasket adhesive and set the valve covers onto the cylinder heads. Install the valve cover bolts with a 7/16-inch socket and tightened to 8 ft-lbs with a 3/8-inch-drive torque wrench. If additional clearance is needed, Fel-Pro also offers a 1/4-inch-thick gasket for this purpose.

Precision Measurement,
Torque Fasteners

4 Install Spark Plugs

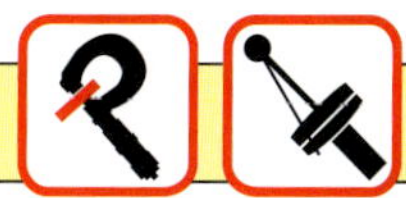

A high-voltage ignition system with an electronic distributor replaces the original contact-points distributor. Set the gap on the AC Delco R45S spark plugs at 0.050 inch. Install the gasket-seat spark plugs with a 13/16-inch socket and tighten them to 25 ft-lbs with a 3/8-inch-drive torque wrench. Later cylinder heads use tapered seat plugs, which are tightened to 15 ft-lbs with a 5/8-inch socket.

Torque Fasteners

5 Install Oil Filter Housing

Install the oil filter housing and use a new Fel-Pro or similar gasket. Tighten the three bolts to 30 ft-lbs with a 9/16-inch socket and a 3/8-inch-drive torque wrench.

6 Install Fuel Pump

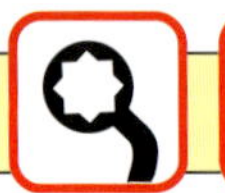 *A new stock-replacement fuel pump from Carter replaces the worn-out original. Install a new Fel-Pro gasket or similar gasket. The bolts securing the fuel pump to the timing cover are tightened to 25 ft-lbs with a 7/16-inch socket and 3/8-inch-drive torque wrench.*

7 Pre-Lube Oil System

Install a high-quality oil filter (ACDelco PF24, NAPA Gold 1258, or Mobil M1-203) onto the housing and tighten it by hand. Fill the crankcase with 6 quarts of oil. I prefer PennGrade 30W break-in oil. A special additive for a flat-tappet camshaft may also be required. For that and the recommended break-in procedure, consult with the camshaft manufacturer. Thread a mechanical oil pressure gauge into the oil-pressure sending unit hole in the oil filter housing. Using a reversible air drill or a high-power electric and an oil system priming tool, spin the oil pump counterclockwise for several seconds, so oil is drawn into the pickup and the entire oiling system is pressurized. The gauge should show steady and consistent pressure while the pump is spinning. Repeat the process several more times to be sure that the oil distributes throughout the entire engine. Some hobbyists feel that oil must be present at every pushrod or rocker arm. I've found that it's not always possible, depending on lifter position. If steady oil pressure occurs and you can see oil flowing by looking in the valve covers, then there is rarely any issue if the oil system plugs were properly installed.

8 Install Distributor

A points-type distributor can provide sufficient performance, and breaker-less conversion kits to convert it from mechanical to electronic operation are available from many companies. However, I sourced a new HEI from PerTronix instead of salvaging a worn original. Its fit and function is identical to an original Pontiac HEI. If using a roller camshaft, replace the distributor gear supplied by PerTronix with a polymer gear from BOP Engineering that is compatible with the steel roller camshaft. With the number-1 piston at TDC on the compression stroke, a spark plug wire terminal is designated as number-1. Align the rotor tip so it points at the corresponding terminal when dropping the distributor in place. You may need to rotate the oil pump shaft with a large screwdriver so it aligns with the distributor drive. After the distributor is fully seated in the block and the rotor tip is pointing at the designated number-1 terminal, rotate the distributor clockwise slightly, which advances timing for initial start-up. Install the distributor hold-down clamp with a 9/16-inch socket. Firmly tighten it, but it doesn't receive final torque until after the break-in procedure, so timing adjustments can be made after initial start-up. Using a counterclockwise pattern, install the distributor cap and route new spark plug wires to the cylinders. The firing order is 1-8-4-3-6-5-7-2. I prefer stock-replacement ACDelco plug wires in applications where original appearance is a concern and Taylor plug wires elsewhere. ACDelco plug wires can be sourced from a local parts store. Taylor wires are readily available from any large mail-order supplier.*

9 Install Flywheel/Flexplate

If your Pontiac uses a manual transmission, a new flywheel may be required during a rebuild. I prefer the steel units produced by Centerforce. New stock replacement flexplates (for automatic transmission) are readily available from many OEM suppliers. Any new flywheel or flexplate should be balanced with the reciprocating assembly. Attach an engine lift plate to the carburetor flange with 5/16-18 x 1-inch bolts. Tighten the bolts very tightly with a 1/2-inch socket. It's lifted slightly with an engine hoist and removed from the engine stand. With a helper holding the engine steady, install the flywheel or flexplate onto the crankshaft flywheel flange. The flange features a unique bolt pattern, so the flywheel may need to be rotated to properly align the bolt holes. Place a drop of blue thread lock on the bolts and install them. Have a helper prevent the crankshaft from turning by using a 15/16-inch socket on the harmonic balancer bolt and supporting it with a long breaker bar. Tighten the bolts to 95 ft-lbs with a 5/8-inch socket and 1/2-inch-drive torque wrench. It's unlikely that your machinist removed the bellhousing locating dowels, but be sure the two 5/8 x 1-1/8 inch dowels protrude from the back of the block. If they are missing, Dura-Bond replacements (number-AD-009-P) are readily available from a local parts store. The engine is now ready for transportation or installation into the vehicle.

10 Prepare for Transportation

If the engine is transported, an engine cradle like this from Butler Performance should be installed. It bolts to the motor mount and bellhousing flanges and safely supports the engine from below. Its low-slung design helps prevent the engine from tipping over while being transported. The original motor mount bolts to the engine stand with a pair of 3/8-16 x 1½-inch bolts. The bolts are installed very tightly using 11/16-inch and 9/16-inch sockets, respectively.

11 Engine Assembly Complete

It's almost ready to run! The 400 is nearly complete and is ready for initial start-up and break-in on an engine dyno, test stand, or in the vehicle. Only a few remaining components need to be installed, and those parts are bolted on either just before or after installation into the vehicle. Those include the engine mount brackets, exhaust manifolds, carburetor and fuel lines, the various wiring and vacuum harnesses, and all accessories and associated brackets.

START-UP, BREAK-IN, AND TUNING

Your newly rebuilt engine is just about ready to fire! If everything was assembled correctly, it should start up relatively easily, and the sound of the exhaust pulsations smoothly bellowing out the exhaust is the best reward for your hard work. If all goes well, the improved operational and performance characteristics of your new engine should give you a great sense of self-satisfaction.

Before starting your engine, determine how to handle initial start-up and camshaft break-in. Will it be performed on a test stand, an engine dyno, or in the vehicle? I much prefer a test stand or engine dyno to vehicle installation. The former gives you a chance to closely inspect for leaks or abnormalities and easily perform any necessary adjustments or repairs within minutes of detecting them. The latter is much more involved, however, and repairs may require several hours of frustrating work of uninstalling the engine.

Engine Test Stand or Dyno

An engine test stand is designed to safely cradle an engine for start-up and operation. Commercially available units are available for purchase, or it can be homemade. Either should be constructed of heavy steel tubing and include a control panel with a starter button, master kill switch, complete instrumentation to monitor the engine's vital functions during operation, a radiator, and an electric fan. A full exhaust can be added to provide quiet operation. The engine can be run normally and closely checked for leaks to break in a flat-tappet camshaft, etc. If the engine checks out fine after initial start-up, it's ready to install into the vehicle and seat the piston rings.

There are two popular types of dynos commonly used to measure engine output. An engine dyno looks similar to a test stand but contains a hydrostatic brake. It directly connects to the crankshaft and measures how much full-throttle horsepower and torque an engine generates. The computer is programmed to let the engine accelerate at a certain number of RPM per second. The specific RPM that the computer begins recording output at is also adjustable. Output values recorded on an engine dyno are generally referred to as "at the flywheel."

A chassis dyno measures the amount of output a vehicle generates through its entire drivetrain. With the engine installed in the vehicle and the break-in process already performed, the vehicle's drive wheels are placed on a large, fixed-weight roller drum and output is recorded as the drum rotates. Values attained

An engine dyno is a common sight at higher-end engine shops. It's an excellent tool to start-up and break-in a new engine while checking for oil and coolant leaks. Its primary use, however, is to measure the full-throttle horsepower and torque an engine generates. A complete dyno session should include adjusting the carburetor and distributor to find the settings that produce peak power.

on a chassis dyno are usually significantly lower than those of an engine dyno—sometimes by 15 to 30 percent. The difference between the two is the amount of engine power consumed by transmission and rear axle operation. Results recorded "at the tire" can be converted into an approximated flywheel value. But because each vehicle's drivetrain is slightly different than the next, there are too many variables to generate an exact flywheel conversion factor.

Engine Reinstallation

The engine installation process varies for each Pontiac model, and can even vary from one year to another on similar models. I feel the best method is simply reversing the process used for engine removal. Refer to your photographs and notes for assistance, and your Pontiac service manual for torque specifications for any bolts, brackets, and accessories. I also strongly suggest having a capable helper assist you throughout the entire installation process. Your newly rebuilt engine is very heavy and must be handled with care. Any mistake can seriously injure you, your engine, or your vehicle.

1 Install Motor Mounts

When the engine is ready for installation into the vehicle, install the motor mounts. Depending on the year, Pontiac used rubber isolators on the engine or on the frame with a corresponding bracket on the other. New stock-replacement motor mounts were sourced from a Pontiac vendor and installed. The bolts are tightened to 70 ft-lbs with an 11/16-inch socket and 1/2-inch-drive torque wrench.

2 Install Exhaust Manifolds

Some models allow the engine to be installed into the vehicle with the exhaust manifolds in place. Whether installing them before or after engine installation, use new exhaust gaskets. The steel shim-type may be sufficient, but I recommend Fel-Pro coated gaskets; both types are included in the Fel-Pro gasket kit. Round port gaskets are sold separately. The bolts are installed with a 9/16-inch socket and tightened to 30 ft-lbs with a 3/8-inch-drive torque wrench. I generally apply a light coating of anti-seize lubricant to the bolt threads to aid future removal.

3 Install Engine

The excited owner is ready to install his freshly rebuilt 400 into his GTO. Actual installation may vary for different vehicles, and different tools and torque specs may be required. Refer to your Pontiac service manual for the exact procedure. Generally, if the engine is resting between the frame rails, the transmission bellhousing dowels are aligned, and the engine is bolted to the transmission. The motor mount bolts are installed and torqued accordingly, and the exhaust is connected.

Torque Fasteners

4 Install Carburetor

Once the engine has been securely attached to the frame rails, remove the carburetor flange adapter from the intake manifold and install the carburetor. Its bolts are tightened to 5 ft-lbs with a 1/2-inch socket and 3/8-inch wrench. The remaining fuel lines and vacuum hoses are also installed.

5 Install Accessory Brackets

The engine is nearly ready to start! Install all accessories and any associated brackets, hook up the electrical connections, and install the radiator and coolant lines. Then fill the cooling system with fresh coolant. After a thorough check to be sure everything is assembled correctly, the engine is ready to start!

Final Preparations

With the engine completely installed in the vehicle, recheck your work to ensure that every nut and bolt is tight and that the coolant hoses, fuel and vacuum lines, and all electrical wiring are properly installed. Be sure that the crankcase is full of your machinist's recommended brand and weight of oil. Usually it is 30W premium-brand oil specifically designed for the break-in process. Such oil contains high quantities of anti-wear additives to protect surfaces and prevent scuffing. It isn't intended for long-term use, though. Plan to replace it after the break-in process is complete.

Preventing Coolant System Air Pockets

Immediately before the initial start-up, the coolant system should be completely filled with a fresh 50/50 mix of coolant and distilled water. Any air pockets trapped within the cooling system can create undesirable hot spots in the block or cylinder heads. To bleed the system of trapped air, I leave the heater core hose disconnected from its nipple at the rear of the passenger-side cylinder head and pack several old rags around it.

I pour the coolant mix directly into the radiator. The open hole allows trapped air to escape. As the cooling system nears its capacity, I begin adding small amounts of coolant while closely watching for it to trickle out of the nipple on the cylinder head. Don't be concerned if a little bit pushes out; the rags are there to soak it up. As soon as coolant is visible at the nipple, the hose is connected and its clamp tightened. The cooling system is now primed and ready for start-up.

Start-Up

The engine is nearly ready for start-up. The oiling system still must be primed from the assembly process. Verify that the number-1 piston is at TDC on the compression stroke and the distributor rotor tip is pointing at the number-1 terminal of the cap. Verify that the spark plug wires are oriented correctly for a firing order of 1-8-4-3-6-5-7-2 in counterclockwise rotation.

The carburetor should be primed with fuel. With a Quadrajet, I use a disposable animal feed syringe to gently squirt some fuel into the well that houses the secondary metering rods. It provides a direct route to the float bowl. Be sure the fuel is going into the float bowl and not into the secondary barrels. The carburetor is pumped until two shots of fuel are discharged from the accelerator pump holes. If you don't see any discharged fuel after several attempts, you may need to squirt more fuel into the float bowl. After the engine receives two pump shots of fuel, it is ready to fire.

Your helper should be nearby with a pressurized garden hose to extinguish any flame that could occur from a backfire. Connect the battery, twist the ignition key to engage the starter, and your engine should roar to life within a couple of revolutions. As soon as it starts,

The Dyno Session

I had the opportunity to use WAM's Land & Sea Dynomite engine dynamometer to break in the 400 and measure its output. WAM's dyno has been used on a number of Pontiac engines in the past. Based on the types of combinations measured on it, the numbers it generates seem to fall in line with similar combinations tested on similar dynos. That simply means that similar combinations can produce similar results when tested on other dynos.

Chuck Willard installed the 400 onto the dyno. He added a pair of 2.5-inch Ram Air manifolds from RARE, a pair of mandrel-bent 2.5-inch downpipes constructed of stainless steel from Pypes Performance Exhaust, and primed the carburetor. The engine fired immediately and engine timing was adjusted to 10 degrees. With the coolant and oil at normal operating temperature, Willard began varying engine load and RPM to seat the piston rings. After a successful break-in period, he made several full-throttle pulls, recording engine output each time.

Pontiac's 400 HO was originally rated at 360 hp and 445 ft-lbs for the 1967 model year. This 400 had been upgraded with HO components during past rebuilds and should've performed similarly to an original 400 HO. But because of the significant crankshaft issue found during the blueprinting process it's unlikely that this 400 had ever generated anywhere near that amount.

After the rebuild, the GTO's engine displaced 408 ci. With the addition of a mild hydraulic roller camshaft, the otherwise stock-rebuilt engine peaked at an astounding 396 hp at 5,300 rpm and 444 ft-lbs at 4,400 rpm, after adjusting the carburetor and distributor. The careful selection of parts to complement the GTO's optional equipment proved to be very successful; the 400 generates more than 400 ft-lbs at 3,000 rpm. That makes the GTO a pleasure to cruise on the highway! ∎

The 400 was started and broken in on WAM's Land & Sea Dynomite engine dynamometer. A complete dyno tuning session followed, which included closely monitoring the fuel and ignition curves to ensure the engine was generating peak horsepower and torque. The relatively mild combination produced 396 hp and 444 ft-lbs of torque. This is an astounding number, considering how many of the original components were used.

400-ci Dyno Results		
RPM	HP	TQ
3000	240	421
3100	255	430
3200	262	430
3300	271	430
3400	279	431
3500	288	434
3600	301	436
3700	310	438
3800	318	438
3900	323	435
4000	336	437
4100	347	442
4200	355	444
4300	358	437
4400	364	434
4500	368	431
4600	370	422
4700	375	418
4800	380	416
4900	382	409
5000	383	402
5100	384	395
5200	389	392
5300	396	392
5400	384	376
AVG	337	423

Some oil companies produce 30W oil that's specifically designed for engine break-in. Penn Grade and Joe Gibbs Driven lubricants are quite popular with machinists and engine builders. Either lubricant provides excellent protection for initial start-up and is ideal for the first few miles of driving. They aren't intended for long-term use, so plan to change the oil shortly after the break-in process is complete.

immediately begin the camshaft break-in procedure.

Don't panic if your engine doesn't immediately fire. An engine requires only fuel and spark for normal operation. If you saw fuel squirt from the accelerator pump discharge holes earlier, then check for spark with a timing light on the number-1 spark plug wire while cranking. But do not continue pumping the carburetor. You do not want to flood your new engine and wash the assembly oil from the cylinder walls! Retrace your steps to locate and correct your electrical glitch.

Flat-Tappet Camshaft Break-In

A flat-tappet camshaft requires a very specific break-in process that includes specific lubricants and oil additives, and as much as 30 minutes of increased-RPM operation. The cast-iron lobe and lifter face of any flat-tappet camshaft is surface hardened. A specific break-in procedure is used to polish the two contact surfaces. The surfaces receive no direct lubrication during normal operation but instead are indirectly lubricated by oil seepage from the lifter bores and splash oiling from the crankshaft.

During camshaft installation, the lifter and lobe surfaces are thoroughly coated with a specific camshaft break-in lubricant, which is designed to prevent scuffing that occurs before oil circulation begins at initial start-up. If prolonged cranking occurs during the initial start-up process, seriously consider removing the valley pan and recoating the lifters and lobes with break-in lubricant. A failed lifter or lobe sends metallic filings throughout the engine and makes for a complete teardown, a thorough cleaning, and new bearings required, at the minimum.

Immediately after the engine fires, its speed should be increased toward 2,500 rpm by adjusting the carbure-

Flat-tappet camshafts can experience lobe and/or lifter failure if not properly broken in. In addition to a specific break-in procedure, some camshaft manufacturers offer a thick paste that's applied directly to the lobe and lifter contact surfaces during installation to prevent scuffing at initial start-up. I feel that a paste is better than a liquid because it's less likely to drip off or be wiped away spinning the engine. Ask your camshaft supplier for a recommendation.

tor idle speed screw. The added RPM is necessary because it increases pressurized oil circulation and splash lubrication. It also lessens the overall inertial load on the lifters, allowing them to rotate quicker on the lobes and enhance the polishing effect. The distributor vacuum advance can be connected to full manifold vacuum to further advance spark lead and reduce the risk of overheating. There's no risk of detonation because there is no load on the engine.

Your camshaft supplier provides you with specific break-in instructions. It might also suggest specific lubricants or physical steps be taken for the process. Follow them closely if you expect any camshaft company to honor a warranty claim. The entire flat-tappet camshaft break-in procedure should take 20 to 30 minutes to complete. Remember: The engine should never be run at idle speed during that time.

Your helper should be watching oil pressure and coolant temperature throughout the break-in process. The engine can be shut down if coolant temperature rises above about 230°F or if any operational concerns are detected. The process can continue once the engine has had ample time to cool back into the 160 to 180°F range. If shutdown is required, simply restart the engine and pick up where you left off until the manufacturer's suggested run time has elapsed.

Roller Camshaft Break-In

Roller camshaft break-in is much simpler than flat-tappet camshaft break-in. The steel camshaft and roller lifters do not need to mate like flat-tappet components. There is, however, metal-to-metal contact upon initial start-up, particularly within the hydraulic roller lifter body and plunger. If your camshaft manufacturer doesn't provide you with specific break-in instructions, simply increase RPM to about 1,500 for a few minutes to allow the engine oil to circulate throughout the engine. Check for leaks and listen intently for any abnormal noises. Engine speed can then be reduced to where the engine doesn't die, and the carburetor and distributor can be adjusted accordingly.

Engine Break-In

After the camshaft break-in process is complete, the engine should be driven for several miles to give the piston rings a chance to properly seat. The process should never include operating at a constant speed or at full throttle for any extended

General Motors Engine Oil Supplement (E.O.S.) is a heavily concentrated lubricant that's packed full of desirable anti-wear additives (left). It is readily available from your nearest GM dealer (part number 88862586). Most camshaft manufacturers, such as Comp Cams, offer a proprietary oil additive specifically designed for flat-tappet camshaft break-in (right). Either is an excellent choice that can be mixed with oil at regular change intervals to provide sufficient flat-tappet camshaft protection during normal operation.

length of time. The proper procedure consists of varying engine speed and engine load by continually accelerating and decelerating on an open road. Accelerate briskly and then let off the throttle. It's best to leave the transmission in a lower gear, allowing for engine braking while decelerating. The process allows the rings to properly seat under acceleration and deceleration.

Engine Oil and Additives

Specific break-in oil is recommended for initial engine start-up and during break-in. Before running your new engine very hard, you should change the engine oil to rid it of any filings that result from component wear-in. It can be very thick as it cleans the heavy assembly lubricants from the internal surfaces used during assembly. Pontiac originally specified 20W oil during winter months and 30W oil during summer months. I routinely use 10W-30, 10W-40, and 15W-40 oils

in our street-driven Pontiacs without any issue. The type of engine oil used depends greatly on the type of camshaft being used.

Oil companies have reduced the levels of desirable anti-wear additives present in modern-spec passenger car oil. A zinc-phosphorus compound (ZDDP) provides a high-pressure lubrication to prevent two metallic surfaces from contacting one another when the oil film is squeezed away. It's a beneficial additive that protects such high-pressure internal engine surfaces as a flat-tappet camshaft lobe and lifter.

Modern auto manufacturers are required to warrant certain components of the emissions system of new vehicles for 8 years or 80,000 miles. It was determined that the phosphorus found in ZDDP was negatively reacting with the exhaust catalytic converter, causing premature failure. The additive is essential when using a flat-tappet camshaft, but because modern production engines use a steel camshaft and roller lifters, oil companies could remove a significant amount of the additive without any negative effects.

The reduction of ZDDP seems to have contributed to the unusually high number of flat-tappet camshaft failures in vintage engines in recent

American Petroleum Institute (API) rates oil quality and regulates additives. Its ratings for oils are found in the "donut" on the back label of any oil container. Modern-spec oil carries an "SN" rating, and its lubricating qualities may be the best ever. It has less of the desirable anti-wear additives than past oils, however, and that can lead to premature flat-tappet camshaft failure in older engines. If using SN-spec oil, be sure to use an additive in any engine with a flat-tappet camshaft.

years. As the lifter or lobe wears through the hardened portion of the cast iron, whether during initial break-in or normal operation, complete failure results. That usually requires a complete teardown to clean all traces of iron filings from the engine, which might otherwise imbed into the bearings.

Many companies, including camshaft manufacturers, produce specific oil or additive packages that contain a concentrated amount of anti-wear additives, which are intended to combat flat-tappet camshaft failure. But they are generally not readily available at local auto parts stores. They must be sourced through local speed shops, machine shops, or mail-order vendors. Though these products effectively reduce the failure risk, they are simply not required when using a roller camshaft, which is constructed of steel.

In addition to any benefit related to reduced friction and slightly more aggressive lobe profiles, a hydraulic roller camshaft is an excellent choice for a street-driven Pontiac, if the budget allows. Not only is there no real break-in process, there is no risk of failure and you can use most modern-spec oils that are readily available from the nearest auto parts store. I liken flat-tappet camshafts in modern engines and the associated oil concerns to high-compression engines that cannot operate on pump fuel. You just never know when you won't be able to find what you need if you're in a pinch, and that could potentially lead to some type of damage or failure.

Carburetor Tuning

The Quadrajet may be the most popular carburetor used for street-driven Pontiacs today. Not only does it offer an excellent balance of low-speed throttle response and full-throttle performance, Pontiac used the Quadrajet for its performance applications in 1967 and as its only 4-barrel carburetor from 1968 forward. With the high number produced over the years, there are a number of original castings available today. They look completely original while providing excellent performance when modified correctly.

A carburetor must provide the correct mixture of atomized fuel and air for maximum performance in every operating condition. Each Quadrajet was specifically calibrated for its intended applications. Three specific fuel circuits—idle, primary (or main), and secondary—provide strong performance throughout the entire powerband. Significant engine modifications, such as camshaft or compression ratio changes, or cylinder-head port work, can require altering carburetor fueling.

When a hobbyist attempts to use a Quadrajet that was originally intended for a mild 301 on a highly modified 455, for instance, the carburetor simply cannot handle the fuel demand of the larger engine. While metering jet and/or rod changes can improve part-throttle and full-throttle fueling, the engine often struggles to stay running or requires an exces-

Effective Quadrajet modifications are more involved than simply changing metering jets and rods. Enlarging certain passages with a small drill bit often is the only way to improve idle quality and the off-idle transition. CarTech's How to Rebuild and Modify Rochester Quadrajet Carburetors, *by Cliff Ruggles, is an excellent resource that clearly describes which holes must be drilled and how large to make them. It's one any hobbyist should have before working on any Quadrajet.*

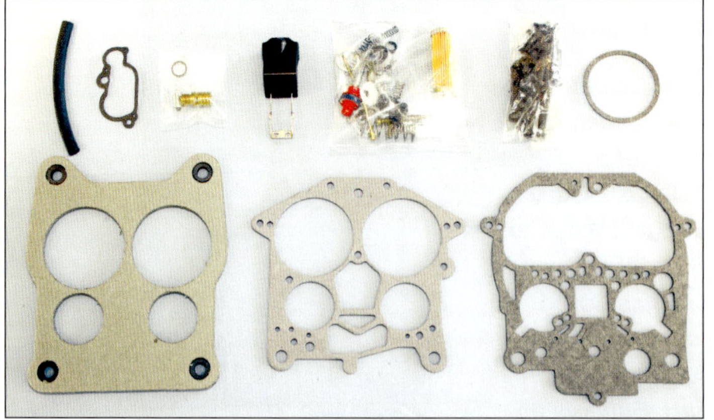

Cliff's High Performance offers complete rebuild kits that contain virtually every piece needed to properly restore the functionality of a Rochester Quadrajet carburetor. Cliff's kits may be more costly than those available at local auto parts stores, but his are full of top-quality components and include new gaskets, a float and filter, various small parts, and even new fasteners. The rubber parts are specially designed for use with ethanol-blend fuel.

Finding complete rebuild kits for Rochester 2-barrel carburetors can be difficult enough, but finding the correct kits to properly rebuild a Pontiac Tri-Power setup can be discouraging. Pontiac Tri-Power offers complete rebuild kits for each Tri-Power carburetor. The kits include the required gaskets and a plethora of small parts. Even better, Pontiac Tri-Power offers an informative DVD that walks you through the Tri-Power rebuild and tuning process. Pontiac Tri-Power is an excellent resource for all your Tri-Power needs.

sive amount of initial timing to produce suitable idle quality. It is this instance that lends the Quadrajet its negative reputation. The proper repair is to completely disassemble the Quadrajet and enlarge the fixed orifices within the carburetor that control idle fueling.

That process and all the necessary information required for proper calibration can be found in CarTech's *How to Rebuild and Modify Rochester Quadrajet Carburetors* by Cliff Ruggles. It's an excellent resource that helps you identify the best Pontiac Quadrajet castings, the proper rebuild technique, and how to correctly calibrate one for most applications. Both Cliff's High Performance and The Carburetor Shop can provide you with top-quality components compatible with ethanol-blend fuel for your project.

Tri-Power induction remains very popular with Pontiac hobbyists. The unique wail the Rochester 2-barrel trio makes at full-throttle is a sound

unmatched by any 4-barrel carburetor. It is a sound that many attempt to mimic by adding a Tri-Power intake manifold to their Pontiac. Many are hesitant to adjust or modify a somewhat-properly working Tri-Power setup, fearing that it may operate worse than before. Tri-Power may seem complicated, but it is much easier to tune if the carburetors are functioning properly.

Pontiac TriPower and The Carburetor Shop are companies that are capable of handling all your Tri-Power needs. Both stock a complete line of components required to properly rebuild a Rochester 2-barrel carburetor, including rubber components compatible with ethanol-blend fuel. In addition to carburetor parts, Pontiac TriPower also carries an entire line of restoration components to properly restore your original Tri-Power setup. Both companies offer knowledgeable tech support that's sure to help you diagnose and correct any operational issue you may experience.

Distributor Types

There are two basic types of ignition systems that Pontiac used over the years: One uses contact points, and the other is electronically controlled.

The contact points set in a distributor transfers electrical energy from the coil to the spark plugs. Energy builds while the points are closed, and the duration that the points are closed is referred to as "dwell angle," which is a degree of distributor rotation. An intense electrical spark travels the air gap across the spark plug electrode and ground strap as the points open.

Contact points distributors are quite simple and operate reliably. Dwell angle does change as the contact points wear during normal operation, however, degrading spark intensity over time. Periodic dwell angle adjustments to return it to the

A contact points set was a common sight inside most new car distributor wells into the 1970s. The coil saturates with current while the points are closed, and the resistance that occurs when the points open is released as an electrical spark that jumps the spark plug gap. New contact points sets are available at local auto parts stores. I recommend Echlin number CS89 from NAPA. Most hobbyists elect to convert from mechanical operation to an electronic conversion.

28- to 32-degree range Pontiac suggests is required to maintain peak performance and minimal emissions. Once dwell exceeds that range and cannot be adjusted accordingly, the points set must be replaced, which is a relatively easy process.

Pontiac began offering its transistorized electronic distributor on a larger scale during the 1960s. An electronic ignition module that automatically adjusted dwell replaced the contact points set. Another electronic distributor was introduced late in the 1971 model year. The Unitized ignition system was marketed as a fully self-contained unit that featured an in-cap coil and required a single 12-volt power lead for

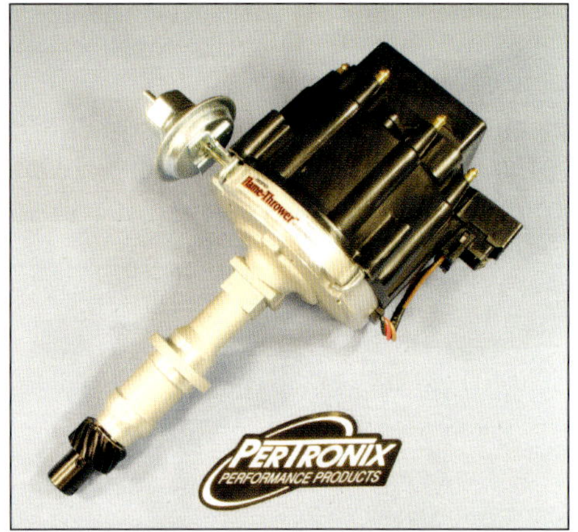

The HEI was Pontiac's most common electronic ignition system. It debuted in the mid-1970s and became standard equipment on all GM vehicles shortly after. Used units are easily found at swap meets or salvage yards, but it's often easier to purchase a brand new HEI as opposed to salvaging a worn original. The PerTronix D-1200 is an excellent choice when looking to purchase a new HEI. It contains top-quality components and an adjustable vacuum advance unit. PerTronix also offers a few different Ignitor kits to convert a points-type distributor to electronic operation.

normal operation. Plagued by expensive replacement parts, it was used more often during the 1972 to 1974 model years before it was replaced by high energy ignition (HEI), which made its debut in May 1974.

HEI functioned similarly to Unitized, but its design was much simpler and more reliable. Produced by the Delco-Remy division of GM, HEI became standard equipment on most Pontiac engines toward the end of the 1974 model year. It was standard equipment on all Pontiac engines beginning in 1975. HEI remains a widely popular ignition-system choice for most GM vehicles. Some aftermarket companies produce modern interpretations of the HEI to replace worn originals or to simply replace a points-type distributor all together. The only real drawback to an HEI distributor is its compatibility with certain Pontiac platforms and intake manifolds. Its large-cap design sometimes interferes with the firewall on such models as the first-generation Firebird or certain years of the

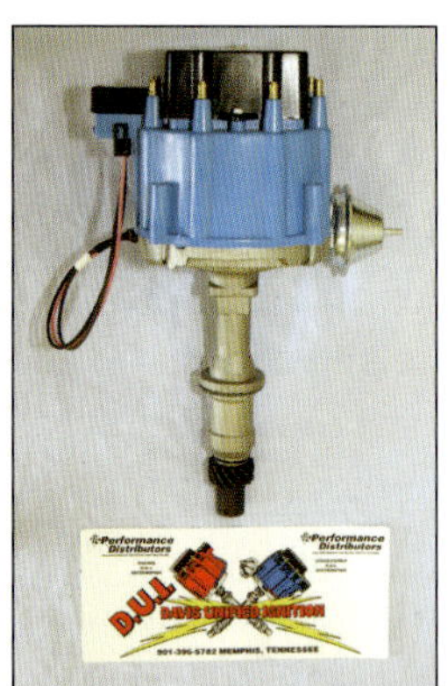

Most low-end HEIs available on the aftermarket contain generic mechanical advance curves that use low-quality pieces and may need to be re-curved to produce peak engine output. Performance Distributors offers new top-quality HEIs that feature custom-calibrated mechanical and vacuum advance curves for your individual combination. They are delivered ready to run and offer proven success.

Ventura. If a slight amount of clearance is required, a hammer can be used to lightly "massage" the firewall.

HEI is not compatible with any type of original Tri-Power intake manifold. The runners simply extend too far rearward to allow the use of an original-type HEI. Companies, such as DAVE's small-body HEI's, can produce an HEI-type distributor

M&H Electric Fabricators' breakerless electronic conversion kit allows owners to eliminate the contact points set within a conventional distributor and install an electronic triggering system. The complete M&H kit fits completely within the points-type distributor cap. Its one-wire hookup lends to easily installation, while maintaining a completely original appearance. The M&H kit comes with a 3-year manufacturer warranty.

MSD has developed a new HEI ignition module with rev limiting capability (part number 83645) that replaces the original electronic module found within an HEI distributor. It features increased output and full adjustability over its rev limiter, which can be set from 5,000 to 10,000 rpm. The MSD module installs relatively easily and retains a stock-type appearance.

that uses a points-type housing at a very reasonable cost. Other companies offer complete electronic conversions for hobbyists who want to reuse a points-type distributor but use an electronic triggering system.

Spark Advance Tuning

An internal combustion engine generates torque by applying the combustion force as leverage, which rotates the crankshaft. Maximum torque occurs when cylinder pressure peaks at a crankshaft angle between 10 and 20 degrees after top dead center (ATDC). That range allows combustion pressure to exert as much of its force as possible over the entire length of the crankshaft's stroke.

The crankshaft is in constant motion and total combustion takes a fixed amount of time. As engine speed increases, ignition must be initiated at an earlier crankshaft angle before top dead center (BTDC) for peak pressure to occur within the desired ATDC crankshaft angle.

There are three basic terms often used when speaking of spark advance initial timing, mechanical advance, and vacuum advance. Each plays a distinct role in engine performance and each is very adjustable. Finding the right combination of the three can be difficult, but peak engine performance occurs only when combustion pressure is applied at the right time under every RPM and engine load.

Initial timing is the base amount of spark lead an engine sees at idle with the distributor's vacuum advance canister disconnected from any vacuum source. Initial timing is measured by connecting a timing light to the number-1 spark plug wire. The timing light is aimed at

The XR-i conversion kit from Crane Cams allows owners to easily convert a conventional distributor to electronic operation. Unlike the others, Crane's kit includes an adjustable rev limiter, and the unit specific to Pontiac is number 750-1720. I've installed several XR-i modules into distributors over the years and have found them easy to use and quite reliable.

the harmonic balancer. The strobe produced makes the harmonic balancer's TDC timing mark appear stationary with the graduated hash marks on the timing cover. Most Pontiacs are in the 8- to 12-degree range. Initial timing can be adjusted by simply loosening the hold-down clamp and rotating the distributor. Clockwise rotation advances timing; counterclockwise retards it.

A distributor is equipped with a mechanical advance system that automatically advances spark timing in relation to engine speed. Also called "centrifugal advance," it uses a pair of weights that overcome spring tension as engine speed increases to press on a center cam and advance the spark timing. The factory-designed advance curves are often an excellent compromise of emissions, performance, and reliable operation on questionable-quality fuel.

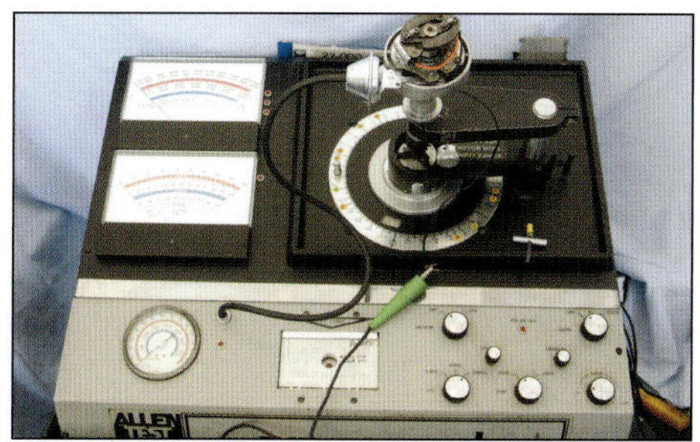

Electronics companies, such as Sun and Allen, offered a number of different distributor testers like this Allen Syncrograph, which was produced in the early 1980s. They were once used by service professionals to test complete functionality of a distributor. Speed shops used them to adjust the mechanical advance curve for optimum performance. Fully functional units are quite rare. If you have a distributor that you need re-curved, you may be able to find someone who has one locally simply by asking around.

Modifying the centrifugal advance curve is a popular way to increase the low-speed street manners and full-throttle performance of a particular combination. It usually involves more spark advance and/or a quicker rate of advance. The advance curve can be tested on professional equipment or with an adjustable timing light. The goal is to tailor the advance curve for peak performance by replacing weights, center cam, and/or springs. Though each combination must be addressed individually, 22 to 24 crankshaft degrees of mechanical advance that peaks between 3,000 and 3,500 rpm is an excellent starting point for a street-driven application.

Total timing is the sum of static initial timing plus mechanical advance. For instance, 10 degrees of static initial plus 24 degrees of mechanical advance produces 34 degrees of total advance. I've found

Not everyone has access to professional distributor testing equipment. Not to worry! Bob Davis Distributors can provide you with a high-quality re-curve kit that contains everything required to properly adjust your HEI's mechanical advance.

The Crane Cams Adjustable Vacuum Advance kit offers complete and independent adjustability of the amount of vacuum advance and the vacuum actuation point. Crane Cams produces separate kits for points-type and HEI distributors. They install easily and are quite simple to use. I recommend using a Crane Cams kit in any application where vacuum advance testing is planned.

that most Pontiacs with cast-iron cylinder heads seem to perform best with 34 to 38 degrees of total timing. Experiment to determine the amount of timing that works best for your particular application, but listen very intently for any high-speed "ticking" or "rattling" at full throttle. Too much timing can cause engine-damaging detonation, and any testing should be immediately halted until timing can be adjusted accordingly.

Vacuum Advance Tuning

A carburetor is designed to provide the required amount of fuel to produce peak power at every engine speed under every type of load. In light-load conditions such as at part-throttle cruise, the throttle plates are almost closed, and it provides minimal amounts of fuel and air. Cylinder volume doesn't change, however, so the fuel and air molecules within the combustion chamber aren't as tightly compacted during the compression stroke, resulting in a less combustible mixture.

The flame front of a less combustible mixture spreads slower. Spark must be initiated much earlier for peak cylinder pressure to occur at the optimum time. This is sometimes in excess of 50 degrees BTDC depending upon the condition. It's impossible to have a distributor mechanical advance curve properly set to provide peak performance for both part-throttle and full-throttle conditions, so a load-sensing device that uses engine vacuum to advance spark in light-load conditions was added to the distributor.

Vacuum advance tuning should be performed only after the initial and mechanical advance curves have been modified to produce peak performance. I have found that most Pontiac engines respond favorably to 10 to 15 degrees of vacuum advance, which increases the amount of spark lead to nearly 50 degrees at part throttle. Some engines may actually tolerate even more vacuum advance without detonating, but it seems the effects appear to diminish beyond about 15 degrees.

I feel that the adjustable vacuum advance kit produced by Crane Cams is the best available choice. It allows the tuner to adjust the amount of vacuum advance and the vacuum actuation point independently of one another. Too much vacuum advance can produce audible detonation at light part-throttle conditions. If any detonation is detected, remove 2 degrees of vacuum advance and test again. Continue the process until detonation subsides.

There are two types of engine vacuum that the vacuum advance canister can be connected to. Ported vacuum provides available engine vacuum only when the throttle plates are open. Manifold vacuum provides engine vacuum at all times, including idle and deceleration. One type isn't necessarily better than the other and not all carburetors are equipped to provide ported vacuum.

If your carburetor contains a ported vacuum source, I recommend performing your own testing session to determine which type of vacuum advance is best suited for an application. Connect the vacuum advance canister to one type first, adjust the idle speed accordingly, trim the carburetor mixture screws to provide peak vacuum, and perform a thorough test drive.

After establishing a baseline, connect the vacuum canister to the other type. Adjust the idle speed and carburetor mixture screws accordingly, and perform another test drive.

You should find that a proper amount of vacuum advance is immediately noticeable at part-throttle driving conditions. The engine should be more responsive to throttle angle changes at low speed, and the improved engine efficiency can translate into a slight fuel economy increase as well as possibly reduce normal operating temperature. I have yet to find any negative results when using a reasonable amount of vacuum advance in any combination.

A Final Note

Your rebuild is complete! If everything went as planned, your newly rebuilt Pontiac V-8 should perform better than ever before in any driving condition. It should start easily, idle smoothly, and accelerate effortlessly. It should not run hot and should be free of any oil or coolant leaks. If you can find any spare time to dedicate to finely tuning the carburetor and distributor, you may be able to extract a few more horsepower and further improve its street manners.

The owner of the 400 rebuilt in these pages was very pleased with the result. After the 400-hp engine was reinstalled into the GTO, the car's performance was outstanding. The 400's operating characteristics are much different than before. It starts easily, operates reliably on 91-octane pump gas, and has provided the owner with a few thousand miles of issue-free performance so far. The car is much easier to drive in any condition, and the 400-hp engine otherwise looks just like any other beautifully detailed, original 1967 400. That's the exact result we were after. Hopefully your rebuild is as successful!

If your rebuild was successful, your Pontiac is running better than ever before in every driving condition. Any operating concern that existed before the rebuild should no longer be an issue. It should start quickly and easily and operate very consistently. It should run better and better as more miles are added, so drive your Pontiac often!

Torque Specifications

Original Fastener Torque Specifications (refer to manufacturer instructions for aftermarket pieces)

Component	Required Wrench/Socket Size	Torque Spec in ft-lbs	Lubricant	Thread Sealer
Block Engine Mount	11/16	70	dry	
Block Main Journal Cap	3/4	100	30W oil	
Block Rear Main Journal Cap	15/16	120	30W oil	
Camshaft Thrust Plate	1/2	20	dry	blue thread locker
Camshaft Timing Gear	3/4	40	dry	blue thread locker
Carburetor to Intake Manifold	1/2	5	dry	
Connecting Rods (stock 3/8 inch fasteners)	9/16	43	30W oil	
Cylinder Head Bolt	3/4	100	30W oil	
Distributor Clamp	9/16	30	dry	
Exhaust Manifolds	9/16	30	anti-seize	
Fan To Water Pump Hub	1/2	20	dry	
Flywheel to Crankshaft	5/8	95	dry	blue thread locker
Fuel Pump	7/16	25	dry	
Harmonic Balancer	15/16	160	dry	
Intake Manifold to Cylinder Head	9/16	40	dry	
Intake Manifold to Timing Cover	7/16	15	dry	
Oil Filter Housing to Block	9/16	30	dry	
Oil Pan Drain Plug	11/16	22	dry	
Oil Pan to Block	7/16	12	dry	
Oil Pan to Block (rear corners with straps)	7/16	20	dry	
Oil Pan to Timing Cover	7/16	12	dry	
Oil Pump Bottom Cover Plate	1/2	15	dry	blue thread locker
Oil Pump Regulator Spring	13/16	15	dry	
Oil Pump To Block	9/16	30	dry	blue thread locker
Rocker Arm (stock bottleneck studs)	5/8	20	dry	
Rocker Arm Stud	11/16	50	dry	
Spark Plug (gasket seat)	13/16	25	dry	
Spark Plug (tapered seat)	5/8	15	dry	
Thermostat Housing	9/16	30	dry	
Timing Cover to Block	9/16	15	dry	
Valley Pan (Pushrod Cover)	7/16	3.5	dry	
Valve Cover (Rocker Cover)	7/16	8	dry	
Water Pump to Timing Cover	1/2	15	dry	
Windage Tray to Main Caps	1/2	15	dry	blue thread locker

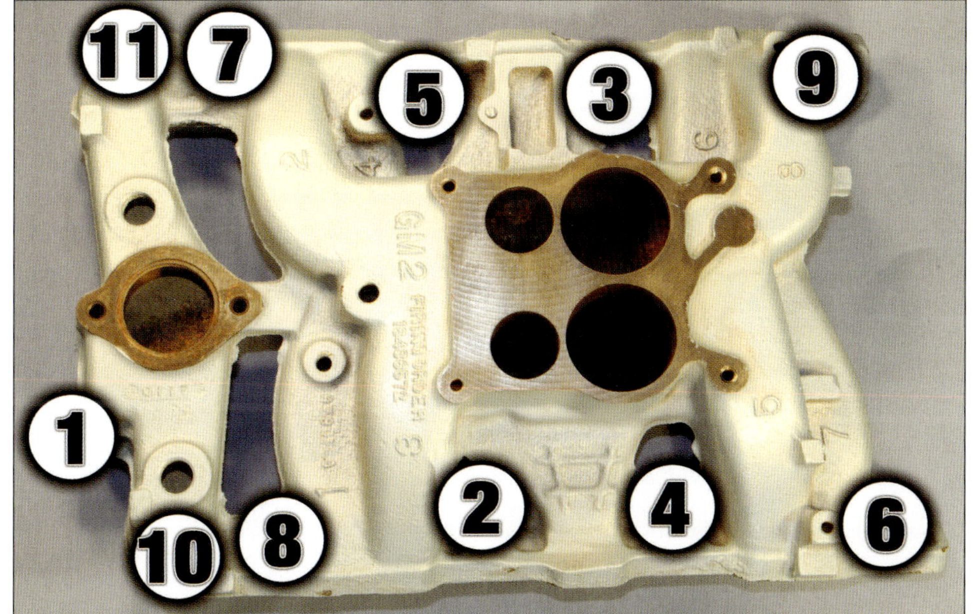

Intake Manifold

Use this torque sequence to tighten the intake manifold bolts in 10 ft-lb increments to 40 ft-lbs.

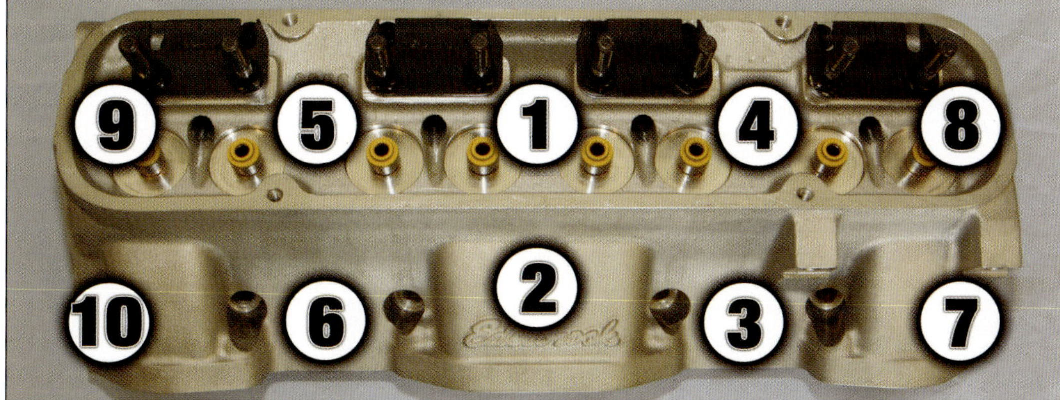

Cylinder Head

Use this torque sequence to tighten all cylinder head bolts to 100 ft-lbs in 20 ft-lb increments and use 30W oil for lubrication. Follow the manufacturer's spec if aftermarket fasteners are used.

Main Bearing Cap

Place the main caps on the block in their designated registers and in the correct orientation. Make sure they fit down into their registers. Next, torque the main bearing cap bolts according to the sequence in the photo. Starting from the center cap and working outward helps prevent crankshaft distortion during main cap installation. If the crankshaft is straight and the block's main saddles were machined properly, working front to back shouldn't be an issue, but it can be if certain components were reused without machining or machined incorrectly. With original fasteners, torque all main cap bolts except the rear journal cap, are torqued to 100 ft-lbs. Torque the rear main journal cap bolts to 120 ft-lbs. Use 30W oil for lubrication on all. If aftermarket fasteners are used, refer to the manufacturer's recommended lubrication and torque specs.

The correct cylinder firing order is designated on this distributor.

Cylinder Location

This shows the location of cylinder numbers-1 through -8.

Engine Codes

Year	Block Code	CI	HP	Head Casting	Advertised Compression Ratio (:1)	Camshaft	Carburetor	Distributor	Transmission	Body	Notes 1	Notes 2
1967	WA	400	265	142	8.6	E	2-barrel	1111242	M	B		
1967	WB	400	265	142	8.6	E	2-barrel	1111242	M	B		
1967	WC	326	250	140	9.2	U	2-barrel	1111164	M	F		
1967	WD	400	333	143	10.5	P	AFB	1111254	M	B	With A.I.R.	Replaced by XT
1967	WE	400	333	143	10.5	P	AFB	1111253 or 1111255	M	B		Replaced by WY
1967	WF	400	350	670	10.5	N	AFB	Presently unknown	M	GP	A/C	
1967	WG	428	360	670	10.5	P	7027263	1111183, 1111243, or 1111180	M	B		
1967	WH	326	250	140	9.2	U	2-barrel	1111119	M	F	With A.I.R.	
1967	WI	400	325	97/997	10.75	H	7037276	1111250	M	F		Ram Air I
1967	WJ	428	376	670	10.75	S	7027263	1111250, 1111183, 1111243, or 1111180	M	B		
1967	WK	326	285	141	10.5	U	AFB	1111165	M	F		326 H.O.
1967	WM	400	265	142	8.6	U	2-barrel	Presently unknown	M	B	With A.I.R.	
1967	WN	400	265	142	8.6	U	2-barrel	Presently unknown	M	B	With A.I.R.	
1967	WO	326	285	141	10.5	U	AFB	1111238	M	F	With A.I.R.	326 H.O.
1967	WP	326	250	140	9.2	U	2-barrel	1111164	M	F		
1967	WQ	400	325	97/997	10.75	H	7037276	1111252	M	F	With A.I.R.	Ram Air I
1967	WR	326	285	141	10.5	U	AFB	1111165 or 1111166	M	A		326 H.O.
1967	WS	400	360	670	10.75	S	7027263	1111183 or 1111180	M	A		
1967	WT	400	335	670	10.75	P	7027263	1111183 or 1111180	M	A		
1967	WU	400	325	670	10.75	P	7037273	1111252	M	F	With A.I.R.	
1967	WV	400	360	670	10.75	S	7037263	1111237	M	A	With A.I.R.	
1967	WW	400	335	670	10.75	P	7037263	1111237	M	A	With A.I.R.	
1967	WX	326	250	140	9.2	U	2-barrel	1111199	M	F	With A.I.R.	
1967	WY	400	333	061	10.5	P	AFB	1111261	M	B		Replaced WE
1967	WZ	400	325	670	10.75	P	7027273	1111250	M	F		
1967	XA	400	350	143	7.6	U	2-barrel	Presently unknown	M	B		
1967	XB	400	260	143	7.6	E	2-barrel	1111242	A	B		
1967	XC	400	293	142	7.6	N	AFB	1111242	A	B		
1967	XD	428	360	670	10.5	P	7037262	Presently unknown	A	B	With A.I.R.	
1967	XF	326	250	140	9.2	U	2-barrel	1111199	A	F	With A.I.R.	
1967	XG	326	285	141	10.5	U	AFB	1111238	A	A	With A.I.R.	326 H.O.
1967	XH	400	350	670	10.5	N	AFB	1111243 or 1111245	A	GP		
1967	XI	326	250	140	9.2	U	2-barrel	1111199	A	F	With A.I.R.	
1967	XJ	400	350	140	10.5	N	AFB	1111243 or 1111245	A	GP	A/C	
1967	XK	428	376	670	10.75	S	7037263	1111237, 1111252, or 1111244	M	B	With A.I.R.	
1967	XL	400	255	142	8.6	U	2-barrel	1111261	A	A	With A.I.R.	
1967	XM	400	255	142	8.6	U	2-barrel	1111242	A	A		
1967	XN	400	325	97/997	10.75	H	7027276	1111250	A	F	After 646619	Ram Air I
1967	XO	326	285	141	10.5	U	AFB	1111238	A	F	With A.I.R.	326 H.O.
1967	XP	400	360	670/ 97/ 997	10.75	H	7027262 or 7037271	1111183 or 1111180	A	A	After 646618	Ram Air I
1967	XR	326	285	141	10.5	U	AFB	1111238	M	A	With A.I.R.	326 H.O.
1967	XS	400	360	670/ 97/997	10.75	H	7027263 or 7037271	1111183 or 1111180	M	A		Ram Air I
1967	XT	400	333	061	10.5	P	AFB	1111269	M	B		Replaced WD
1967	XU	400	290	061	10.5	E	AFB	1111261	A	B	A/C	Replaced YD
1967	XV	400	290	061	10.5	E	AFB	1111261	A	B	Non-A/C	Repalced YC
1967	XW	400	325	061	10.5	N	AFB	1111261	A	B		Replaced YE

Year	Block Code	CI	HP	Head Casting	Advertised Compression Ratio (:1)	Camshaft	Carburetor	Distributor	Transmission	Body	Notes 1	Notes 2
1967	XX	400	325	061	10.5	N	AFB	1111261	A	B		Repalced YF
1967	XY	400	350	670	10.5	P	AFB	1111244	M	GP	With A.I.R.	
1967	XZ	400	350	670	10.5	P	AFB	1111243 or 1111245	M	GP		
1967	Y2	428	360	670	10.5	P	7027262	1111183 or 1111243	A	B		
1967	Y3	428	376	670	10.75	S	7027262	1111250, 1111183, 1111243, or 1111180	A	B	With A.I.R.	
1967	YA	400	265	142	8.6	E	2-barrel	1111242	A	B		
1967	YB	400	265	142	8.6	E	2-barrel	1111261	A	B	With A.I.R.	
1967	YC	400	290	143	10.5	E	2-barrel	1111253 or 1111255	A	B	Non-A/C	Replaced by XV
1967	YD	400	290	143	10.5	E	2-barrel	1111253 or 1111255	A	B	A/C	Replaced by XU
1967	YE	400	325	143	10.5	N	AFB	1111253 or 1111255	A	B	Non-A/C	Rdplaced by XW
1967	YF	400	325	143	10.5	N	AFB	1111253 or 1111255	A	B	A/C	Replaced by XX
1967	YH	428	360	670	10.5	P	7027262	1111183, 1111243, or 1111180	A	B		
1967	YJ	326	250	140	9.2	U	2-barrel	1111164	A	F		
1967	YK	428	376	670	10.75	S	7027262	1111250, 1111183, 1111243, or 1111180	A	B		
1967	YL	400	350	670	10.5	N	AFB	Presently unknown	A	GP	With A.I.R.	
1967	YM	326	285	141	10.5	U	AFB	1111165	A	F		326 H.O.
1967	YN	326	250	140	9.2	U	2-barrel	1111164	A	F		
1967	YO	326	250	140	9.2	U	2-barrel	1111164	A	F		
1967	YP	326	285	141	10.5	U	AFB	1111165 or 1111166	M	A		326 H.O.
1967	YR	400	360	670/97/997	10.75	H	7027263 or 7037271	1111237	M	A	With A.I.R.	Ram Air I
1967	YS	400	335	670	10.75	P	7027262	1111180 or 1111183	A	A		
1967	YT	400	325	670	10.75	P	7027272	1111250	A	F		
1967	YU	400	290	143	10.5	U	2-barrel	Presently unknown	A	B	With A.I.R.	
1967	YV	400	290	143	10.5	U	2-barrel	Presently unknown	A	B	A/C	
1967	YX	400	325	143	10.5	N	AFB	Presently unknown	A	B	With A.I.R.	
1967	YY	428	360	670	10.5	P	7037263	1111237 or 1111244	M	B	With A.I.R.	
1967	YZ	400	360	670	10.75	S	7027262	1111183 or 1111180	A	A		
1968	WA	400	290	15	10.5	N	2-barrel	1111448	M	B		
1968	WB	400	290	15	10.5	N	2-barrel	1111448	M	B		
1968	WC	350	265	17	9.2	U	2-barrel	1111281	M	F		
1968	WD	350	265	17	9.2	U	2-barrel	1111281	M	A		
1968	WG	428	375	16	10.5	S	7028267	1111450	M	B		
1968	WI	400	335	31	10.75	H	7028277	1111449	M	F		Ram Air I
1968	WJ	428	390	16	10.75	P	7028267	1111449	M	B, GP		428 H.O.
1968	WK	350	320	18	10.5	P	7028269	1111447	M	F		350 H.O.
1968	WP	350	265	17	9.2	U	2-barrel	1111281	M	A, F		
1968	WQ	400	335	16	10.75	S	7028271	1111449	M	F		400 H.O.
1968	WR	350	320	18	10.5	P	7028269	1111447	M	A		350 H.O.
1968	WS	400	360	16	10.75	S	7028267	1111449	M	GTO		400 H.O.
1968	WT	400	360	16	10.75	P	7028263	1111449	M	GTO		
1968	WU	400	340	96	10.75	T	7028273	1111941	M	F		Ram Air II
1968	WY	400	366	96	10.75	T	7028273	1111941	M	GTO		Ram Air II
1968	WZ	400	330	16	10.75	P	7028265	1111449	M	F		
1968	XA	400	265	14	8.6	U	2-barrel	1111272 or 1111940	A	B, GP		
1968	XH	400	350	16	10.5	N	7028262	1111300 or 1111253	A	B, GP		
1968	XM	400	265	14	8.6	U	2-barrel	1111272 or 1111940	A	GTO		
1968	XN	400	335	31	10.75	S	7028276	1111270	A	F		Ram Air I
1968	XP	400	360	31	10.75	S	7028274	1111270	A	GTO		Ram Air I
1968	XS	400	360	31	10.75	H	7028275	1111449	M	GTO		Ram Air I
1968	XT	400	360	96	10.75	S	7028270	1111941	A	F		Ram Air II
1968	XW	400	366	96	10.75	S	7028270	1111941	A	GTO		Ram Air II
1968	XZ	400	350	16	10.5	P	7028263	1111300	M	B, GP		
1968	YA	400	265	14	8.6	U	2-barrel	1111272 or 1111940	A	B, GP		

     HOW TO REBUILD PONTIAC V-8s

Year	Block Code	CI	HP	Head Casting	Advertised Compression Ratio (:1)	Cam-shaft	Carburetor	Distributor	Trans-mission	Body	Notes 1	Notes 2
1968	YC	400	290	15	10.5	N	2-barrel	1111253	A	B		
1968	YE	400	340	15	10.5	N	7028262	1111253	A	B		
1968	YE	400	340	15	10.5	E	7028262	1111937	A	B		
1968	YF	400	340	15	10.5	N	7028262	1111937	A	B, GP		
1968	YH	428	375	16	10.5	P	7028268	1111435	A	B, GP		
1968	YJ	350	265	17	9.2	U	2-barrel	1111281 or 1111165	A	F		
1968	YK	428	390	16	10.75	P	7028268	1111270	A	B, GP		428 H.O.
1968	YM	350	320	18	10.5	N	7028266	1111282	A	F		350 H.O.
1968	YN	350	265	17	9.2	U	2-barrel	1111281 or 1111165	A	A, F		
1968	YP	350	320	18	10.5	N	7028266	1111282	A	A		350 H.O.
1968	YS	400	350	16	10.75	P	7028268	1111270	A	GTO		
1968	YT	400	330	16	10.75	P	7028264	1111270	A	F		
1968	YW	400	330	16	10.75	P	7028264	1111270	A	F		400 H.O.
1968	YZ	400	350	16	10.75	P	7028268	1111270	A	GTO		400 H.O.
1968	ZR	400	290	15	10.5	U	2-barrel	1111253	A	B		
1969	WA	400	290	15	10.5	N	2-barrel	1111952	M	B		Replaced by WD
1969	WB	400	290	15	10.5	N	2-barrel	1111952	M	B		Replaced by WE
1969	WC	350	265	17	9.2	U	2-barrel	1111960	M	F		Replaced by WM
1969	WD	400	290	46	10.5	N	2-barrel	1111952	M	B		Replaced WA
1969	WE	400	290	46	10.5	N	2-barrel	1111952	M	B		Replaced WB
1969	WF	428	370	62	10.5	P	7029263	1111960	M	G		
1969	WG	428	360	62	10.5	P	7029263	1111960	M	B		
1969	WH	400	345	722	10.75	T	7029273	1111941	M	F		Ram Air IV
1969	WJ	428	390	48	10.75	S	7029263	1111952	M	B		428 H.O.
1969	WL	428	390	48	10.75	S	7029263	1111952	M	G		428 H.O.
1969	WM	350	265	47	9.2	U	2-barrel	1111960	M	F		Replaced WC
1969	WN	350	325	48	10.5	S	7029263	1111966	M	F		350 H.O.
1969	WP	350	265	17	9.2	U	2-barrel	1111960	M	A		Repalced by WU
1969	WQ	400	335	48	10.75	S	7029273	1111952	M	F		400 H.O./Ram Air III
1969	WS	400	366	48	10.75	H	7029273	1111952	M	GTO		Ram Air III (S cam after ESN 709185)
1969	WT	400	350	48	10.75	S	7029263	1111952	M	GTO		
1969	WU	350	265	47	9.2	U	2-barrel	1111960	M	A		Replaced WP
1969	WV	350	330	48	10.5	S	7029263	1111966	M	A		350 H.O.
1969	WW	400	370	722	10.75	T	7029273	1111952	M	GTO		Ram Air IV
1969	WX	400	350	62	10.5	P	7029263	1111952	M	G		
1969	WZ	400	330	62	10.75	P	7029263	1111952	M	F		
1969	XB	350	265	47	9.2	U	2-barrel	1111942	A	F		Replaced XL
1969	XC	350	325	48	10.5	P	7029268	1111965	A	F		350 H.O.
1969	XE	428	360	15	10.5	P	7029268	1111959	A	B (Police Highway Enforcer)		Replaced by XJ
1969	XF	428	370	62	10.5	N	7029268	1111959	A	G		
1969	XG	428	390	62	10.75	P	7029268	1111946	A	G		428 H.O.
1969	XH	400	350	62	10.5	S	7029268	1111253	A	F, G		
1969	XJ	428	360	46	10.5	P	7029268	1111959	A	B (Police Highway Enforcer)		Replaced XE
1969	XK	428	360	62	10.5	P	7029268	1111959	A	B (Police Freeway Enforcer)		
1969	XL	350	265	17	9.2	U	2-barrel	1111942	A	F		Replaced by XB
1969	XM	400	265	14	8.6	U	2-barrel	1111940	A	All		Replaced by XX
1969	XN	400	345	722	10.75	T	7029270	1111941	A	F		Ram Air IV
1969	XP	400	370	722	10.75	T	7029270	1111952	A	A		Ram Air IV
1969	XR	350	265	17	9.2	U	2-barrel	1111942	A	A		Replaced by XS
1969	XS	350	265	47	9.2	U	2-barrel	1111942	A	A		Replaced XR
1969	XU	350	330	48	10.5	P	7029268	1111965	A	A		350 H.O.
1969	XX	400	265	45	8.6	U	2-barrel	1111940	A	GTO		Replaced XM

Year	Block Code	CI	HP	Head Casting	Advertised Compression Ratio (:1)	Camshaft	Carburetor	Distributor	Transmission	Body	Notes 1	Notes 2
1969	XZ	400	340	46	10.5	U	7029268	1111253	A	B		
1969	YA	400	265	14	8.6	U	2-barrel	1111940	A	B		Replaced by YB
1969	YB	400	265	45	8.6	U	2-barrel	1111940	A	B		Replaced YA
1969	YC	400	290	15	10.5	U	2-barrel	1111253	A	B		Replaced by YD
1969	YD	400	290	45	8.6	U	2-barrel	1111253	A	B		Replaced YC
1969	YE	350	265	47	9.2	U	2-barrel	1111942	A	F		Replaced YJ
1969	YF	400	265	45	8.6	U	2-barrel	1111940	A	G		
1969	YH	428	360	46	10.5	N	7029268	1111959	A	B		Replaced by YL
1969	YJ	350	265	17	9.2	U	2-barrel	1111942		A, F		Replacd by YE
1969	YK	428	390	62	10.75	P	7029268	1111946	A	B		
1969	YL	428	360	15	10.5	N	7029268	1111959	A	B		Replaced YH
1969	YN	350	265	17	9.2	U	2-barrel	1111942	A	A		Replaced by YU
1969	YS	400	350	62	10.75	P	7029268	1111946	A	A		
1969	YT	400	330	62	10.75	P	7029268	1111946	A	F		
1969	YU	350	265	47	9.2	U	2-barrel	1111942	A	A		Replaced YN
1969	YW	400	335	62	10.75	P	7029270	1111946	A	F	400 H.O./Ram Air III	
1969	YZ	400	366	48	10.75	S	7029270	1111946	A	A	400 H.O./Ram Air III	
1970	W7	350	5	11	8.6	U	2-barrel	1112008	M	B		
1970	WA	455	370	64	10.5	S	7040267 (or 7040279 with Ram with A.I.R.)	1112012	M	A		
1970	WE	400	290	16	10.0	N	2-barrel	1112008	A	B		
1970	WG	455	370	64	10.5	S	7040267	1112012	M	B, G		
1970	WH	400	370	614	10.5	T	7040273	1112013	M	F	Non-Production Ram Air Super Duty	
1970	WS	400	366	12	10.5	S	7040273	1112024	M	A, F		Ram Air III
1970	WT	400	350	12	10.25	P	7040263	1111176	M	A, F		
1970	WU	350	255	11	8.8	U	2-barrel	1112008	M	A, F		
1970	WW	400	370	614	10.5	T	7040273	1112011	M	A, F		Ram Air IV
1970	WX	400	350	13	10.25	P	7040263	1111176	M	G		
1970	X7	350	255	11	8.8	U	2-barrel	1112008	A	B		
1970	XF	455	370	64	10.5	P	7040268	1112012	A	B, G		
1970	XH	400	350	13	10.25	N	7040264	1111148	A	G		
1970	XN	400	370	614	10.5	T	7040270	1112013	A	F	Non-Production Ram Air Super Duty	
1970	XP	400	370	614	10.5	T	7040270	1112011	A	A, F		Ram Air IV
1970	XV	400	330	16	10.0	N	7040264	1112007	A	A		
1970	XX	350	265	11	8.8	U	2-barrel	1112007	A	A, F		
1970	XY	400	330	16	10.0	N	7040264	1112007	A	A, B		
1970	XZ	400	330	16	10.0	N	7040264	1112007	A	B		
1970	YA	455	370	64	10.25	P	7040268 (or 7040278 with Ram with A.I.R.)	1112012	A	A		
1970	YB	350	265	11	8.6	U	2-barrel	1112007	A	B, G		
1970	YC	455	370	64	10.25	P	7040268	1112012	A	A		
1970	YD	400	290	16	10.0	U	2-barrel	1112007	A	B		
1970	YH	455	360	15	10.5	P	7040262	1111105	A	B		
1970	YS	400	350	13	10.25	P	7040264	1111148	A	A, F		
1970	YU	350	265	11	8.8	U	2-barrel	1112008	A	A, F		
1970	YZ	400	366	12	10.5	S	7040270	1112009	A	A, F		Ram Air III
1971	WC	455	335	197	8.4	S	7041263	1112073	M (4spd)	A, F		455 H.O.
1971	WG	455	280	99	8.2	N	2-barrel	1112071	M (3spd)	B		
1971	WJ	455	325	66	8.2	P	7041263	1112072	M (3spd)	B		
1971	WK	400	300	96	8.2	P	7041263	1112070	M (4spd)	A, F, G		
1971	WL	455	335	197	8.4	S	7041267 or 7041273	1112073	M (3spd)	A, F		455 H.O.
1971	WN	350	250	94	8.0	W	2-barrel	1112090	M (3spd)	A, B, F		

HOW TO REBUILD PONTIAC V-8s

Year	Block Code	CI	HP	Head Casting	Advertised Compression Ratio (:1)	Camshaft	Carburetor	Distributor	Transmission	Body	Notes 1	Notes 2
1971	WP	350	250	94	8.0	W	2-barrel	1112090	M (4spd)	A, F		
1971	WR	350	250	94	8.0	W	2-barrel	1112083	M (3spd)	A, B, F		
1971	WS	400	265	98	8.2	W	2-barrel	1112068	M	A, B, F		
1971	WT	400	300	96	8.2	P	7041263	1112070	M (3spd)	A, F, G		
1971	WU	350	250	94	8.0	W	2-barrel	1112083	M (4spd)	A, F		
1971	WX	400	265	98	8.2	W	2-barrel	1112089	M (3spd)	B		
1971	XR	350	250	94	8.0	N	2-barrel	1112069	A (M38)	A, B, F		
1971	XX	400	265	98	8.2	W	2-barrel	1112068	A	A, B, F		
1971	YA	455	335	66	8.2	P	7041262	1112035 (Unitized)	A	B, G		
1971	YC	455	325	66	8.2	P	7041262	1112072	A	A, B, F, G		
1971	YE	455	335	197	8.4	S	7041268 or 7041270	1112073	A	A, F		455 H.O.
1971	YG	455	280	99	8.2	N	2-barrel	1112071	A	B		
1971	YN	350	250	94	8.0	N	2-barrel	1112090	A (M38)	A, B, F		
1971	YP	350	250	94	8.0	W	2-barrel	1112090	M (4spd)	A, B, F		
1971	YS	400	300	96	8.2	P	7041264	1112070	A	A, B, F, G		
1971	YU	350	250	94	8.0	W	2-barrel	1112069	A (M35)	A, B, F		
1971	YX	400	265	98	8.2	W	2-barrel	1112089	A	A, B, F		
1972	WD	455	300	7F6	8.4	S	7042273	1112126	M	F		455 H.O.
1972	WK	400	250	7K3	8.2	P	7042263	1112121	M (4spd)	A, F		
1972	WM	455	300	7F6	8.4	S	7042273	1112133 (Unitized)	M	A, F		455 H.O.
1972	WR	350	175	7H1	8.0	W	2-barrel	1112140	M	A, F		
1972	WS	400	250	7K3	8.2	P	7042263	1112121	M (3spd)	A		
1972	Y3	400	250	7K3	8.2	P	7042274	1112121	A	-		
1972	Y4	455	250	7M5	8.2	P	7042272	1112145	A	G		
1972	Y5	455	250	7M5	8.2	P	7042272	1112127 (Unitized)	A	G		
1972	YA	455	250	7M5	8.2	P	7042262	1112127 (Unitized)	A	B, G		
1972	YB	455	300	7F6	8.4	S	7042270	1112133 (Unitized)	A	A, F		455 H.O.
1972	YC	455	250	7M5	8.2	P	7042262	1112145	A	A, B, G		
1972	YD	455	250	7M5	8.2	P	7042276	1112188	A	-	High altitude	455 H.O.
1972	YE	455	300	7F6	8.4	S	7042270	1112126	A	F		
1972	YH	455	250	7L4	8.2	N	2-barrel	1112122 (1112190 late)	A	B		
1972	YK	455	250	7M5	8.2	P	7042276	1112187	A	-	High altitude	
1972	YR	350	175	7H1	8.0	W	2-barrel	1112118 (1112143 late)	A	A, F, B		
1972	YS	400	250	7K3	8.2	P	7042264	1112121	A	A, B, F, G		
1972	YT	400	250	7K3	8.2	P	7042278	1112186	A	-	High altitude	
1972	YU	350	175	7H1	8.0	W	2-barrel	1112143	A	A, F, (B Calif)		
1972	YV	350	175	7H1	8.0	W	2-barrel	1112118	A	X		
1972	YW	455	200	7L4	8.2	N	2-barrel	1112185	A	-	High altitude	
1972	YX	400	200	7J2	8.2	W	2-barrel	1112119 (1112189 late)	A	A, F, B		
1972	YZ	400	200	7J2	8.2	W	2-barrel	1112184	A	-	High altitude	
1972	ZH	455	250	7L4	8.2	P	2-barrel	1112122 (1112190 late)	A	B	California	
1972	ZK	400	200	7J2	8.2	N	2-barrel	1112119 (1112189 late)	A	A, B, F	California	
1972	ZS	400	250	7K3	8.2	P	7042278	1112121	A	A, B, F, G		Replaced by YS
1972	ZX	400	200	7J2	8.2	N	2-barrel	1112189	A	-		
1973	W5	400	170	4X-4H	8.0	5	2-barrel	1112809	A	A, B (exc wagon), F	High altitude	
1973	W8	455	310	16	8.4	K	7043273	1112218	M	A, F, G		SD-455 (non-production)
1973	WA	350	150	4C-5	7.6	W	2-barrel	1112804	A	A (exc wagon), F	With A.I.R. California	
1973	WC	350	150	4C-5	7.6	W	2-barrel	1112804	A	X	With A.I.R. California	

Year	Block Code	CI	HP	Head Casting	Advertised Compression Ratio (:1)	Camshaft	Carburetor	Distributor	Transmission	Body	Notes 1	Notes 2
1973	WD	350	150	46	7.6	W	2-barrel	1112804	A	A (exc wagon), F		
1973	WF	350	150	46	7.6	W	2-barrel	1112804	A	B		
1973	WK	400	230	4X-3H	8.0	P	7043263	1112239	M (4spd)	A, F		
1973	WL	350	150	46	7.6	W	2-barrel	1112808	A	A (exc wagon), F	High altitude	
1973	WN	350	150	46	7.6	W	2-barrel	1112808	A	X	High altitude	
1973	WO	350	150	46	7.6	W	2-barrel	1112234	A	A, F, X		
1973	WP	400	230	4X-3H	8.0	P	7043263	1112233 (Unitized)	M (4spd)	A, F		
1973	WS	400	230	4X-3H	8.0	P	7043263	1112231	M (3spd)	A		
1973	WT	455	250	4X-1H	8.0	P	7043265	1112203 (Unitized)	M	F		
1973	WW	455	250	4X-1H	8.0	P	7043265	1112191	M	F		
1973	X2	350	150	46	7.6	W	2-barrel	1112804	A	A (wagon)		
1973	X3	400	170	4X-4H	8.0	5	2-barrel	1112805	A	A, F	California	
1973	X4	400	170	4X-4H	8.0	5	2-barrel	1112805	A	A, B (exc wagon), F		
1973	X5	400	230	4X-7H	8.0	N	7043266	1112813	A	B (exc wagon), G		
1973	X7	455	250	4X-1H	8.0	P	7043272	1112220 or 1112242	A	A (wagon), B (exc wagon)	High altitude	
1973	XA	455	250	4X-1H	8.0	P	7043262	1112513	A	A (wagon), B (exc wagon)		
1973	XC	350	150	46	7.6	W	2-barrel	1112804	A	X		
1973	XD	455	290	16	8.4	Y	7043270	1112205	A	F		SD-455 (production)
1973	XE	455	250	4X-1H	8.0	P	7043262	1112191 or 1112241	A	A (exc wagon), F, G		
1973	XF	350	150	4C-5	7.6	W	2-barrel	1112804	A	A (wagon), B	With A.I.R. California	
1973	XH	400	170	4C-8	8.0	5	2-barrel	1112805	A	B	With A.I.R. California	
1973	XI	400	170	4X-4H	8.0	5	2-barrel	1112805	A	B (wagon)		Replaced YI
1973	XJ	455	250	4X-1H	8.0	P	7043262	1112513	A	B		
1973	XK	400	230	4X-3H	8.0	N	7043274	1112814	A	A, B (exc wagon), F, G	High altitude	
1973	XL	455	250	4X-1H	8.0	P	7043262	1112203 (Unitized)	A	A (exc wagon), F, G		
1973	XM	455	250	4X-1H	8.0	P	7043272	1112507	A	A (wagon), B (exc wagon)	High altitude	
1973	XN	400	230	4X-3H	8.0	N	7043266	1112813	A	A, F		
1973	XO	455	250	4X-1H	8.0	P	7043262	1112810 (Unitized)	A	A (wagon), B (exc wagon)		
1973	XR	350	150	4C-5	7.6	W	2-barrel	1112202	M	A, F	With A.I.R.	
1973	XT	455	250	4X-1H	8.0	P	7043262	1112810	A	A (exc wagon), F, G		
1973	XV	350	150	4C-5	7.6	W	2-barrel	1112202	M	X	With A.I.R	
1973	XW	350	150	4C-5	7.6	W	2-barrel	1112202	M	F		

 HOW TO REBUILD PONTIAC V-8s

Year	Block Code	CI	HP	Head Casting	Advertised Compression Ratio (:1)	Camshaft	Carburetor	Distributor	Transmission	Body	Notes 1	Notes 2
1973	XX	400	230	4X-3H	8.0	N	7043266	1112812 (Unitized)	A	A, B (exc wagon), F, G		
1973	XY	455	250	4X-1H	8.0	P	7043272	1112811	A	A (exc wagon), B, F, G	High altitude	
1973	XZ	400	230	4X-7H	8.0	N	7043266	1112813	A	B (wagon)		
1973	Y2	350	150	46	7.6	W	2-barrel	1112510	A	A		
1973	Y3	400	230	4X-7H	8.0	N	7043266	1112233 (Unitized)	A	A, B, F, G		
1973	Y4	400	170	4X-4H	8.0	5	2-barrel	1112511	A	B		
1973	Y6	400	230	4X-3H	8.0	P	7043263	1112231 or 1112239	M	A (exc wagon), F		
1973	Y7	350	150	46	7.6	W	2-barrel	1112510	A	B		
1973	Y8	455	310	16	8.4	K	7043270	1112218	A	A, F, G	SD-455 (non-production)	
1973	YA	455	250	4X-1H	8.0	P	7043262	1112203 (Unitized)	A	A, B, F, G		
1973	YC	455	250	4X-1H	8.0	P	7043262	1112191	A	A, B, F, G		
1973	YD	455	250	4X-1H	8.0	P	7043272	1112507	A	A, B, F, G	High altitude	
1973	YF	400	230	4X-3H	8.0	P	7043263	1112231 or 1112239	M	A (exc wagon)		
1973	YG	400	230	4X-3H	8.0	P	7043263	1112233 (Unitized)	M	A (exc wagon), F		
1973	YI	400	170	4X-4H	8.0	5	2-barrel	1112511	A	B (wagon)		Replaced XI
1973	YK	455	250	4X-1H	8.0	P	7043272	1112220	A	A, B, F, G	High altitude	
1973	YL	350	150	46	7.6	W	2-barrel	1112216	A	A, F	High altitude	
1973	YM	350	150	46	7.6	W	2-barrel	1112216	A	X	High altitude	
1973	YN	400	230	4X-7H	8.0	N	7043264	1112231	A	B, G		
1973	YO	350	150	46	7.6	W	2-barrel	1112510	A	A, B, F		
1973	YP	400	170	4X-4H	8.0	5	2-barrel	1112199	A	A (wagon)		
1973	YR	350	150	46	7.6	W	2-barrel	1112510	A	A, F		
1973	YS	400	230	4X-7H	8.0	N	7043264	1112231	A	A, F		
1973	YT	400	230	4X-7H	8.0	N	7043274	1112232	A	A, B, G	High altitude	
1973	YV	350	150	46	7.6	W	2-barrel	1112201	A	X		
1973	YW	350	150	46	8.0	W	2-barrel	1112199	A	F		
1973	YX	400	170	4X-4H	8.0	5	2-barrel	1112511	A	A, F		
1973	YY	400	230	4X-7H	8.0	N	7043264	1112233 (Unitized)	A	A		
1973	YZ	400	170	4X-4H	8.0	5	2-barrel	1112224	A	A, B, F	High altitude	
1973	ZA	455	250	4X-1H	8.0	P	7043262	1112203 (Unitized)	A	A, B		
1973	ZB	350	150	4C-5	7.6	W	2-barrel	1112806	M	A (exc wagon), F	With A.I.R.	
1973	ZC	455	250	4X-1H	8.0	P	7043262	1112191	A	A, B		
1973	ZD	350	150	4C-5	7.6	W	2-barrel	1112806	M	X	With A.I.R.	
1973	ZE	455	250	4H-1H	8.0	P	7043262	1112203 (Unitized)	M	F		
1973	ZJ	455	290	16	8.4	Y	7043273	1112205	M	F	SD-455 (production)	
1973	ZK	400	170	4C-9	8.0	5	2-barrel	1112199	A	A, B, F	California	
1973	ZN	400	230	4X-7H	8.0	N	7043264	1112231	A	B	California	
1973	ZR	350	150	4C-5	7.6	W	2-barrel	1112201	A	A, B, F	With A.I.R. California	
1973	ZS	400	230	4X-7H	8.0	N	7043264	1112231	A	A		
1973	ZT	350	150	4C-5	7.6	W	2-barrel	1112201	A	A, B, F	With A.I.R. California	
1973	ZV	350	150	4C-5	7.6	W	2-barrel	1112201	A	X	With A.I.R. California	
1973	ZX	400	170	4X-4H	8.0	5	2-barrel	1112199	A	A, F	California	
1973	ZZ	455	250	4X-1H	8.0	P	7043262	1112191 or 1112241	M	F		
1974	A3	400	225	4X-7H	8.0	N	7044274	1112213 (HEI)	A	A, B, F, G	High altitude	
1974	A4	455	250	4X-1H	8.0	P	7044272	1112878 (HEI)	A	A, B, F, G	High altitude	
1974	AA	350	155	46	7.6	W	2-barrel	1112808 or 112235	A	A, F	High altitude	
1974	AD	400	175	4X-4H	8.0	5	2-barrel	1112547 (HEI)	A	A, B, F	High altitude	

Year	Block Code	CI	HP	Head Casting	Advertised Compression Ratio (:1)	Camshaft	Carburetor	Distributor	Transmission	Body	Notes 1	Notes 2
1974	AH	400	175	4X-4H	8.0	5	2-barrel	1112809 or 1112238	A	A, B, F	High altitude	
1974	AT	400	225	4X-7H	8.0	N	7044274	1112814 or 1112240	A	A, B, F, G	High altitude	
1974	AU	455	250	4X-1H	8.0	P	7044272	1112859 or 1112860	A	A, B, F, G	High altitude	
1974	W8	455	290	16	8.4	Y	7044273	1112205	M	F		
1974	WA	350	155	4C-5	7.6	W	2-barrel	1112806 or 1112236	M	A, F	With A.I.R.	
1974	WB	350	155	4C-5	7.6	W	2-barrel	1112806 or 1112236	M	X	With A.I.R.	
1974	WN	350	155	46	7.6	W	7044269	1112857 or 1112856	M	A		
1974	WP	350	155	46	7.6	W	7044269	1112857 or 1112856	M	X	California	
1974	WR	400	225	4X-3H	8.0	P	7043263	1112871 (HEI)	M	A, F		
1974	WT	400	225	4X-3H	8.0	P	7043263	1112231 or 1112239	M	A, F		
1974	Y3	400	225	4X-7H	8.0	N	7044276	1112812 (Unitized)	A	A, B, F, G		
1974	Y4	455	250	4X-1H	8.0	P	7044262	1112210 (HEI)	A	B		
1974	Y6	455	250	4X-1H	8.0	P	7044262	1112210 (HEI)	A	B		
1974	Y8	455	290	16	8.4	Y	7044270	1112205	A	F		
1974	Y9	455	250	4X-1H	8.0	P	7044262	1112210 (HEI)	A	A, B, F, G		
1974	YA	350	155	46	7.6	W	2-barrel	1112804 or 1112234	A	A, F		
1974	YB	350	155	46	7.6	W	2-barrel	1112804 or 1112234	A	X		
1974	YC	350	155	46	7.6	W	2-barrel	1112804 or 1112234	A	A		
1974	YF	400	175	4X-4H	8.0	5	2-barrel	1112546 (HEI)	A	A, B, F		
1974	YH	400	175	4X-4H	8.0	5	2-barrel	1112805 or 1112237	A	A, B, F		
1974	YJ	400	175	4X-4H	8.0	5	2-barrel	1112805 or 1112237	A	A, B, F		
1974	YK	400	225	4X-7H	8.0	5	2-barrel	1112546 (HEI)	A	B		
1974	YL	400	225	4X-7H	8.0	N	7044276	1112212 (HEI)	A	A, B, F, G		
1974	YM	400	225	4X-7H	8.0	N	7044276	1112813 or 1112512	A	A, B, F, G		
1974	YN	350	155	46	7.6	W	7044268	1112821 or 1112822	A	A		
1974	YP	350	155	46	7.6	W	7044268	1112821 or 1112822	A	X		
1974	YR	455	250	4X-1H	8.0	P	7044267	1112859 or 1112860	A	B		
1974	YS	350	155	46	7.6	W	7044268	1112821 or 1112822	A	X		
1974	YT	400	225	4X-7H	8.0	N	7044266	1112813 or 1112512	A	A, B, F, G		
1974	YU	455	250	4X-1H	8.0	P	7044262	1112807 or 1112513	A	B		
1974	YW	455	250	4X-1H	8.0	P	7044262	1112810 (Unitized)	A	A, B, F, G		
1974	YX	455	250	4X-1H	8.0	P	7044262	1112807 or 1112513	A	B		
1974	YY	455	250	4X-1H	8.0	P	7044262	1112807 or 1112513	A	A, B, F, G		
1974	YZ	400	225	4X-7H	8.0	N	7044266	1112812 (Unitized)	A	A, B, F, G		
1974	Z4	455	250	4X-1H	8.0	P	4-barrel	1112210 (HEI)	A	A, B, F, G	California	
1974	Z6	455	250	4X-1H	8.0	P	4-barrel	1112210 (HEI)	A	B	California	
1974	ZA	350	155	4C-5	7.6	3	2-barrel	1112804 or 1112234	A	A, F	With A.I.R. California	
1974	ZB	350	155	4C-5	7.6	3	2-barrel	1112804 or 1112234	A	X	With A.I.R. California	
1974	ZD	400	175	4X-4H	8.0	Z	2-barrel	1112876 (HEI)	A	A, B	California	
1974	ZH	400	175	4C-8	8.0	Z	2-barrel	1112833 or 1112834	A	A	With A.I.R. California	
1974	ZJ	400	175	4C-8	8.0	Z	2-barrel	1112833 or 1112834	A	A, F	With A.I.R. California	
1974	ZK	400	175	4X-4H	8.0	Z	2-barrel	1112876 (HEI)	A	A, F	California	
1974	ZP	350	155	46	7.6	3	7044568	1112805 or 1112237	A	X	California	
1974	ZS	400	225	4X-7H	8.0	N	4-barrel	1112212 (HEI)	A	A, F, G	California	
1974	ZT	400	225	4X-7H	8.0	N	7044266	1112813 or 1112512	A	A, F, G	California	
1974	ZU	455	250	4X-1H	8.0	P	7044562	1112807 or 1112513	A	A, B, F, G	California	
1974	ZW	455	250	4X-1H	8.0	P	7044262	1112810 (Unitized)	A	A, B, F, G		
1974	ZX	455	250	4X-1H	8.0	P	7044560	1112807 or 1112513	A	B	California	
1975	WN	350	155	5C-4/6X-4	7.6	W	7045269	1112946	M	A, F		
1975	WT	400	185	5C-8/6X-8	7.6	P	7045263	1112495	M	F		
1975	WX	455	200	51-6/6H-6	7.6	P	7045261	1112923	M	F		
1975	Y9	400	185	5C-8/6X-8	7.6	5	2-barrel	1112500	A	-		Replaced YJ

     HOW TO REBUILD PONTIAC V-8s

Year	Block Code	CI	HP	Head Casting	Advertised Compression Ratio (:1)	Camshaft	Carburetor	Distributor	Transmission	Body	Notes 1	Notes 2
1975	YA	350	155	5C-4/6X-4	7.6	W	2-barrel	1112950	A	A		
1975	YB	350	155	5C-4/6X-4	7.6	W	2-barrel	1112950	A	F, X		
1975	YC	350	155	5C-4/6X-4	7.6	W	2-barrel	1112950	A	-		
1975	YH	350	155	5C-4/6X-4	7.6	Z	2-barrel	1112500	A	-		Replaced by YJ
1975	YJ	350	155	5C-4/6X-4	7.6	Z	2-barrel	1112500	A	-		Replaced YH at MUN 151826 on 11/5/74 and by Y9
1975	YK	350	155	5C-4/6X-4	7.6	W	2-barrel	1112950	A	-		
1975	YL	400	185	5C-8/6X-8	7.6	N	7045264	1112958	A	-		
1975	YM	400	185	5C-8/6X-8	7.6	N	7045264	1112928	A	B		
1975	YN	350	175	5C-4/6X-4	7.6	W	7045268	1112498	A	A, F		
1975	YS	400	185	5C-8/6X-8	7.6	N	7045266/7045274	1112928	A	F		
1975	YT	400	185	5C-8/6X-8	7.6	N	7045264	1112928	A	A, B, G		
1975	YU	455	200	51-6/6H-6	7.6	P	7045562	1112930	A	B (wagon)		
1975	YW	455	200	51-6/6H-6	7.6	P	7045562	1112930	A	A, B, G (exc wagon)		
1975	YY	455	200	51-6/6H-6	7.6	P	7045260	1112949	A	-		
1975	YZ	400	185	5C-8/6X-8	7.6	N	7045266	1112929	A	-		
1975	ZP	350	175	5C-9/6S-9	7.6	W	7045568	1112947	A	A, F	With A.I.R.	
1975	ZS	400	185	5C-7/6S-7	7.6	N	7045564	1112949	A	-		
1975	ZT	400	185	5C-7/6S-7	7.6	N	7045564	1112949	A	A, B, F, G	With A.I.R.	
1975	ZU	455	200	51-6/6H-6	7.6	P	7045566	1112960	A	A, B, G (exc wagon)	With A.I.R.	
1975	ZW	455	200	51-6/6H-6	7.6	P	7045566	1112960	A	B (wagon)	With A.I.R.	
1975	ZY	400	185	5C-7/6S-7	7.6	N	7045564	1112948	A	-	With A.I.R.	
1976	WT	400	185	6X-8	7.6	P	17056263	1112495	M	F		10.4-inch clutch
1976	WX	455	200	6H-6	7.6	P	17056261 or 17056263	1112923	M	F		
1976	WY	400	185	6X-8	7.6	P	17056263	1112495	M	F		11-inch clutch
1976	X3	350	165	6X-4	7.6	Star	4-barrel	1103223	A	A, G		With hub
1976	X6	400	185	6X-8	7.6	N	17056264	1112928	A	A, B, G	Non-A/C	With hub, replaced Y6
1976	X7	400	185	6X-8	7.6	N	17056264	1112928	A	A, B, G	A/C	With hub, replaced Y7
1976	X9	400	185	6X-8	7.6	N	17056274	1112958	A	F		With hub, replaced Y9
1976	XA	400	185	6X-8	7.6	W	2-barrel	1103214	A	A, B, G	Export	Replaced by XB near 12/1/75

Year	Block Code	CI	HP	Head Casting	Advertised Compression Ratio (:1)	Camshaft	Carburetor	Distributor	Transmission	Body	Notes 1	Notes 2
1976	XB	400	185	6X-8	7.6	W	2-barrel	1103214	A	A, B, G	Export	Replaced XA near 12/1/75
1976	XC	400	185	6X-8	7.6	W	2-barrel	1112500	A	A, B, G	A/C	Replaced YC near 12/1/75
1976	XH	350	160	6X-4	7.6	W	2-barrel	1112500	A	A (wagon), B (exc wagon)	Non-A/C	Introduced 1/15/76
1976	XJ	400	185	6X-8	7.6	W	2-barrel	1112500	A	A, B, G	Non-A/C	Replaced YJ near 12/1/75
1976	XK	350	160	6X-4	7.6	U	2-barrel	1103216	A	A, G	Non-A/C	Replaced YK
1976	XL	350	160	6X-4	7.6	U	2-barrel	1103216	A	A, G	A/C	
1976	XM	350	160	6X-4	7.6	U	2-barrel	1112950	A	A (wagon), B (exc wagon)		With hub, replaced XN
1976	XN	350	160	6X-4	7.6	U	2-barrel	1112950	A	A (wagon), B (exc wagon)	A/C	Introduced 1/15/76 and replaced by XM
1976	XP	350	160	6X-4	7.6	U	2-barrel	1112950	A	A, G	A/C	With hub
1976	XR	350	160	6X-4	7.6	U	2-barrel		A	F	A/C	With hub
1976	XS	400	185	6X-8	7.6	N	17056274	1112928	A	F	Non-A/C	With hub, replaced YS
1976	XT	400	185	6X-8	7.6	N	17056264	1112928	A	A, G	Non-A/C	With hub, replaced YT
1976	XY	400	185	6X-8	7.6	N	17056264	1112928	A	A, G	A/C	With hub, replaced YY
1976	XZ	400	185	6X-8	7.6	N	17056274	1112928	A	F	A/C	With hub, replaced YZ
1976	Y3	455	200	6H	7.6	P	17056262	1112930	A	A (wagon), B (exc wagon)		
1976	Y4	455	200	6H	7.6	P	17056262	1112930	A	B (wagon)		
1976	Y6	400	185	6X-8	7.6	N	17056264	1112928	A	A (wagon), B, G	Non-A/C	
1976	Y7	400	185	6X-8	7.6	N	17056264	1112928	A	A (wagon), B, G	A/C	
1976	Y8	455	200	6H	7.6	P	17056262	1112930	A	A (exc wagon), G		
1976	Y9	400	185	6X-8	7.6	N	17056274	1112958	A	F		
1976	YA	350	160	6X-4	7.6	U	2-barrel	1112950	A	A, G		Replaced by YK at MUN 80793
1976	YB	350	160	6X-4	7.6	U	2-barrel	1112797	A	F	Non-A/C	
1976	YC	400	160	6X-8	7.6	W	2-barrel	1112500	A	A, B, G	A/C	Replaced by XC near 12/1/75
1976	YD	350	165	6X-4	7.6	Star	4-barrel	1103223	A	A, G		
1976	YJ	400	165	6X-8	7.6	W	2-barrel	1112500	A	A, B, G	Non-A/C	Replaced by XJ near 12/1/75
1976	YK	350	160	6X-4	7.6	U	2-barrel	1103216	A	A, G	Non-A/C	Replaced YA and replaced by XK
1976	YL	350	160	6X-4	7.6	U	2-barrel	1103216	A	A, G	A/C	Replaced YP and replaced by XL
1976	YP	350	160	6X-4	7.6	U	2-barrel	1112950	A	A, G	A/C	Replaced by YL at MUN 80704
1976	YR	350	160	6X-4	7.6	U	2-barrel	1112797	A	F	A/C	Replaced by XR
1976	YS	400	185	6X-8	7.6	N	17056274	1112928	A	F	Non-A/C	Replaced by XS
1976	YT	400	185	6X-8	7.6	N	17056264	1112928	A	A	Non-A/C	Replaced by XT
1976	YY	400	185	6X-8	7.6	N	17056264	1112928	A	A	A/C	Replaced by XY
1976	YZ	400	185	6X-8	7.6	N	17056274	1112928	A	F	A/C	Replaced by XZ

HOW TO REBUILD PONTIAC V-8s

Year	Block Code	CI	HP	Head Casting	Advertised Compression Ratio (:1)	Camshaft	Carburetor	Distributor	Transmission	Body	Notes 1	Notes 2
1976	Z3	455	200	6H	7.6	P	17056566	1103207	A	B (exc wagon)	California	
1976	Z4	455	200	6H	7.6	P	1705568	1112960	A	B (wagon)	California	
1976	Z6	455	200	6H	7.6	P	17056566	1112960	A	A, G	With A.I.R. California	
1976	Z8	400	185	6X-8	7.6	W	2-barrel	1112500	A	A, B, G	Export	
1976	ZA	400	185	6S-7	7.6	N	17056564	1103205	A	A (wagon), B, G	With A.I.R. California	
1976	ZB	455	200	6H	7.6	P	17056562	1112960	A	B	California	
1976	ZC	350	165	6S-9	7.6	W	17056568	1103206	A	F	With A.I.R. California	Replaced ZX
1976	ZK	400	185	6S-7	7.6	N	17056564	1103205	A	A, F	With A.I.R. California	Replaced by ZL
1976	ZL	400	185	6S-7	7.6	N	17056564	1103205	A	A, F		
1976	ZX	350	165	6S-9	7.6	W	17056568	1103206	A	A, F, G	With A.I.R. California	Replaced by ZC on 10/1/75
1977	WA	400	200	6X-4	8.0	Square	17057263	1103271	M	F		T/A 6.6
1977	WB	301	135	01	8.25	Crescent	2-barrel	1103273	M	F, X		
1977	WM	301	135	01	8.25	Crescent	2-barrel	1103273	M	F		
1977	XA	400	180	6X-8	7.6	Star	17057274	1103269	A	F		
1977	XB	350	170	6X-4	7.6	Star	17057262	1103276	A	B		
1977	XC	350	170	6X-4	7.6	Star	17057262	1103276	A	B		
1977	XD	400	180	6X-8	7.6	Star	17057274	1103269	A	B		
1977	XF	400	180	6X-8	7.6	Star	17057274	1103269	A	B		
1977	XH	400	180	6X-8	7.6	Star	17057274	1103269	A	B		
1977	XJ	400	180	6X-8	7.6	Star	17057274	1103269	A	B		
1977	XK	400	180	6X-8	7.6	Star	17057274	1103278	A	-		
1977	XL	301	135	01	8.25	F	2-barrel	1103272	A	B		
1977	XN	301	135	01	8.25	F	2-barrel	1103272	A	All		
1977	XP	301	135	01	8.25	F	2-barrel	1103272	A	B		
1977	XR	301	135	01	8.25	F	2-barrel	1103272	A	G		
1977	Y4	400	180	6X-8	7.6	Star	17057274	1103269	A	A		
1977	Y6	400	200	6X-4	8.0	O	17057266	1103271	A	A (Can Am), F		T/A 6.6
1977	Y7	400	180	6X-8	7.6	Star	17057274	1103278	A	A		Police
1977	Y9	350	170	6X-4	7.6	Star	17057262	1103257	A	F		
1977	YA	350	170	6X-4	7.6	Star	17057262	1103276	A	A, G		
1977	YB	350	170	6X-4	7.6	Star	17057262	1103276	A	A, G		
1977	YC	400	180	6X-8	7.6	Star	17057274	1103269	A	A, G		
1977	YD	400	180	6X-8	7.6	Star	17057274	1103269	A	A, G		
1977	YH	301	135	01	8.25	F	2-barrel	1103272	A	A, F, G, X		
1977	YK	301	135	01	8.25	F	2-barrel	1103272	A	F, G, X		
1977	YU	400	180	6X-8	7.6	Star	17057274	1103269	A	A		
1977	YW	301	135	01	8.25	F	2-barrel	1103272	A	B		
1977	YX	301	135	01	8.25	F	2-barrel	1103272	A	B		
1978	WC	400	220	6X-4	8.0	Circled A	17058263	1103315	M	F		T/A 6.6
1978	X7	400	220	6X-4	8.0	Circled A	17058266	1103315	A	F		T/A 6.6
1978	X9	400	180	6X-8	7.6	Star	17058274	1103316	A	B		
1978	XA	301	135	01	8.25	M	2-barrel	1003310	A	A, B, G		
1978	XC	301	135	01	8.25	M	2-barrel	1003310	A	A, B, G		
1978	XF	301	150	01	8.25	7	17058272	1103310	A	A, B, G		
1978	XH	301	150	01	8.25	7	17058272	1103310	A	A, B, G		

Year	Block Code	CI	HP	Head Casting	Advertised Compression Ratio (:1)	Camshaft	Carburetor	Distributor	Transmission	Body	Notes 1	Notes 2
1978	XJ	400	180	6X-8	7.6	Star	17058274	1103343	A	B		
1978	XK	400	180	6X-8	7.6	Star	17058274	1103343	A	B		
1978	YA	400	180	6X-8	7.6	Star	17058276	1103359	A	F (early)		
1978	YH	400	180	6X-8	7.6	Star	17058274	1103343	A	B		
1978	YJ	400	180	6X-8	7.6	Star	17058274	1103316	A	B		
1978	YK	400	180	6X-8	7.6	Star	17058274	1103343	A	B		
1978	YR	400	180	6X-8	7.6	Star	17058264 or 17058274	1103316	A	B		
1978	YS	400	180	6X-8	7.6	Star	17058264 or 17058274	1103343	A	B		
1978	YT	400	180	6X-8	7.6	Star	17058264 or 17058274	1103343	A	B		
1978	YU	400	180	6X-8	7.6	Star	17058278	1103359	A	F (late)		
1978	YW	400	180	6X-8	7.6	Star	17058264 or 17058274	1103316	A	B		
1979	WA	301	150	01	8.1	M	17059271	1003400	M	F		
1979	WB	301	150	01	8.1	M	17059271	1003400	M	A, G		
1979	WH	400	220	6X-4	8.0	Circled A	17059263	1103315	M	F		T/A 6.6
1979	X4	301	150	01	8.1	7	17059272	1103399	A	F		
1979	X6	301	150	01	8.1	7	17059272	1103399	A	F		
1979	X7	301	135	01	8.1	M	2-barrel	1103314	A	-		
1979	X9	301	135	01	8.1	M	2-barrel	1103314	A	-		
1979	XF	301	135	01	8.1	M	2-barrel	1103314	A	A, B		
1979	XH	301	135	01	8.1	M	2-barrel	1103314	A	A, B		
1979	XL	301	150	01	8.1	7	17059272	1103399	A	A, G		
1979	XN	301	150	01	8.1	7	17059272	1103399	A	A, G		
1979	XP	301	135	01	8.1	M	2-barrel	1103314	A	A, B, F		
1979	XR	301	135	01	8.1	M	2-barrel	1103314	A	A, B, F		
1979	XS	301	150	01	8.1	7	17059272	1103399	A	B		
1979	XT	301	150	01	8.1	7	17059272	1103399	A	B		
1979	XU	301	150	01	8.1	7	17059272	1103399	A	B		
1979	XW	301	150	01	8.1	7	17059272	1103399	A	B		
1980	X3	301	150	01	8.1	7	17080272	1103425	A	B		
1980	X7	301	150	01	8.1	7	17080272	1103425		B		
1980	X9	301	150	01	8.1	7	8.3	1103425	A	B		
1980	XG	265	120	01	8.3	M	2-barrel	1103450	A	B		
1980	XH	265	120	01	8.3	M	2-barrel	1103450	A	A, G		
1980	XN	301	150	01	8.1	7	17080272	1103425	A	F		
1980	XR	265	120	01	8.3	M	2-barrel	1103450	A	A, F		
1980	XT	301	150	01	8.1	7	17080272	1103425	A	G		
1980	XW	301	150	01	8.1	7	17080272	1103425	A	-		
1980	XX	301	150	01	8.1	7	17080272	1103425	A	B		
1980	YL	301	210	01	7.5	7	17080274	1103444	A	F		Turbo 4.9
1980	YN	301	170	01	8.1	E	17080270	1103407	A	F		T/A 4.9
1980	YR	301	170	01	8.1	E	17080270	1103407	A	F, G		T/A 4.9
1981	WBO	301	200	01	7.5	7	17081273	1103453	A	F		Turbo 4.9
1981	WAU	265	119	01	8.3	M	2-barrel	1103453	A	All		
1981	WAV	265	119	01	8.3	M	2-barrel	1103453	A	All		
1981	WAZ	265	119	01	8.3	M	2-barrel	1103453	A	All		
1981	WBA	265	119	01	8.3	M	2-barrel	1103453	A	All		
1981	WBD	301	155	01	8.1	7	17081272	1103453	A	All		
1981	WBJ	301	155	01	8.1	7	17081270	1103453	A	F		
1981	WDB	265	119	01	8.3	M	2-barrel	1103453	A	All		
1981	WDC	265	119	01	8.3	M	2-barrel	1103453	A	All		
1981	WDH	265	119	01	8.3	M	2-barrel	1103453	A	All		
1981	WDJ	265	119	01	8.3	M	2-barrel	1103453	A	All		

HOW TO REBUILD PONTIAC V-8s

Crankshafts

Casting Number	Year	Application	Stroke (inches)	Main Journal (inches)	Material
9770488	1963	421	4.00	3.00	ArmaSteel
9773383	1964–1965	389	3.75	3.00	ArmaSteel
9773384	1964–1965	421	4.00	3.25	ArmaSteel
9782770	1966–1967	326	3.75	3.00	ArmaSteel
9782646	1966	389	3.75	3.00	ArmaSteel
9783787	1966	421	4.00	3.25	ArmaSteel
9782769	1966	421	4.00	3.25	Nodular Iron
9783787	1967–1969	428	4.00	3.25	ArmaSteel
9782769	1967–1969	428	4.00	3.25	Nodular Iron
9773524	1967–1968	400	3.75	3.00	Nodular Iron
9793573	1968	350	3.75	3.00	Nodular Iron
9794054	1968	Ram Air II	3.75	3.00	ArmaSteel
9795479	1969–1970	350	3.75	3.00	Nodular Iron
9795480	1969–1970	400	3.75	3.00	Nodular Iron
9795481	1969–1970	Ram Air IV	3.75	3.00	Nodular Iron
9799103	1970–1974	455	4.21	3.25	Nodular Iron
481379	1971–1973	350	3.75	3.00	Nodular Iron
481380	1971–1973	400	3.75	3.00	Nodular Iron
495030	1973–1974	SD-455	4.21	3.25	Nodular Iron
495268	1974	350	3.75	3.00	Nodular Iron
495201	1974	400	3.75	3.00	Nodular Iron
496413	1975	350	3.75	3.00	Nodular Iron
496414	1975	400	3.75	3.00	Nodular Iron
496415	1975–1976	455	4.21	3.25	Nodular Iron
496453	1975–1976	455	4.21	3.25	Nodular Iron
496452	1976–1977	350	3.75	3.00	Nodular Iron
499863	1976–1977	350	3.75	3.00	Nodular Iron
499864	1976–1979	400	3.75	3.00	Nodular Iron
525887	1977	301	3.00	3.00	Nodular Iron
10000590	1978–1981	301	3.00	3.00	Nodular Iron
10009545	1980–1981	265	3.00	3.00	Nodular Iron
10016646	1980–1981	301 Turbo	3.00	3.00	Nodular Iron

Camshafts

Part Number	Stamped Code	Advertised Intake Duration	Advertised Exhaust Duration	0.050-inch Intake Duration	0.050-inch Exhaust Duration	Intake Centerline	Lobe Separation Angle	Valve Overlap	Intake Lobe Lift	Exhaust Lobe Lift	Gross Intake Valve Lift at 1.5	Gross Exhaust Valve Lift at 1.5
480737	K	308	320	230	240	112	113.5	87	0.313	0.313	0.470	0.470
483555	W	269	277	189	202	109	111	51	0.249	0.266	0.374	0.399
491255	5	269	277	189	203	108.5	109	54	0.249	0.266	0.374	0.399
491266	Z	269	282	189	209	109	108.5	58	0.249	0.266	0.374	0.399
493323	Y	301	313	225	236	113	115.5	76	0.271	0.271	0.407	0.407
494957	3	264	273	189	198	106	107.5	54	0.243	0.269	0.365	0.404
525471	O	274	298	190	213	116	114.5	54	0.243	0.271	0.365	0.407
526793	*	264	264	189	189	103	106.5	51	0.243	0.243	0.365	0.365
527471	F	274	274	190	190	105	107.5	59	0.243	0.243	0.365	0.365
537441	E	269	277	189	203	112.5	113	47	0.249	0.271	0.374	0.407
547868	Crescent	274	292	209	190	115	113.5	61	0.252	0.243	0.378	0.365
549112	O	274	298	190	213	116	114.5	55	0.243	0.271	0.365	0.407
549431	Square	274	298	190	213	111	111	62	0.243	0.271	0.365	0.407
9770543	L	288*	302	213	266	113	115.5	63	0.273	0.273	0.410	0.410
9777254	U	269	277	190	201	113	113.5	47	0.249	0.271	0.374	0.407
9779066	N	273	282	198	210	106	111	55	0.272	0.270	0.408	0.405
9779067	P	273	289	198	213	113	113	54	0.269	0.271	0.404	0.407
9779068	S	288	302	212	225	113	115.5	63	0.272	0.271	0.408	0.407
9785744	H	301	313	225	236	113	115.5	76	0.271	0.271	0.407	0.407
9794041	T	308	320	230	240	112	113.5	87	0.313	0.313	0.470	0.470
10002464	7	248	248	183	183	110	103.5	41	0.245	0.245	0.368	0.368
10002977	M	274	274	190	190	105	107.5	59	0.243	0.243	0.365	0.365
10003402	Circled A	273	289	198	213	118	113	54	0.270	0.271	0.404	0.407
10007424	B	250	250	181	181	108	106	38	0.233	0.233	0.350	0.350
10012185	E	274	274	190	190	115	110	59	0.243	0.243	0.365	0.365

Cylinder Heads

Casting Number	Year	Application	Intake Valve (inches)	Exhaust Valve (inches)	Rocker Studs	Chamber Volume
140	1967	326 2-barrel	1.94	1.64	Pressed	67 cc
141	1967	326 H.O.	1.94	1.64	Pressed	58 cc
142	1967	400 2-barrel (low compression)	1.94	1.64	Pressed	92 cc
143	1967	400 B-car	1.94	1.64	Pressed	76 cc

Casting Number	Year	Application	Intake Valve (inches)	Exhaust Valve (inches)	Rocker Studs	Chamber Volume
670	1967	400 4-barrel/428 4-barrel	2.11	1.77	Threaded	72 cc
061	1967	400 4-barrel B-car	2.11	1.77	Pressed	72 cc
670	1967	Ram Air I	2.11	1.77	Threaded	72 cc
97	1967	Ram Air I	2.11	1.77	Threaded	72 cc
997	1967	Ram Air I	2.11	1.77	Threaded	72 cc
16	1968	400 4-barrel	2.11	1.77	Threaded	74 cc
18	1968	350 H.O.	1.96	1.66	Pressed	66 cc
31	1968	Ram Air I	2.11	1.77	Threaded	72 cc
96	1968	Ram Air II	2.11	1.77	Threaded	71 cc
14	1968–1969	400 2-barrel (low compression)	1.96	1.66	Pressed	92 cc
15	1968–1969	400 2-barrel	1.96	1.66	Pressed	76 cc
17	1968–1969	350 2-barrel	1.96	1.66	Pressed	83 cc
45	1969	400 2-barrel (low compression)	1.96	1.66	Pressed	92 cc
46	1969	400 2-barrel/428 4-barrel	1.96	1.66	Pressed	76 cc
47	1969	350 2-barrel	1.96	1.66	Pressed	83 cc
48	1969	350 H.O./400 4-barrel manual transmission/428 H.O. manual transmission	2.11	1.77	Threaded	66 cc
62	1969	400 4-barrel	2.11	1.77	Threaded	77 cc
722	1969	Ram Air IV	2.11	1.77	Threaded	71 cc
11	1970	350/400 2-barrel	1.96	1.66	Pressed	87 cc
12	1970	Ram Air III	2.11	1.77	Threaded	70 cc
13	1970	400 4-barrel	2.11	1.77	Threaded	76 cc
15	1970	455 4-barrel	1.96	1.66	Pressed	99 cc
16	1970	400 2-barrel	1.96	1.66	Pressed	78 cc
64	1970	455 4-barrel	2.11	1.77	Threaded	90 cc
614	1970	Ram Air IV	2.11	1.77	Threaded	70 cc
66	1971	455 4-barrel	2.11	1.77	Threaded	112 cc
94	1971	350 2-barrel	1.96	1.66	Pressed	90 cc
96	1971	400 4-barrel	2.11	1.77	Threaded	96 cc
98	1971	455 2-barrel	1.96	1.66	Pressed	113 cc
99	1971	400 2-barrel	1.96	1.66	Pressed	97 cc
197	1971	455 H.O.	2.11	1.77	Threaded	108 cc
7F6	1972	455 H.O.	2.11	1.77	Threaded	108 cc
7H1	1972	350 2-barrel	1.96	1.77	Pressed	90 cc
7J2	1972	400 2-barrel	1.96	1.77	Pressed	96 cc
7K3	1972	400 4-barrel	2.11	1.77	Threaded	96 cc
7L4	1972	455 2-barrel	1.96	1.77	Pressed	113 cc
7M5	1972	455 4-barrel	2.11	1.77	Pressed	112 cc
16	1973–1974	SD-455	2.11	1.66	Threaded	111 cc
46	1973–1974	350	1.96	1.66	Both	96 cc
4C-5	1973–1974	350 with A.I.R.	1.96	1.66	Threaded	96 cc
4C-9	1973–1974	400 with A.I.R.	1.96	1.66	Threaded	98 cc
4X-1H	1973–1974	455	2.11	1.66	Both	112 cc
4X-3H	1973–1974	400 4-barrel manual transmission	2.11	1.66	Threaded	98 cc
4X–4H	1973–1974	400 2-barrel	2.11	1.66	Both	98 cc
4X-7H	1973–1974	400 4-barrel auto transmission	2.11	1.66	Both	98 cc
51-6	1975	All 455	2.11	1.66	Threaded	124 cc
5C-4	1975	All 350	2.11	1.66	Threaded	94 cc
5C-7	1975	400 with A.I.R.	2.11	1.66	Threaded	100 cc
5C-8	1975	All 400	2.11	1.66	Threaded	100 cc
5C-9	1975	350 with A.I.R.	2.11	1.66	Threaded	94 cc
6H-6	1975–1976	All 455	2.11	1.66	Threaded	124 cc
6S-7	1975–1976	400 with A.I.R.	2.11	1.66	Threaded	100 cc
6S-9	1975–1976	350 with A.I.R.	2.11	1.66	Threaded	94 cc
6X-4	1975–1977	350 4-barrel	2.11	1.66	Threaded	94 cc
6X-8	1975–1978	All 400	2.11	1.66	Threaded	100 cc
6X-4	1977–1979	T/A 6.6	2.11	1.66	Threaded	94 cc
01	1977–1981	301	1.72	1.5	Threaded	71 cc

4-Barrel Intake Manifolds

Casting Number	Year	Application	Material
9786286	1967	400/428	Iron
9790140	1968 (early)	350/400/428	Iron
9794234	1968 (late)	350/400/428	Iron
9794234	1969	350/400/428	Iron
9796614	1969	Ram Air IV	Aluminum
9799068	1970	350/400/455	Iron
9799084	1970	Ram Air IV	Aluminum
481733	1971	400/455	Iron
483674	1971	455 H.O.	Aluminum
485640	1972	455 H.O. (early)	Aluminum
485912	1972	400/455	Iron
488945	1972	455 H.O. (late)	Aluminum

Casting Number	Year	Application	Material
491244	1973	350/400/455	Iron
492706	1973	350/400/455	Iron
492744	1973	350/400/455	Iron
494282	1973	350/400/455	Iron
494405	1973	SD-455	Iron
494419	1973	SD-455	Iron
495106	1974	350/400/455	Iron
495107	1974	SD-455	Iron
496140	1975	350/400/455	Iron
525355	1976–1977	350/400/455	Iron
10003395	1978–1979	400	Iron
10000518	1978–1981	301	Iron

Blocks

Block Casting	Displacement	Years
9773153	326	1964
9786339	326	1967
9778840	326	1965–1966
9790079	350	1968–1969
9799916	350	1970
481990	350	1971–1972
488986	350	1973–1974
500810	350	1975–1977
9773155	389	1964
9778789	389	1965–1966
9786133	400	1967
9792506	Ram Air 400	1967–1969
9790071	400	1968–1969
9799914	400	1970

Block Casting	Displacement	Years
9799915	Ram Air 400	1970
481988	400	1971–1975
500557	400	1975–1978
XX481988	T/A 6.6	1978–1979
9773157	421	1964
9778791	421	1965–1966
9782611	421	1966
9786135	428	1967
9792968	428	1968–1969
9799140	455	1970
483677	455	1971
485428	455	1971–1974
500813	455	1975–1976
490132	SD-455	1973–1974

Distributors

Number	Year	Body Style	Application	Type	Curve RPM Range	Centrifugal Advance Degrees	Vacuum Canister	Vacuum Advance Degrees
1111164	1967	A, F	326 2-barrel	Points	900–4,600	30	1115364	20
1111166	1967	A	326 H.O.	Breakerless	900–4,800	26	1115365	20
1111180	1967	A, B	400 4-barrel/428 4-barrel (including H.O.)	Breakerless	1,000–4,400	30	1115365	20
1111183	1967	A, B	400 4-barrel/428 4-barrel (including H.O.)	Points	1000–4,400	30	1115365	20
1111199	1967	A, F	326 2-barrel with A.I.R.	Points	900–4,600	30	1115366	20
1111237	1967	A, B	400 4-barrel manual transmission/428 H.O. manual transmission	Points	1,000–4,400	30	1115367	20
1111238	1967	A, F	326 H.O. with A.I.R.	Points	1,000–4,800	26	1115367	20
1111242	1967	A, B	400 2-barrel/400 4-barrel	Points	1,000–4,600	22	1115364	20
1111243	1967	B	400 4-barrel/428 4-barrel (including H.O.)	Points	900–4,600	30	1115365	20
1111244	1967	B	400 4-barrel manual transmission/428 4-barrel (including H.O.) manual transmission	Points	900–4,600	30	1115367	20
1111245	1967	GP	400 4-barrel	Breakerless	900–4,400	30	1115365	20
1111250	1967	B, F	400 4-barrel auto transmission (includes Ram Air)/428 H.O.	Points	1,000–4,400	30	1115365	20
1111251	1967	A, B	400 4-barrel manual transmission/428 H.O. manual transmission	Breakerless	1,000–4,400	30	1115365	20
1111252	1967	B, F	400 4-barrel manual transmission (includes Ram Air)/428 H.O. with A.I.R.	Points	1,000–4,400	30	1115367	20
1111254	1967	B	400 4-barrel with A.I.R.	Points	1,000–4,600	22	1115375	20
1111255	1967	B	400 2-barrel/400 4-barrel	Breakerless	1,000–4,600	22	1115374	20
1111261	1967	B	400 2-barrel (low compression)/400 4-barrel	Points	1,000–4,600	22	1115366	20
1111268	1967	B	400 with A.I.R.	Points	1,100–4,400	34	1115365	20

Number	Year	Body Style	Application	Type	Curve RPM Range	Centrifugal Advance Degrees	Vacuum Canister	Vacuum Advance Degrees
1111165	1967–1968	A, F	326 2-barrel/326 H.O./350 2-barrel auto transmission	Points	1,000–4,400	26	1115365	20
1111253	1967–1969	B, G	400 2-barrel/400 4-barrel	Points	1,000–4,600	22	1115374	20
1111270	1968	A, B, F	400 4-barrel auto transmission/428 H.O. auto transmission	Points	1,000–4,600	22	1973412	20
1111272	1968	B	400 2-barrel (low compression)	Points	1,000–4,550	34	1973411	20
1111281	1968	A, F	350 2-barrel (early)	Points	1,100–4,800	26	1973411	20
1111282	1968	A, F	350 H.O. auto transmission	Points	1,400–5,000	20	1973411	20
1111300	1968	B, G	400 4-barrel	Points	1,000–4,600	22	1973412	20
1111435	1968	B	428 4-barrel auto transmission (exc H.O.)	Points	950–4,600	24	1973412	20
1111447	1968	A, F	350 H.O. manual transmission	Points	1,250–4,550	34	1973411	20
1111448	1968	B	400 2-barrel manual transmission	Points	1,400–4,600	24	1973412	20
1111449	1968	A, F	400 4-barrel/428 H.O. manual transmission	Points	1,400–4,600	22	1973411	20
1111450	1968	B	428 manual transmission (exc H.O.)	Points	1,400–4,600	24	1973411	20
1111937	1968	B	400 4-barrel auto transmission (YE)	Points	1,400–5,000	20	1115374	20
1111940	1968–1968	A, B, G	400 2-barrel (low compression)	Points	1,000–4,500	34	1115365	20
1111941	1968–1969	A, F	Ram Air II, Ram Air III (A-auto), Ram Air IV	Points	1,300–4,600	24	1115365	20
1111942	1969	A, F	350 2-barrel	Points	1,100–4,800	26	1115364	20
1111946	1969	A, B, F	400 4-barrel (and F Ram Air III) auto transmission/428 H.O. auto transmission	Points	1,000–4,600	22	1115365	20
1111952	1969	A, B, F, G	400 manual transmission/428 H.O. manual transmission	Points	1,400–4,600	22	1115365	20
1111953	1969	B, G	400 4-barrel auto transmission	Points	1,000–4,600	22	1973412	20
1111959	1969	B, G	428 4-barrel auto transmission (exc H.O.)	Points	1,100–4,600	24	1115365	20
1111960	1969	B, G	350 2-barrel manual transmission/428 4-barrel manual transmission (exc H.O.)	Points	1,400–4,600	24	1115365	20
1111965	1969	A, F	350 H.O. auto transmission	Points	1,000–5,600	20	1115365	20
1111966	1969	A, F	350 H.O. manual transmission	Points	1,300–5,600	20	1115365	20
1111105	1970	B	Bonneville 455 YH	Points	800–4,400	16	1115365	20
1111148	1970	A, F, G	400 4-barrel auto transmission	Points	800–4,600	26	1115365	20
1111176	1970	A, F, G	400 4-barrel manual transmission	Points	1,100–4,700	26	1115365	20
1112007	1970	A, B, F, G	350 2-barrel/400 2-barrel auto transmission	Points	800–4,600	26	1115365	20
1112008	1970	A, B, F	350 2-barrel, manual transmission	Points	1,100–4,700	26	1115364	20
1112009	1970	A, F	Ram Air III auto transmission	Points	800–4,600	22	1115365	20
1112010	1970	A, F	Ram Air III manual transmission	Points	1,100–4,600	22	1115365	20
1112011	1970	A, F	Ram Air IV	Points	1,200–6,100	28	1115365	20
1112012	1970	A, B, G	455 4-barrel	Points	800–4,400	16	1115365	20
1112013	1970	F	Ram Air Super Duty (not used)	Points	1,200–6,100	28	1115365	20
1112024	1970	A, F	Ram Air III manual transmission	Points	1,100–4,600	22	1115365	20
1112035	1971	B, G	455 4-barrel (YA)	Unitized	1,300–4,600	22	1115365	20
1112068	1971	A, B, F	400 2-barrel (late)	Points	1,700–4,600	28	1115364	20
1112069	1971	A, B, F	350 2-barrel auto transmission	Points	1,700–4,600	22	1115364	20
1112070	1971	A, B, F, G	400 4-barrel	Points	1,300–4,600	22	1115364	20
1112071	1971	B	455 2-barrel auto transmission	Points	1,800–4,600	24	1115365	20
1112072	1971	A, B, F, G	455 4-barrel	Points	1,300–4,600	22	1115364	20
1112073	1971	A, F	455 H.O.	Points	1,100–4,500	26	1115364	20
1112083	1971	A, B, F	350 2-barrel manual transmission (late)	Points	1,400–4,600	22	1115364	20
1112089	1971	A, B, F	400 2-barrel (early)	Points	1,600–4,600	24	1115364	20
1112090	1971	A, B, F	350 2-barrel auto transmission (late)	Points	1,600–4,600	18	1115364	20
1112118	1972	A, B, F	350 2-barrel auto transmission (early)	Points	1,600–4,600	20	1115364	20
1112119	1972	A, B, F	400 2-barrel auto transmission (early)	Points	1,600–4,600	26	1115365	20
1112121	1972	A, B, F, G	400 4-barrel	Points	1,400–4,600	26	1115364	20
1112122	1972	B	455 2-barrel auto transmission (early)	Points	1,600–4,600	26	1115365	20
1112126	1972	A, F	455 H.O.	Points	1,150–4,600	30	1115346	20
1112127	1972	B, G	455 4-barrel auto transmission	Unitized	1,400–4,600	22	1115365	20
1112133	1972	A, F	455 H.O.	Unitized	1,150–4,600	30	1115346	20
1112140	1972	A, F	350 2-barrel manual transmission	Points	1,600–4,600	24	1115346	20
1112143	1972	A, B, F	350 2-barrel auto transmission	Points	1,600–4,600	20	1115364	20

 HOW TO REBUILD PONTIAC V-8s

Number	Year	Body Style	Application	Type	Curve RPM Range	Centrifugal Advance Degrees	Vacuum Canister	Vacuum Advance Degrees
1112145	1972	B, G	455 4-barrel auto transmission	Points	1,400–4,600	22	1115365	20
1112184	1972	A, B, F	400 2-barrel auto transmission altitude	Points	1,700–4,600	26	1973444	20
1112185	1972	B	455 2-barrel auto transmission altitude	Points	1,600–4,600	26	1973444	20
1112186	1972	A, B, F, G	400 4-barrel auto transmission altitude	Points	1,800–4,600	26	1973444	20
1112187	1972	A, B, F, G	455 4-barrel auto transmission altitude	Points	1,600–4,200	22	1973444	20
1112189	1972	A, B, F	400 2-barrel auto transmission (late)	Points	1,400–4,600	26	1115365	20
1112190	1972	B	455 2-barrel auto transmission (late)	Points	1,500–4,600	26	1115365	20
1112191	1973	A, B, F, G	455 4-barrel	Points	1,150–3,900	18	1973470	25
1112199	1973	A, B, F	350 2-barrel (Firebird), 400 2-barrel (wagon)	Points	1,200–3,750	24	1973455	25
1112201	1973	A, B, F, X	350 2-barrel auto transmission	Points	1,200–3,600	24	1973491	25
1112202	1973	A, F, X	350 2-barrel manual transmission with A.I.R.	Points	1,400–3,500	26	1973491	25
1112203	1973	A, B, F, G	455 4-barrel	Unitized	1,200–4,000	18	1973470	25
1112205	1973	F	SD-455	Points	1,200–4,600	22	1973458	25
1112216	1973	A, B, F, X	350 2-barrel auto transmission altitude	Points	1,200–3,600	24	1973444	20
1112218	1973	F	SD-455	Points	1,200–3,300	20	1973643	20
1112220	1973	A, B, F, G	455 4-barrel auto transmission altitude	Points	1,150–3,900	18	1973464	25
1112224	1973	A, B, F	400 2-barrel altitude	Points	1,200–3,750	24	1973464	25
1112232	1973	A, B, F, G	400 4-barrel auto transmission altitude	Points	1,200–4,600	22	1973454	25
1112233	1973	A, B, F, G	400 4-barrel	Unitized	1,200–4,600	22	1973458	25
1112241	1973	A, B, F, G	455 4-barrel	Points	1,150–3,900	18	1973470	25
1112242	1973	A, B, F, G	455 4-barrel auto transmission altitude	Points	1,150–3,900	18	1973464	25
1112510	1973	A, G	350 2-barrel auto transmission	Points	1,000–3,800	24	1973471	25
1112511	1973	A, B, F	400 2-barrel auto transmission (exc A wagon)	Points	1,000–3,800	24	1973455	25
1112811	1973	A, B, F, G	455 4-barrel auto transmission altitude	Points	1,150–3,800	18	1973471	25
1112817	1973	A, B	455 4-barrel auto transmission altitude	Points	1,300–3,900	20	1973471	25
1112231	1973–1974	A, F	400 4-barrel manual transmission	Points	1,200–4,600	22	1973428	25
1112234	1973–1974	A, F, X	350 2-barrel auto transmission with A.I.R., California	Points	1,200–3,600	24	1115364	20
1112235	1973–1974	A, F, X	350 2-barrel auto transmission altitude	Points	1,200–3,450	26	1973464	25
1112236	1973–1974	A, F, X	350 2-barrel manual transmission with A.I.R.	Points	1,300–3,450	26	1115364	20
1112237	1973–1974	A, B, F, X	350 2-barrel Calif/400 2-barrel auto transmission	Points	1,200–3,750	24	1115365	20
1112238	1973–1974	A, B, F	400 2-barrel auto transmission altitude	Points	1,200–3,750	24	1973471	24
1112239	1973–1974	A, F	400 4-barrel manual transmission	Points	1,200–4,600	22	1973428	25
1112240	1973–1974	A, B, F, G	400 4-barrel auto transmission altitude	Points	1,200–4,600	22	1973471	25
1112243	1973–1974	F	SD–455	Points	1,200–4,600	22	1973428	25
1112507	1973–1974	A, B, F, G	455 4-barrel auto transmission altitude	Unitized	1,200–4,000	18	1973464	25
1112512	1973–1974	A, B, F, G	400 4-barrel auto transmission	Points	1,200–4,600	22	1115365	20
1112513	1973–1974	A, B, F, G	455 4-barrel auto transmission (including California)	Points	1,150–3,900	18	1115365	20
1112804	1973–1974	A, B, F, X	350 2-barrel auto transmission with A.I.R. California	Points	1,200–3,600	24	1115364	20
1112805	1973–1974	A, B, F, X	350 2-barrel auto transmission, California, 400 2-barrel	Points	1,200–3,750	24	1115365	20
1112806	1973–1974	A, F, X	350 2-barrel manual transmission with A.I.R.	Points	1,300–3,450	26	1115364	20
1112807	1973–1974	A, B, F, G	455 4-barrel auto transmission (including California)	Points	1,150–3,900	18	1115365	20
1112808	1973–1974	A, F, X	350 2-barrel auto transmission altitude	Points	1,200–3,450	26	1973464	25
1112809	1973–1974	A, B, F, G	400 2-barrel auto transmission altitude	Points	1,200–3,750	24	1973471	24
1112810	1973–1974	A, B, F, G	455 4-barrel auto transmission altitude	Unitized	1,200–4,000	18	1115365	20
1112812	1973–1974	A, B, F, G	400 4-barrel auto transmission	Unitized	1,200–4,600	22	1115365	20
1112813	1973–1974	A, B, F, G	400 4-barrel auto transmission	Points	1,200–4,600	22	1115365	20
1112814	1973–1974	A, B, F, G	400 4-barrel auto transmission altitude	Points	1,200–4,600	22	1973471	25
1112205	1974	F	SD-455	Points	1,200–4,600	22	1973428	25
1112210	1974	A, B, F, G	455 4-barrel auto transmission	HEI	1,200–3,900	18	1973494	20
1112212	1974	A, B, F, G	400 4-barrel auto transmission	HEI	1,200–4,600	22	1973494	20
1112213	1974	A, B, F, G	400 4-barrel auto transmission altitude	HEI	1,200–4,600	22	1973493	25
1112546	1974	A, B, F	400 2-barrel auto transmission	HEI	1,200–3,600	24	1973494	20
1112547	1974	A, B, F	400 2-barrel auto transmission altitude	HEI	1,200–3,600	24	1973493	25
1112821	1974	A, F, X	350 4-barrel auto transmission	Points	1,000–3,800	24	1115364	20
1112822	1974	A, F, X	350 4-barrel auto transmission	Points	1,000–3,800	24	1115364	20
1112824	1974	A	350 4-barrel auto transmission altitude	Points	1,100–3,800	26	1973464	20
1112833	1974	A, F	400 2-barrel auto transmission California	Points	1,200–4,000	24	1973464	20

Number	Year	Body Style	Application	Type	Curve RPM Range	Centrifugal Advance Degrees	Vacuum Canister	Vacuum Advance Degrees
1112834	1974	A, F	400 2-barrel auto transmission, California	Points	1,200–4,000	24	1973464	20
1112856	1974	A, X	350 4-barrel manual transmission	Points	1,200–3,800	24	1115364	20
1112857	1974	A, X	350 4-barrel manual transmission	Points	1,200–3,800	24	1115364	20
1112859	1974	All	455 4-barrel auto transmission altitude	Points	1,150–3,900	18	1115364	20
1112860	1974	A, B, F, G	455 4-barrel auto transmission altitude	Points	1,150–3,900	18	1115364	20
1112871	1974	A, F	400 4-barrel manual transmission	HEI	1,200–4,600	22	1973512	25
1112876	1974	A, B, G	400 2-barrel auto transmission, California	HEI	1,200–3,800	24	1973494	20
1112878	1974	A	455 4-barrel auto transmission altitude	HEI	1,200–3,900	18	1973515	20
1112498	1975	A, F	350 4-barrel auto transmission	HEI	1,200–3,600	17	1973546	24
1112929	1975	A, F, G	400 4-barrel auto transmission (export?)	HEI	1,000–4,400	20	1973513	20
1112946	1975	F	350 4-barrel manual transmission	HEI	1,000–3,600	21	1973561	24
1112947	1975	A, F	350 4-barrel auto transmission, California	HEI	1,200–,3800	20	1973562	20
1112948	1975	All	400 4-barrel auto transmission, California	HEI	1,200–4,400	22	1973562	20
1112495	1975–1976	F	400 4-barrel manual transmission	HEI	1,000–4,400	20	1973513	20
1112497	1975–1976	A, F, G	350 2-barrel auto transmission	HEI	1,200–3,800	20	1973514	25
1112500	1975–1976	A, B, G	400 2-barrel auto transmission	HEI	1,200–4,400	20	1973493	25
1112923	1975–1976	F	455 4-barrel manual transmission	HEI	1,000–4,400	14	1973493	25
1112928	1975–1976	All	400 4-barrel auto transmission, exc California	HEI	1,200–4,400	16	1973493	25
1112930	1975–1976	A, B, G	455 4-barrel auto transmission	HEI	1,400–4,400	10	1973493	25
1112950	1975–1976	A, F, X	350 2-barrel auto transmission	HEI	1,200–3,800	20	1973453	20
1112958	1975–1976	All	400 4-barrel auto transmission	HEI	1,200–4,400	16	1973514	25
1112960	1975–1976	A, B, G	455 4-barrel auto transmission, California	HEI	1,200–4,400	14	1973545	20
1103205	1976	All	400 4-barrel auto transmission, California	HEI	1,200–4,400	16	1973545	20
1103207	1976	A, B, G	455 4-barrel auto transmission, California	HEI	1,000–4,400	14	1973562	20
1103214	1976	All	400 2-barrel auto transmission	HEI	1,400–4,400	22	1973562	20
1103216	1976	A, F, G	350 2-barrel auto transmission without A/C	HEI	1,200–3,800	20	5–12”	20
1103223	1976	A, D, G	350 4-barrel auto transmission	HEI	700–3,600	16	1973514	25
1103206	1976–1977	A, F	350 4-barrel auto transmission, California	HEI	1,200–3,600	17	1973543	20
1103257	1977	F	350 4-barrel auto transmission	HEI	1,200–3,600	17	1973607	20
1103269	1977	All	400 4-barrel auto transmission	HEI	1,000–4,600	17	1973607	20
1103271	1977	A, F	400 4-barrel (T/A 6.6)	HEI	1,000–4,400	20	1973514	25
1103272	1977	All	301 2-barrel auto transmission	HEI	825–3,450	21.5	1982765	25
1103273	1977	All	301 2-barrel manual transmission	HEI	1,000–3,600	19	1982765	25
1103276	1977	A, G	350 4-barrel auto transmission	HEI	1,000–3,600	20	1963607	20
1103278	1977	A	400 4-barrel (wagon) auto transmission	HEI	1,200–4,400	16	1973607	20
1103310	1978	All	301 4-barrel	HEI	1,000–4,400	14	1973635	25
1103314	1978	All	301 2-barrel	HEI	900–3,400	21	1973635	25
1103315	1978	F	400 4-barrel (T/A 6.6)	HEI	1,000–4,400	20	1973636	25
1103316	1978	B	400 4-barrel auto transmission	HEI	1,000–4,600	17	1973636	25
1103343	1978	B	400 4-barrel auto transmission	HEI	800–3,650	16.5	1973649	25
1103359	1978	F	400 4-barrel auto transmission	HEI	1,000–4,600	17	1973637	20
1103315	1979	F	400 4-barrel (T/A 6.6)	HEI	1,000–4,600	17	1973636	25
1103399	1979	All	301 4-barrel auto transmission	HEI	1,150–4,400	20	1973635	25
1103400	1979	All	301 4-barrel manual transmission	HEI	1,050–4,700	17	1973636	25
1103407	1980	F	301 4-barrel (T/A 4.9) YN YR	HEI	1,200–4,400	23	1973716	20
1103425	1980	All	All 301 (exc T/A 4.9)	HEI	1,250–4,600	18	1973716	20
1103444	1980	F	301 Turbo auto transmission	HEI	1,200–4,400	14	1973725	19
1103450	1980	F	265 2-barrel	HEI	1,050–5,000	18	1973727	20
1103453	1981	A, F	265 and 301 all	HEI	computer			

HOW TO REBUILD PONTIAC V-8s

Bore Stroke

Year	Displacement	Bore (inches)	Stroke (inches)	Main Journal Diameter (inches)
1955	287	3.75	3.25	2.50
1956	316	3.94	3.25	2.50
1957	347	3.94	3.56	2.62
1958	370	4.06	3.56	2.62
1959–1966	389	4.06	3.75	3.00
1963–1966	421	4.09	4.00	3.25
1963–1967	326	3.72	3.75	3.00
1967–1969	428	4.12	4.00	3.25
1967–1979	400	4.12	3.75	3.00
1968–1977	350	3.88	3.75	3.00
1970–1976	455	4.15	4.21	3.25
1977–1981	301	4.00	3.00	3.00
1980–1981	265	3.75	3.00	3.00

Quadrajets

Number	Year	Body Style	Application	Primary Jet	Primary Rod	Secondary Rod	Notes
7027260	1967	A, F	OHC-6 auto transmission (early)	71	44	BF 0.0397 inch	
7027261	1967	A, F	OHC-6 manual transmission (early)	71	42	BF 0.0397 inch	
7027262	1967	A, B, GP	400/428 auto transmission	70	41	BF 0.0397 inch	
7027263	1967	A, B, GP	400/428 manual transmission	70	39	BF 0.0397 inch	
7027268	1967	A, F	OHC-6 auto transmission (late)	71	44	BF 0.0397 inch	
7027269	1967	A, F	OHC-6 manual transmission (late)	71	42	BF 0.0397 inch	
7027272	1967	F	400 auto transmission	70	41	BF 0.0397 inch	
7027273	1967	F	400 manual transmission	70	39	BF 0.0397 inch	
7037260	1967	A, F	OHC-6 auto transmission with A.I.R. (early)	71	43	BF 0.0397 inch	
7037261	1967	A, F	OHC-6 manual transmission with A.I.R. (early)	71	41	BF 0.0397 inch	
7037262	1967	B	400/428 auto transmission with A.I.R.	70	40	BF 0.0397 inch	
7037263	1967	A, B	400/428 manual transmission with A.I.R.	70	38	BF 0.0397 inch	
7037268	1967	A, F	OHC-6 auto transmission with A.I.R. (late)	72	44	BF 0.0397 inch	
7037269	1967	A, F	OHC-6 manual transmission with A.I.R. (late)	71	44	BF 0.0397 inch	
7037271	1967	GTO	Ram Air I (late)	70	38	BF 0.0397 inch	
7037272	1967	F	400 auto transmission with A.I.R.	70	40	BF 0.0397 inch	
7037273	1967	F	400 manual transmission with A.I.R.	70	38	BF 0.0397 inch	
7037276	1967	F	Ram Air I	70	38	BF 0.0397 inch	
7028260	1968	A, F	OHC-6 auto transmission	70	42	BF 0.0397 inch	
7028261	1968	A, F	OHC-6 manual transmission	70	41	BF 0.0397 inch	
7028262	1968	A, B, GP	400 auto transmission	73	43	BE 0.0410 inch	
7028263	1968	A	400 manual transmission	72	40	BE 0.0410 inch	
7028264	1968	F	400 auto transmission	73	42	BE 0.0410 inch	
7028265	1968	F	400 manual transmission	73	40	BE 0.0410 inch	
7028266	1968	A, F	350 H.O. auto transmission	73	42	BE 0.0410 inch	
7028267	1968	A, B, GP	400/428 manual transmission	72	41	BE 0.0410 inch	
7028268	1968	A, B, GP	400/428 auto transmission	73	42	BE 0.0410 inch	
7028269	1968	A, F	350 H.O. manual transmission	72	41	BE 0.0410 inch	
7028270	1968	A, F	400 Ram Air II auto transmission	72	41	BE 0.0410 inch	
7028271	1968	F	400 H.O. manual transmission	72	41	BE 0.0410 inch	
7028273	1968	A, F	400 Ram Air II manual transmission	72	42	BE 0.0410 inch	
7028274	1968	A	400 Ram Air I auto transmission	73	41	BE 0.0410 inch	
7028275	1968	A	400 Ram Air I manual transmission	72	40	BE 0.0410 inch	
7028276	1968	F	400 Ram Air I auto transmission	73	41	BE 0.0410 inch	
7028277	1968	F	400 Ram Air I manual transmission	72	40	BE 0.0410 inch	
7029260	1969	A, F	OHC-6 auto transmission	70	41	BL 0.0410 inch	
7029261	1969	A, F	OHC-6 manual transmission	69	40	BL 0.0410 inch	
7029262	1969	B	428 auto transmission	72	45	BE 0.0410 inch	
7029263	1969	A, B, F, G	350/400/428 manual transmission	71	44	BE 0.0410 inch	
7029268	1969	A, B, F, G	350/400/428 auto transmission	71	44	BE 0.0410 inch	
7029270	1969	A, F	400 H.O./Ram Air III/Ram Air IV auto transmission	69	38	BP 0.0397 inch	

Number	Year	Body Style	Application	Primary Jet	Primary Rod	Secondary Rod	Notes
7029273	1969	A, F	400 H.O./Ram Air III/Ram Air IV manual transmission	69	37	BP 0.0397 inch	
7040262	1970	B	455 auto transmission	72	44	BE 0.0410 inch	
7040263	1970	A, F, G	400 manual transmission	71	44	CC 0.030 inch	
7040264	1970	A, F, G	400 auto transmission	70	41	BP 0.0397 inch	
7040267	1970	A, G	455 manual transmission	71	42	CC 0.030 inch	
7040268	1970	A, G	455 auto transmission	71	42	CC 0.030 inch	
7040270	1970	A, F	Ram Air III/Ram Air IV auto transmission	70	39	CC 0.030 inch	
7040273	1970	A, F	Ram Air III/Ram Air IV manual transmission	70	39	CC 0.030 inch	
7040278	1970	A	455 auto transmission with Ram Air	-	-	-	Assigned but not produced
7040279	1970	A	455 manual transmission with Ram Air	-	-	-	Assigned but not produced
7040562	1970	B	400/455 auto transmission, California	68	37	BP 0.0397 inch	
7040563	1970	A, F, G	400 manual transmission, California	68	36	BU 0.0547 inch	
7040564	1970	A, F, G	400 auto transmission, California	68	38	BU 0.0547 inch	
7040567	1970	A, G	455 manual transmission, California	70	40	BU 0.0547 inch	
7040568	1970	A, G	455 auto transmission, California	69	37	BU 0.0547 inch	
7040578	1970	A	455 auto transmission with Ram Air, California	-	-	-	Assigned but not produced
7040579	1970	A	455 manual transmission with Ram Air, California	-	-	-	Assigned but not produced
7040570	1970	A, F	Ram Air III/Ram Air IV auto transmission, California	67	33	CC 0.030 inch	
7040573	1970	A, F	Ram Air III/Ram Air IV manual transmission, California	67	33	CC 0.030 inch	
7041262	1971	A, B, F, G	455 auto transmission	71	43	BU 0.0547 inch	
7041263	1971	A, B, F, G	400/455 manual transmission	75	47	BU 0.0547 inch	
7041264	1971	A, B, F, G	400 auto transmission	71	46	BP 0.0397 inch	
7041267	1971	A, F	455 H.O. manual transmission without Ram Air	73	38	BP 0.0397 inch	
7041268	1971	A, F	455 H.O. auto transmission without Ram Air	74	43	BP 0.0397 inch	
7041270	1971	A, F	455 H.O. auto transmission with Ram Air	74	43	BP 0.0397 inch	
7041271	1971	A, B, F, G	400/455 auto transmission, high alt	69	43	BP 0.0397 inch	
7041273	1971	A, F	455 H.O. manual transmission with Ram Air	73	38	BP 0.0397 inch	
7042262	1972	A, B, G	455 auto transmission	72	43	CR 0.0547 inch	
7042263	1972	A, F, G	400 manual transmission	72	45	CS 0.0397 inch	
7042264	1972	A, B, F, G	400 auto transmission, California	74	47	CR 0.0547 inch	
7042270	1972	A, F	455 H.O. auto transmission	71	45	CR 0.0547 inch	
7042272	1972	A, B, G	455 auto transmission	72	43	CR 0.0547 inch	
7042273	1972	A, F	455 H.O. manual transmission	71	43	CR 0.0547 inch	
7042274	1972	A	400 auto transmission	74	47	CS 0.0397 inch	
7042276	1972	A, G	455 auto transmission, high alt	71	43	CR 0.0547 inch	
7042278	1972	A, F, G	400 auto transmission, high alt	72	46	CS 0.0397 inch	
7043262	1973	A, B, F, G	455 auto transmission	71	41	CR 0.0547 inch	
7043263	1973–1974	A, F	400 manual transmission	71	43	CS 0.0397 inch	
7043264	1973	A, F, G	400 auto transmission	72	43	DB 0.0697 inch	Replaced by 7043266
7043265	1973	F	455 manual transmission	71	44	CR 0.0547 inch	
7043266	1973	A, F, G	400 auto transmission	72	45	DB 0.0697 inch	Replaced 7043264
7043270	1973	F	SD-455 auto transmission	76	51	BV 0.0297 inch	
7043272	1973	A, B, F, G	455 auto transmission, high alt	70	41	CR 0.0547 inch	
7043273	1973	F	SD-455 manual transmission	75	49	BV 0.0297 inch	
7043274	1973	A, F, G	400 auto transmission, high alt	72	45	DB 0.0697 inch	
7044262	1974	A, B, F, G	455 auto transmission	71	41	CR 0.0547 inch	
7044266	1974	A, B, F, G	400 auto transmission	72	45	DB 0.0697 inch	Replaced by 7044276
7044267	1974	B	455 auto transmission	68	33	CR 0.0547 inch	
7044268	1974	A, X	350 auto transmission	72	43	DB 0.0697 inch	
7044269	1974	A, X	350 manual transmission	68	35	DB 0.0697 inch	

Number	Year	Body Style	Application	Primary Jet	Primary Rod	Secondary Rod	Notes
7044270	1974	F	SD-455 auto transmission	70	38	DM 0.0393 inch	
7044272	1974	A, B, F, G	455 auto transmission high alt	70	41	CR 0.0547 inch	
7044273	1974	F	SD-455 manual transmission	70	38	DM 0.0393 inch	
7044274	1974	A, B, F, G	400 auto transmission high alt	72	45	DB 0.0697 inch	
7044276	1974	A, B, F, G	400 auto transmission	72	45	DB 0.0697 inch	Replaced 7044266
7044560	1974	B	455 auto transmission, California	71	41	CR 0.0547 inch	
7044568	1974	X	350 auto transmission, California	72	43	DB 0.0697 inch	
7044568	1974	X	350 auto transmission, California	72	43	DB 0.0697 inch	
7045261	1975	F	455 manual transmission	67	40	DB 0.0697 inch	
7045263	1975	F	400 manual transmission	70	38	DB 0.0697 inch	
7045264	1975	A, B, G	400 auto transmission	72	40	DB 0.0697 inch	
7045268	1975	A, F	350 auto transmission	66	38	DE 0.0874 inch	
7045269	1975	A, F	350 manual transmission	66	42	DE 0.0874 inch	
7045274	1975	F	400 auto transmission	72	40	DB 0.0697 inch	
7045562	1975	A, B, G	455 auto transmission	66	40	DB 0.0697 inch	
7045564	1975	A, B, F, G	400 auto transmission, California	67	40	DB 0.0697 inch	
7045566	1975	A, B, G	455 auto transmission, California	65	36	DB 0.0697 inch	
7045568	1975	A, F	350 auto transmission, California	66	38	DE 0.0874 inch	
17056261	1976	F	455 manual transmission	70	42	DB 0.0697 inch	
17056262	1976	A, B, G	455 auto transmission	72	46	DB 0.0697 inch	
17056263	1976	F	400/455 manual transmission	70	42	DB 0.0697 inch	
17056264	1976	A, B, G	400 auto transmission	72	46	DB 0.0697 inch	
17056266	1976	A, F, G	400 transmission	71	43	DB 0.0697 inch	
17056274	1976	F	400 auto transmission	72	46	DB 0.0697 inch	
17056562	1976	B (wagon)	455 auto transmission, California	69	43	DB 0.0697 inch	
17056564	1976	A, B, F, G	400 auto transmission, California	71	43	DB 0.0697 inch	
17056566	1976	A, B, G	455 auto transmission, California	69	39	DB 0.0697 inch	
17056568	1976	A, F, G	350 auto transmission, California	71	41	DB 0.0697 inch	
17057262	1977	A, B, F, G	350 auto transmission	71	43	DB 0.0697 inch	
17057263	1977	F	400 T/A 6.6 manual transmission	70	42	DB 0.0697 inch	
17057266	1977	F (and Can Am)	400 T/A 6.6 auto transmission	71	45	DB 0.0697 inch	
17057274	1977	A, B, F, G	400 auto transmission	71	45	DB 0.0697 inch	
17058263	1978	F	400 T/A 6.6 manual transmission	70	39	DB 0.0697 inch	
17058264	1978	B	400 auto transmission (late)	72	45	DB 0.0697 inch	Replaced 17058274
17058266	1978	F	400 T/A 6.6 auto transmission	72	45	DB 0.0697 inch	
17058272	1978	A, B	301 auto transmission	72	51	CH 0.0567 inch	
17058274	1978	B	400 auto transmission (early)	72	45	DB 0.0697 inch	Replaced by 17058264
17058276	1978	F	400 auto transmission (early)	72	45	DB 0.0697 inch	Replaced by 17058278
17058278	1978	F	400 auto transmission (late)	72	45	DB 0.0697 inch	Replaced 17058276
17059263	1979	F	400 T/A 6.6 manual transmission	70	40	DB 0.0697 inch	
17059271	1979	A, F, G	301 manual transmission	71	44	CH 0.0567 inch	
17059272	1979	A, B, F, G	301 auto transmission	72	52	CH 0.0567 inch	
17080272	1980	A, F, G	301 auto transmission	71	49	CH 0.0567 inch	
17080274	1980	F	301 Turbo auto transmission	71	48	CM 0.0397 inch	
17080270	1980	F	301 T/A 4.9 auto transmission	71	50	CH 0.0567 inch	
17081272	1981	A, F, G	301 auto transmission	computer			
17081273	1981	F	301 Turbo auto transmission	computer			
17081276	1981	F	301 Turbo auto transmission export	computer			

All Pontiac
11010 Trade Rd.
Richmond, VA 23236
804-794-6777
allpontiac.com

Ames Performance
10 Pontiac Dr.
PO Box 572
Spofford, NH 03462
800-421-2637
amesperf.com

Best Gasket Company
9230 Norwalk Blvd.
Santa Fe Springs, CA 90670
888-333-2378
bestgasket.com

Bill Hirsch Auto
396 Littleton Ave.
Newark, NJ 07103
800-828-2061
hirschauto.com

Billet Speedworks
(formerly Pro-Gram Engineering)
475 5th St. NE
Barberton, Ohio 44203
330-745-1004
billetspeedworks.com

Bob Davis Distributors
660 Tamburlaine Cove
Collierville, TN 38017
tn47@aol.com
901-412-4414

BOP Engineering
N3651 Schmidt Rd.
Jefferson, WI 53549
920-674-6058
bopengineering.com

Butler Performance
2786 Hwy. 43 North
Lawrenceburg, TN 38464
866-762-7527
butlerperformance.com

The Carburetor Shop LLC
204 E. 15th St.
Eldon, MO 65026
573-392-7378
thecarburetorshop.com

Centerforce Clutches
c/o Midway Industries, Inc.
2266 Crosswind Dr.
Prescott, AZ 86301
800-932-5882
centerforce.com

Cliff's High Performance
20579 Berry Rd.
Mount Vernon, OH 43050
740-397-2921
cliffshighperformance.com

Comp Cams
3406 Democrat Rd.
Memphis, TN 38118
800-999-0853
compcams.com

Crower Cams and Equipment
Co., Inc.
6180 Business Center Court
San Diego, CA 92154
619-661-6477
crower.com

The Cruisin' Tigers Pontiac Club
PO Box 2712
Orland Park, IL 60462
cruisintigers.com

DAVE's Small-Body HEI's
24 Buffalo Lane
Yerington, NV, 89447
775-722-3294
davessmallbodyheis.com

DCI Motorsports
2477 Ohio 44
Atwater, OH 44201
330-628-3354
dcimotorsports.com

Dura-Bond Industries
3200 Arrowhead Dr.
Carson City, NV 89706
800-227-8360
dura-bondbearing.com

Eagle Specialty Products
8530 Aaron Lane
Southaven, MS 38671
662-796-7373
eaglerod.com

Edelbrock
2700 California St.
Torrance, CA 90503
310-781-2222
edelbrock.com

Federal-Mogul
26555 Northwestern Hwy.
Southfield, MI 48033
248-354-7700
federalmogul.com

FlowKooler
500 Linne Rd., Unit I
Paso Robles, CA 93446
802-239-2501
flowkooler.com

Gardner Exhaust
15 Glenn Pond Dr.
Red Hook, NY 12571
845-758-8003
gardnerexhaust.com

GM of Canada
1189 Colonel Sam Dr.
Oshawa, ON L1H 8P7
905-440-7697
vintagevehicleservices.com

GTO Association of America
PO Box 213
Timnath, CO 80547
gtoaa.org

Howards Cams
280 West 35th Ave.
Oshkosh, WI 54902
howardscams.com

Inline Tube
15066 Technology Dr.
Shelby Twp, MI 48315
800-385-9452
inlinetube.com

Kauffman Racing Equipment
22280 Temple Rd.
Glenmont, OH 44628
740-599-5000
krepower.com

Keith Black Pistons
c/o UEM Pistons
1040 Corbett St.
Carson City, NV 89706
800-648-7970
eumpistons.com

Len Williams Auto Machine
12722 South Hwy. 48
Bristow, OK 74010
918-352-9711
lenwilliamsautomachine.com

Lunati Cams
8649 Hacks Cross Rd.
Olive Branch, MS 38654
662-892-1500
lunatipower.com

M&H Electric Fabricators
13537 Alondra Blvd.
Santa Fe Springs, CA 90670
562-926-9552
wiringharness.com

Mahle Clevite, Inc.
1240 Eisenhower Place
Ann Arbor, MI 48108
734-975-4777
mahleclevite.com

Max Performance, Inc.
2705 Clemens Rd., Building
105A
Hatfield, PA 19440
800-542-7278
maxperformanceinc.com

Melling Engine Parts
620 Saradan Dr.
Jackson, MI 49204
517-787-8172
melling.com

MSD Ignition
1350 Pullman Dr., Dock No. 14
El Paso, TX 79936
915-857-5200
msdignition.com

Nunzi's Automotive
6315 New Utrecht Ave.
Brooklyn, NY 11219
718-837-1135
nunzi-pontiac-expert.com

OEM Paints
510 Corporate Dr.
Escondido, CA 92029
760-747-2100
oempaints.com

Performance Distributors
2699 Barris Dr.
Memphis, TN 38132
901-396-5782
performancedistributors.com

Performance Trends
PO Box 530164
Livonia, MI 48153
248-473-9230
performancetrends.com

PerTronix Performance Products
440 East Arrow Hwy.
San Dimas, CA 91773
909-599-5955
pertronix.com

PHS Automotive Services
PO Box 183251
Shelby Township, MI 48318
586-781-5164
phs-online.com

Pontiac Oakland Club International
PO Box 421
Long Lake, MN 55356
763-479-2111
poci.org

Pontiac TriPower
6513 No. Fox Chapel Trail
Edwards, IL 61528
309-360-6385
pontiactripower.com

Pypes Performance Exhaust
2705 Clemens Rd., Building
105A
Hatfield, PA 19440
800-421-3890
pypesexhaust.com

Ram Air Restoration (RARE)
1725 Wood St., Suite B
Round Lake, IL 60073
800-421-8455
ramairrestoration.com

RobbMc Performance
Products
1717 La Mirada St.
Carson City, NV 89703
775-885-7411
robbmcperformance.com

RPM International
420 Atlas St.
Brea, CA 92821
714-784-6840
racingpartsmaximum.com

SI Valves
4477 Shopping Lane
Simi Valley, CA 93063
800-564-8258
sivalves.com

SD Performance
44408 Vedder Mountain Rd.
Chilliwack, B.C. V2R 4C4
604-392-2211
sdperformance.com

Spotts Performance
31 N. Maple Ave.
Hatfield, PA 19440
215-362-2336
spottsperformance.com

Supercar Specialties
11817 E. Grand River
Portland, MI 48875
517-647-2433

Taylor Cable Products
301 Highgrove Rd.
Grandview, MO 64030
816-765-5011
taylorvertex.com

Tin Indian Performance
3540 Burbank Rd., #113
Wooster, OH 44691
330-699-1358
tinindianperformance.com

Total Seal
22642 N. 15th Ave.
Phoenix, AZ 85027
800-874-2753
totalseal.com

Waldron's Exhaust
PO Box 99
208 West Main St.
Centreville, MI 49032
800-503-9428
waldronexhaust.com

Wilhite Performance
200 W. Washington St.
Derby, KS 67037
wilhiteperformance.net
316-788-0514

Willard Auto Machine
7620 N. 96th St.
Omaha, NE 68122
402-573-8984
wampowered.com

Year One
PO Box 521
Braselton, GA 30517
800-932-7663
yearone.com